Labor Markets, Gender and Social Stratification in East Asia

Labor Markets, Gender and Social Stratification in East Asia

A Global Perspective

Edited by

Tarohmaru Hiroshi

BRILL

LEIDEN | BOSTON

Originally published in hardback in 2016 as Volume 7 in the series The Intimate and the Public in Asian and Global Perspectives.

First published 2014, in Japanese [Higashi Ajia no Rōdō Shijō to Shakai Kaisō / 東アジアの労働市場と社会階層] by Kyoto University Press, Kyoto University, 69 Konoe-cho Yoshida, Sakyo, Kyoto 〒606-8315, Japan.

Cover illustration: Shibuya crossing in front of Shibuya Station in Shibuya,Tokyo, Japan (2012). © Kiely Ramos (www.kielyramos.com).

The Library of Congress has cataloged the hardcover edition as follows:
Names: Tarohmaru, Hiroshi, 1968- editor.
Title: Labor markets, gender and social stratification in East Asia : a global perspective / edited by Tarohmaru Hiroshi.
Other titles: Higashi Ajia no rōdō shijō to shakai kaisō. English
Description: Leiden ; Boston : Brill, [2016] | Series: The intimate and the public in Asian and global perspectives ; volume 7 | "First published 2014 in Japanese, Higashi Ajia no Rodo Shijo to Shakai Kaiso by Kyoto University Press." | Includes bibliographical references and index.
Identifiers: LCCN 2015040097| ISBN 9789004256101 (hardback : alk. paper) | ISBN 9789004262737 (e-book)
Subjects: LCSH: Labor market--East Asia--Regional disparities. | Social classes.
Classification: LCC HD5826.A6 H5413 2016 | DDC 331.12095--dc23
LC record available at http://lccn.loc.gov/2015040097

This publication has been typeset in the multilingual "Brill" typeface. With over 5,100 characters covering Latin, IPA, Greek, and Cyrillic, this typeface is especially suitable for use in the humanities. For more information, please see www.brill.com/brill-typeface.

ISBN 978-90-04-76460-6 (paperback, 2026)
ISBN 978-90-04-25610-1 (hardback)
ISBN 978-90-04-26273-7 (e-book)

Contents

List of Figures

List of Tables

Shibata Haruka

Oda Akiko, Tarohmaru Hiroshi and Yamato Reiko

Takenoshita Hirohisa

Chang Chin-Fen, Xie Guihua, Takamatsu Rie and Kim Young-Mi

List of Contributors

CHANG Chin-Fen

Ph.D. (1989), is Research Fellow at the Institute of Sociology, Academia Sinica (Taiwan). Her research interests include gender and the labor market, the sociology of labor, and East Asian comparative studies. Her publications include "Gender Inequality in Earnings in Industrialized East Asia" (*Social Science Research,* 2011).

KIM Young-Mi

Ph.D. (2006), is Assistant Professor at Yonsei University (South Korea). Her publications include "Understanding Intra-Regional Variation in Gender Inequality in East Asia" (*International Sociology,* 2014), co-authored with Shirahase Sawako, and "Dependence on Family Ties and Household Division of Labor in Korea, Japan and Taiwan" (*Asian Journal of Women's Studies*, 2013).

ODA Akiko

M.A. (2010), is a Ph.D. candidate in sociology at Kyoto University. She is also a Japan Society For the Promotion of Science Research Fellow at the Faculty of Policy Studies, Doshisha University (Japan). Her research focuses on gender inequality and labor markets in Japan.

PHANG Hanam

Ph.D. (1995), is Senior Research Fellow at the Korea Labor Institute (South Korea). His numerous articles on Korean labor markets include "Opportunity and Inequality: Educational Stratification in Korea" (*Korean Journal of Sociology,* 2002), co-authored with Kim Ki-Hun.

SAKAGUCHI Yusuke

Ph.D. (2011), is Associate Professor at St. Andrew's University (Japan). He has published numerous articles on risk society and risk perception.

SHIBATA Haruka

Ph.D. (2011), is Associate Professor at Ritsumeikan University (Japan). He specializes in the sociology of well-being, personal relationships, social support, and social policies, and his published articles include "The Effect of Active Labor Market Policies on Suicide Rates" (*Japanese Sociological Review*, 2014).

TAKAMATSU Rie
Ph.D. (2013), is Assistant Professor at Osaka University (Japan). She has published on gender, labor market, and education, including "Occupational Gender Segregation and Wages in Japan" (*Kansai Sociological Review*, 2012).

TAKENOSHITA Hirohisa
M.A. (1995), is Professor at Sophia University (Japan). His current research concerns a cross-national comparison of inequality and social stratification, as well as international migration and inequality. His articles have appeared in the *Journal of Ethnic and Migration Studies, International Migration, Comparative Social Research,* and *International Journal of Japanese Sociology*.

TAROHMARU Hiroshi
M.A. (1993), is Associate Professor at Kyoto University (Japan). His research centers on social stratification in Japan, and his many publications include *Sociology of Young Non-Standard Employees: Social Stratification, Gender and Globalization* (Osaka University Press, 2009).

XIE Guihua
Ph.D. (2004), is Associate Professor at Renmin University of China. Her research focuses on social stratification, migration, and the family in China.

YAMATO Reiko
Ph.D. (2008), is Professor at Kansai University (Japan). Her research centers on care, gender and intergenerational relations, and her publications include *The Making of the Life-long Care-giver in Postwar Japan* (Gakubunsha, 2008) and *Childcare for Men and for Women in Contemporary Japan: A Sociological Approach* (Showado, 2008), co-edited with Kiwaki Nachiko and Onode Setsuko.

CHAPTER 1

Labor Markets, Gender, and Social Stratification in East Asia: An Introduction

Tarohmaru Hiroshi

1 Social Stratification in East Asia

The development of capitalism and industrial technology from the 19th century onward brought huge changes to the nature of work and to social inequality. In western Europe, the rise of the working class and the emergence of class conflict became pressing matters that led to numerous social policy debates including ones concerning the welfare state (Marshall and Bottmore 1987). In the post World War II era, the golden age of the welfare state, labor and social stratification were important social and political issues, even though opportunities for social revolution receded gradually. Since the 1990s income inequality has risen in many countries, including countries in East Asia, and the causes are still being debated (McCall and Percheski 2010; Neckerman and Torche 2007). Inequality lives on, in different guises according to the context. Unequal educational opportunities, gender and racial inequalities, and discrimination against immigrants are all closely interrelated with issues of labor and social stratification (McTague et al. 2009).

Two basic and opposing theories on the dynamics of social stratification pertained in the years of the Cold War: Marxism and industrialism. Marxism predicted that as industrialization progresses in a capitalist society the differences between classes expand and the class struggle intensifies, leading to socialist revolution (Marx and Engels 1848; Cohen 2000). Industrialism held that socialism is functionally equivalent to capitalism, and that a transition from one to the other is not inevitable (Kerr et al. 1960). Industrialism held that capitalism and socialism often converge in many aspects, including in increased equality of opportunity, rising educational levels, and improved labor/management relations, and that socialism and capitalism can co-exist (Kerr 1983). The main battlefield for Marxism and industrialism was "social stratification theory," with several debates unfolding around equality of opportunity and class consciousness (Erikson and Goldthorpe 1992).[1] Notwithstanding

1 The term "social stratification theory" is used mainly by industrialists. Marxists prefer the term "class theory." The term "social stratification" here is used to indicate total inequality caused by various attributes such as class, status, gender, and ethnicity.

 | DOI 10.1163/9789004262737_002

this conflict, both Marxism and industrialism predicted that industrialization and economic growth would eventually cause all societies to converge in a common social structure. Both approaches can be considered forms of convergence theory.

The collapse of Soviet-style socialism exposed flaws in the predictions of both Marxism and industrialism. The range of inequalities that remained in all societies and the importance of understanding the conditions and causes of these inequalities led researchers to take a new look at social stratification theory. As comparable data became more available in the 1980s, researchers started turning their attention to international comparisons of social stratification and labor markets in order to clarify the causes of inequalities. Social stratification theory was found to be an effective tool for determining the nature and magnitude of inequalities and clarifying their institutional background.

The countries of East Asia have already undergone considerable industrialization, but in historical and cultural background and social institutions they differ markedly from Western countries. Considerable differences exist in terms of institutions such as the family system, the gendered division of labor, and welfare regimes. These differences have meant that Western researchers have largely refrained from comparing Asian and Western societies. However, the differences between them may in fact be put to good use, and help us gain a more comprehensive understanding of the relationship between institutions and social stratification. Social stratification and labor markets are not determined solely by economic conditions and industrial structure: they are also strongly associated with contexts such as the family system, gendered division of labor, labor policy, and welfare regime. Limiting research to Western societies restricts both the degree of diversity in research subjects and the generality of the findings obtained.

In this book, we focus primarily on the societies of three East Asian countries: Japan, South Korea, and Taiwan. China is dealt with in Chapter 8. This comparative study between industrialized East Asian societies provides an opportunity for quasi-natural experiments because of economic, cultural, geopolitical, and institutional proximities (Brinton 2001). Japan, Korea and Taiwan are highly industrialized societies and their educational level is as high as industrialized societies in Western Europe and North America—such as France and the United States. They have also all been strongly influenced by Chinese culture, in their adoption of Confucianism as the basis of their ethical thinking and in the use of Chinese characters in their writing systems. They were all under the influence of the United States after World War II, and their military, political and economic alliances with the United States continued thereafter and remain to the present day. Japan was democratized in the 1940s, and Korea and Taiwan in the 1980s. In Korea and Taiwan, the colonial governments introduced Japanese institutional systems during the period of Japanese colonial rule. Even after colonial rule ended, some policies in Korea and Taiwan were modeled on Japanese ones due to the fact that economic development had taken place in Japan earlier. These proximities make it easier to interpret the differences of social stratification between Japan, Korea and Taiwan. If they were totally dissimilar, it would be almost impossible to infer possible causes of the differences in social stratification. In view of this, in this study North Korea is excluded because it is simply too different from Japan, South Korea and Taiwan. Singapore and Vietnam are similarly excluded due to their great differences. Even though we do mention China in passing, and focus on it in Chapter 8, it too is in fact very different in terms of its political and economic systems.

This study was planned as part of a research project on the reconstruction of the public and private spheres (Ochiai 2010), and designed to offer an innovative approach to understanding labor markets and social stratification. Labor is a crucial subject for public discussion and policy, but it cannot be divorced from private interpersonal relationships. The expanded role of companies deeply affects not only government policy but private human relations as well (Coleman 1982). Labor markets are influenced by the changing behavior and role of companies and governments, but also by those of households as well. Studying labor markets is therefore essential not only in itself but for any understanding of how to reconstruct the public and private spheres.

To shed light on the reconstruction of the public and private spheres, it is essential to consider the role of gender and its role in labor markets and social stratification. Labor markets and social stratification are closely related to the gendered division of labor and the family system, and so it is unrealistic to ignore gender when studying these topics. As will be discussed later, a focus on gender is crucial when considering the characteristics of East Asia, and this book therefore pays particular attention to the relationship between gender, labor markets, and social stratification.

In the next section we review comparative sociology, and examine in particular how social stratification theory has viewed East Asia. A general overview of the characteristics of labor markets and social stratification in contemporary East Asia is followed by an outline of this book.

2 East Asia and International Comparisons of Labor Markets and Social Stratification

2.1 *Cross-national Comparisons of Intergenerational Mobility*

Cross-national comparative research on social stratification and labor markets began relatively early. From the perspective of industrialism, Lipset and

Bendix's (1959) study on intergenerational mobility was the leading cross-national comparative study in this field. However, no unified classification of occupations existed at the time of their study, and data comparability and available analytical techniques were limited. In the 1970s, research was conducted in several countries, and international networks of researchers began to evolve, creating the necessary conditions for cross-national comparisons (Hout and DiPrete 2006). Common international classification schemes were devised, such as the Comparative Analysis of Social Mobility in Industrial Nations (CASMIN) educational classification,[2] and the Erikson–Goldthorpe–Portocarero class schema (Erikson et al. 1982).

Featherman et al. (1975) played a leading role in cross-national comparative studies of social stratification. They examined the association between the occupations of fathers and sons, and hypothesized that a pattern of intergenerational mobility (now referred to as "relative mobility")[3] is common to societies with market economies and nuclear families. This hypothesis led to the Featherman–Jones–Hauser (FJH) hypothesis, which states that intergenerational mobility patterns are common to industrialized societies. The FJH hypothesis did not explicitly assert that convergence occurs, but the idea of the convergence of the mobility pattern through industrialization could be easily deduced from it. The FJH hypothesis has since been studied and tested by many researchers. As a result, a supporting theory developed, which held that patterns of association were common, but the strength of association was different (Erikson and Goldthorpe 1992).

An examination of changes during the 1970s in eight countries resulted in a finding that not all societies' patterns of relative mobility start to resemble each other as industrialization proceeds, calling into question the idea of the

---

2 The CASMIN research project reconciled different occupational and educational classifications in different societies, allowing for more data comparison than was previously possible.

3 Featherman et al. (1975) called the pattern of mobility "circulation mobility," distinguishing this from forced/structural mobility. However, the idea of dividing total mobility into forced mobility and circulation mobility cannot be accurately expressed within the dominant analytical framework, the log-linear model (Sobel 1983; Sobel et al. 1985); thus, concepts of absolute mobility and relative mobility came into use. Absolute mobility describes movement into a class different from one's original class, and the absolute mobility rate is the number of people who undergo this movement divided by the total population. Relative mobility is expressed as an odds ratio, and represents the degree of mobility between classes after eliminating the effects of marginal distribution of the mobility table. For example, when a class shrinks rapidly, as the agricultural class did after World War II in many industrialized societies, the absolute mobility rate is high, but as most agriculturists were born into the agricultural class, the relative mobility rate is low.

trend toward convergence (Erikson and Goldthorpe 1992). Breen and Luijkx (2004), analyzing the intergenerational mobility of European countries from the 1970s to 1990s, showed that as similarity between class distributions increased, similarity between absolute mobility rates also increased. They also pointed out, however, that there was a tendency during the 1990s for relative mobility to diffuse. Social mobility theory can thus be seen to have delivered the *coup de grâce* to convergence theory. It came to be widely acknowledged that factors other than industrialization influenced social mobility and class structure, and that the next step in social mobility theory was to discover these other factors.

Few East Asian societies have been the subject of comparative studies on intergenerational mobility. Japan has been a frequent subject of comparative research (Erikson and Goldthorpe 1992; Ganzeboom et al. 1989; Grusky and Hauser 1984; Ishida et al. 1995), but Korea, Taiwan, and China have rarely been considered systematically in comparative studies, and single-county research typically predominates (Bian 2002; Cheng and Dai 1995; Park 2004; Wang 2002).

2.2 *Gender, Family, and Labor Markets*

In addition to studies on intergenerational mobility, cross-national comparisons have been carried out of gender or racial segregation, intra-generational mobility, and wage differentials. When Marxism and industrialism were popular as theories, it was believed that the passage of time would solve not only class conflict but also all other social problems. However, as these theories lost credibility, social inequality came to be studied from a number of angles. If inequality due to origin and home environment is an issue, then naturally inequality due to gender or race is likewise, and it is important to consider not only class but also inequality from perspectives such as wages (England 1984), poverty rate (DiPrete 2002), and property (Chang 2012). Discovering the social causes and results of unequal opportunities has thus been recognized as a major task in social stratification research (Hout and DiPrete 2006; Kerckhoff 1995).

Research into gender, family, and labor markets is particularly vital when considering social stratification in East Asia. A longstanding tradition was to exclude women from intergenerational mobility studies, but to exclude women in any studies in labor in East Asia, when they account for half of the population and over 40 percent of the labor force, is unreasonable, at least in research at the individual level (Acker 1973; Sørensen 1994). Even at the household level, it is difficult to imagine doing so for societies where women have high social status, for societies where married couple's statuses are not equal, or for societies with large numbers of single-parent households.

Division of household and childcare labor and household composition cannot be ignored when considering women's employment. As life courses become more diverse, the necessity to analyze them more comprehensively is widely recognized (Mayer 2009). With the fluidization of employment in recent years, research attempting to understand the conditions of the labor market has increased (Davis-Blake and Uzzi 1993; Korpi and Levin 2001; Houseman et al. 2003). Interest in labor market conditions in East Asia is also high (Cao and Hu 2007; Kye 2008; Sakaguchi 2011; Takenoshita 2008).

Most East Asian societies have family systems that differ from those in the West, making inequality in East Asia different from that in the West. For example, the birth order of siblings affects academic achievement in many parts of Asia, but research shows that in the United States the youngest child is likely to receive higher marks than the firstborn, whereas in Taiwan and Japan the firstborn child is likely to receive higher marks than the youngest child, a trend particularly marked in male children (Fujihara 2012; Yu and Su 2006). As will be explained in the next section, the rate of women who leave their jobs when they marry or have children is still high in Korea and Japan, and so research has been done on the causes of this phenomenon and its social background (e.g., Brinton 2001; Brinton et al. 2001; Yu 2005; Yamato 2008).

One characteristic of labor markets and hierarchical structures in societies in East Asia is the relatively high proportion of small businesses, self-employment, and family-owned businesses (Takenoshita 2011). Because this has a strong bearing on female employment, gender inequality and female roles in the self-employed sector have been extensively studied, particularly for the case of Taiwan (Greenhalgh 1994; Stites 1982; Lu 2001). Small businesses have minimal bureaucracy, and often allow for flexible working patterns, and even women who bear the large share of responsibility for housework and childcare can work relatively easily. On the other hand, blatant discrimination often exists in the self-employed sector, and the status of women is ambiguous. Despite the many similarities between Japan, Korea, and Taiwan, there are still differences between them that may differentiate relationships between gender and labor markets. For example, women are less marginalized in labor markets in Taiwan than in Japan and Korea. In addition, the labor force participation rate of females is higher (Brinton 2001; see also Section 3.2 in this chapter), the wage difference between sexes is smaller (Brinton 2001; Chang and England 2011), and the exit rate from labor markets upon marriage is lower in Taiwan than in the others (Lee and Hirata 2001; Yu 2005). Such advantages for Taiwanese women are not based in tradition, since female labor force participation rate was as low in Taiwan as in Japan and Korea until the 1970s (Brinton 2001). One reason lies in the increasing labor shortage in Taiwan owing to the rise of export-oriented economy in the 1970s, which concentrated on labor-intensive industries such as textile industries (Brinton, Lee and Parish 2001). This raised the female labor force participation rate in Taiwan. Japan and Korea in contrast have been more oriented to capital-intensive industries, with the result that the issue of labor shortage was less critical and women stayed home even during the economic boom in the 1980s.

Although Japan and Korea are relatively similar to each other, women's economic status is somewhat higher in Korea than in Japan (Chang and England 2011; Tarohmaru 2014). The difference may derive from differences in the structure of organizations and labor markets in Japan. Although the proportion of small businesses is high in Japan, Korea, and Taiwan, it is especially high in Korea and Taiwan. The preponderance of smaller-sized organizations leads to the relative underdevelopment of internal labor markets.[4] In contrast, in Japan, where internal labor markets are generally widespread, there is the phenomenon of the "transfer," where regular employees in companies are transferred to places in the country that are quite far from home. This phenomenon of job transfer often makes it difficult for women to remain in the workplace in Japan.

Japanese internal labor markets are highly segregated along gender lines. Male employees are expected to work long hours, while women are expected to take part-time jobs. This makes difficult for men to contribute to family life, and for women to keep a fulltime job. In return for high commitment to the job, which may well involve transfers and require geographical flexibility and lengthy work hours, Japanese male employees enjoy relatively high employment protection and salaries that are often sufficient to feed their family with one sole income (Yu 2005). This employment system contributes to the maintenance of patriarchy in Japan.

The recession that ensued after the burst of Japan's so-called "bubble economy" in the early 1990s had the effect of bringing about a reduction in the size of internal labor markets. However, the basic structures of gender segregation and labor markets survived (Sato 2010; see also Chapter 4 of this book). While the labor force participation rate of married women with small children has

4 An internal labor market is a job market within an organization such as an office or factory which has job ladders. New employees usually accede to jobs at the lowest rungs of the ladder, while jobs at the higher rungs are filled by employees within the organization through promotion or transfer. Job-seekers outside the organization are often excluded from competition for vacant positions. Thus, employees in the internal labor market are protected from competition with outsiders and their wage and working conditions determined by the rules of the organization, not by market mechanisms. In contrast, there is no job ladder in external labor markets, where all job seekers compete with each other and their wage is determined by market mechanisms.

risen gradually over the last 30 years, the percentage of nonstandard employees among both female and male workers has also increased. The net result has been that women's status in the workplace is still low in Japan despite their rising labor force participation.

2.3 *Social Institutions, Labor Markets, and Social Stratification*

What factors besides industrialization affect the labor market, social stratification, and social mobility? Recently, researchers have been addressing institutions and systems. While income inequality can be addressed by systems of income redistribution, several other types of institution have a material impact on social mobility. The educational system, for example, has a significant impact. Educational achievement mediates between class origin and class destination, though the strength of that connection varies depending on the characteristics of the education system. According to Müller and Shavit (1998), the relationship between educational attainment and class destination is strong in societies where higher education is not widespread, where there is a high percentage of vocational education, and where the educational system is stratified.[5] It follows that social mobility rates and patterns can be altered through changing the educational system. In addition, intergenerational mobility is mediated by educational attainment, and relative mobility rates increase when there is less inequality in educational opportunities due to class origin (Beller and Hout 2006).

The magnitude of inequality, the rates of social mobility, and the patterns of mobility can also greatly depend on the policy framework of the welfare regime (DiPrete et al. 1997; Esping-Andersen 1990). Various factors—such as the strength of employment protection and active equal opportunity policies, benefits for the elderly, benefits for homemakers, immigration policy, and the severity of regulatory measures against corporations—are believed to affect inequality and social mobility. Here, we will briefly discuss the effects of employment protection.

When employment protection is strong, as indeed it is in Japan and other countries with conservative regimes, those who become unemployed often encounter difficulty in getting re-employed (Mayer 1997). People entering the labor market for the first time, such as young people, may have difficulty finding jobs because few positions are available (Breen and Buchman 2002). An unintended consequence thus emerges that seems to run counter to the original

5 A stratified education system is basically the same as a bifurcated education system. A stratified education system is one in which the tracks in a bifurcated system ultimately lead to class destinations.

intention: employment protection seems to cause unemployment rates to remain high. However, when human capital is measured with higher accuracy, we find that employment protection and low youth unemployment rates are not incompatible (Breen 2005). Requiring employment protection only from companies over a certain size, as is done in Italy, leads to those companies outsourcing various jobs to small companies that are not bound by the regulations. This means that small self-owned businesses are encouraged, but their work is not protected (Castells and Portes 1989). Perverse outcomes such as these can ultimately defeat the purpose of employment protection policies.

How have studies on East Asian social stratification analyzed the effects of such social institutions? Müller and Shavit's (1998) comparative analysis of education and status attainment included Japan in its study of the relationship between education system and social stratification. Even though the Japanese education system has not been stratified and is quite diverse, the relationship between education and status in Japan was stronger than the model predicted, an exception among the countries considered. Arum et al. (2007) examined the relationship between inequality of educational opportunity and higher education systems in 15 countries, and Japan, Korea, and Taiwan were given as cases of diversified systems. Diversified systems are higher education systems that include various types of institutions offering a wide range of content, such as vocational schools and junior colleges as well as research universities. (The United States and Israel, for example, have diversified systems.) In contrast, Europe's higher-education system includes only research universities or research universities and vocational schools. Diversified systems are characterized by high rates of privatization, with significantly higher numbers of people enrolled in higher education. Privatization itself increases inequality in educational opportunities, but as the increase in the enrollment rate reduces inequality, these effects cancel each other out. Diversified systems thus do not show a particularly high level of inequality in educational opportunities.

Regarding the relationship between stratification and the welfare regime in East Asia, much investigation remains to be done. There are several theories about the kinds of welfare regimes that exist in Japan, Korea, and Taiwan; however, they tend to be all mentioned in the context of southern European countries as examples of "familist" regimes (Goodman and Peng 1996; Miyamoto et al. 2003), or all treated as part of the same "East Asian regime" (Lee and Ku 2007). Both categorizations acknowledge that the family is extremely important in welfare in East Asia. The idea that women and younger generations are exploited and subordinated in these regimes remains strong. However, an in-depth comparative study has yet to be conducted.

2.4 *Speed and Timing of Modernization and Post-industrialism*

Several recent theories have focused on the speed and timing of modernization. Japan, Korea and Taiwan underwent industrialization much later than Western countries. This is considered to have had an effect on major industry, the acquisition of technical skills, and industrial relations (Dore 1974; Hattori 2005). Modernization in East Asia was not only late but also more rapid; processes that took centuries in the west occurred here in the space of a few decades, which again considerably affected the nature of modernization, giving rise to the notion of "compressed modernization," used mainly in the context of Korea (Chang 1999). The speed of modernization is thought to affect the timing of demographic transitions, and to be a factor in the rapid aging of the population (Ochiai 2010). In addition, according to Koo (1990), rapid industrialization in Korea impeded the creation of the sense of class culture among industrial workers. In the West the working class was able to maintain its culture of guilds and artisans as industrialization progressed slowly starting in the 16th century. In contrast, the rapid pace of industrialization in Korea, especially from the 1960s, meant that a majority of factory workers came from rural areas and did not identify with artisan culture.

Further, later and rapid modernization had an effect on the development of the welfare system in Korea (Kim 2009). Whereas Western countries were able to experience a golden age of the welfare state, starting at the end of World War II and lasting until the oil shock of the late 1970s, due both to an upgrading of social welfare systems and the high economic growth. Korea was industrialized over a period of approximately 30 years, with democratization coming in 1987. However, just when conditions were finally in place for the provision of social welfare, the Asian economic crisis occurred, and the world economy entered a period of stagnation. Social welfare and neoliberal Western-style policies were thus instituted without a golden age of the welfare state ever occurring (Kim 2009).

The impact of compressed modernization on labor markets and social stratification remains largely unexplored. The higher the rate of change is in industrial structures, the quicker the change in occupational distribution between generations. Consequently, the absolute mobility rate must significantly increase (Park 2004). How the relative mobility rate is affected, however, remains unclear. One theory suggests that the educational system develops rapidly in societies with later modernization because of the necessity to import technology and knowledge from developed countries. Accordingly, a rapidly increasing level of education should also increase equalization of opportunities. However, the results of analysis are mixed and do not show a clear trend in the relative mobility rate in late industrialized societies (Ishida and Miwa 2011; Whelan and Layte 2002).

While the concept of industrialization is given pride of place in social stratification theory, the issue of post-industrialism is important when considering female employment. As will be discussed in Chapter 5, although the expansion of the service industry has increased female employment, it may also have had the effect of locking women into low-wage occupations (Mandel and Semyonov 2006). In addition, post-industrialism is singled out as the main cause of rising wage inequality since the 1980s because it both deprives skilled workers of their jobs and leads to the creation of more low-paid sales and service jobs (Alderson and Nielsen 2002). Some theories also assert that the transformation of these industrial structures is closely related to the development of the global economy (Friedmann 1986; Sassen 1991), even as globalization tends to spread ideals of universalism, meritocracy, and reduced gender inequality (Meyer 2003). Globalization is also connected to the intensification of competition and the mobility of employment (Mills and Blossfeld 2005).

2.5 *Comparative Sociology in East Asia*

One approach in comparative research on East Asian societies is to compare societies within East Asia. In cross-national comparative research, it is typical to compare Japan (or Korea or Taiwan) with Western societies. However, recent years have seen an increase in research that compares Japan, Korea, and Taiwan (in some cases, China as well) with each other. Brinton (2001) was the first to use this approach. She argued that comparing different societies within East Asia with relatively similar histories and institutions allows the characteristics and circumstances of each society to be understood more accurately. This is in essence the same approach as that adopted by Western researchers who limit their comparisons to Western societies. In the 2000s, sufficient comparable data started to be accumulated in East Asia, beginning with the East Asian Social Survey, making it much easier to perform comparisons within East Asia.

In a comparison of the determinants of income and class identification in Japan, Korea, and Taiwan, Arita (2009) has shown that in Korea and Japan company size and employment status (self-, regular, and irregular employment) have the strongest influence, while occupation type has a strong influence in Taiwan. These variations spring from differences in labor markets and the social security system. Chang and England (2011) analyzed the gender wage gap in Japan, Korea, Taiwan, and China, and showed that the wage gap is greatest in Japan (where women receive 49 percent of men's wages), and smallest in Taiwan (where women receive 79 percent of men's wages), with Korea in the middle. Analyzing the factors that cause gender wage disparities, Chang and England found that in Japan gender difference in rates of irregular employment characteristically lead to gender wage disparity, while in Korea differences in years of education have a relatively large effect on wage disparity. In Taiwan, on the other hand, gender differences in years of employment have a relatively large effect. Tarohmaru (2011) analyzed the wage gap between regular and irregular employment in Japan, Korea, and Taiwan and found that the wage disparity between regular and irregular employment is high in Japan and Taiwan but low in Korea. In Japan one of the main factors in disparity is the closed coalition of executives and regular employees, referred to collectively as the "business community," which keeps the wages of irregular employees depressed. The low wages of irregular employees in Taiwan are caused by their concentration in the informal sector.

Several East Asian comparisons of social mobility have been conducted. Takenoshita (2007) compared rates of intergenerational social mobility in Japan, Korea, and China, and found that the mobility rate between white-collar and blue-collar workers in China is high compared with that in Japan and Korea. He argued that this was influenced by the Chinese socialist system. Yu (2005) argued that the differences between the labor markets in Japan and Taiwan explain why the proportion of women leaving the labor force upon marriage is higher in Japan than in Taiwan. In both countries, he argued, the primary reason why married women stop working is the difficulty of balancing work with household and childcare activities. However, Taiwan has an acute labor shortage: female workers are thus sought-after by employers. In Japan there is the expectation that regular employees will work long hours, making it difficult for women to continue working, since they are still considered responsible for taking care of the household. There is a greater number of small enterprises in Taiwan, making it relatively easy for married women there to adopt flexible work patterns.

While various dynamics have emerged with respect to labor markets and social stratification in East Asian societies, there is still an overwhelming lack of comparative research compared with that accumulated in the West. How are globalization and the fluidization of employment progressing in East Asia? Huge changes have taken place in the gendered division of labor and the female employment system over the last one hundred years, but what forms do they presently take? What sort of influence does social stratification have on people's identities? What sort of effects do social institutions and industrial structures have on labor markets and social stratification? These questions have not yet been fully explored. This book will attempt to address these issues.

3 Overview of Labor Markets and Social Stratification in East Asia

This section will present a brief overview on the basic features of labor markets and social stratification in East Asia. We will begin by sketching the characteristics of Japan, Korea, Taiwan, and China using data provided by the International Labour Organization (ILO) and the International Social Survey Programme (ISSP) 2009, supplemented with data from the East Asian Social Survey (EASS) 2008. Although the ILO and Organization for Economic Co-operation and Development (OECD) provide detailed data for Japan and Korea, data on Taiwan are fairly limited, and data on China even more so. The ISSP 2009 and EASS 2008 will therefore be used.

3.1 *Higher Education*

Let us consider the higher education graduation rate as a basic measure indicating the amount of human capital among workers. Figure 1.1 shows the rate of higher education graduates among people aged 18–60 years and the ratio of women among them. Of the countries in East Asia, Korea has the highest rate of graduation from higher education, and China the lowest. However, the popularization of higher education has increased rapidly among the younger generation in Korea, Taiwan, and China. Limiting the calculation to the younger generation would therefore give a much higher ratio. The scatterplot in Figure 1.1 shows a tendency for the proportion of women to rise when the overall percentage of people graduating from higher education rises. In Japan, Korea, and Taiwan, however, the proportion of women is relatively low when compared with societies that have the same overall graduation rate. This tendency for relatively low investment in women's human capital is one characteristic of East Asian economies.

3.2 *Labor Force Participation*

In general, East Asian countries have high labor force participation rates in comparison with Europe and the United States. However, labor force participation rates for women are relatively low. Plotting women's labor force participation rates by age in Japan and Korea still gives an M-shaped curve, and they are the only OECD countries where this is the case. Figure 1.2 shows a scatter plot of labor force participation rates by gender. The higher to the upper right in the diagram a country is, the higher the labor force participation rate is for both men and women. Since the horizontal axis represents women and the vertical axis represents men, a position in the upper left of the figure shows that the male labor force participation rate is high compared with the female labor force participation rate. Looking at their positions on the vertical axis, Korea,

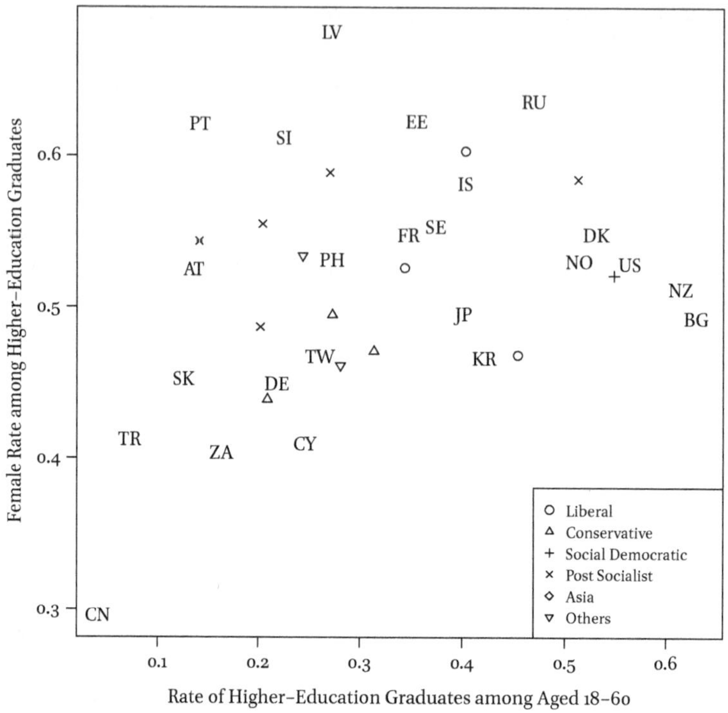

FIGURE 1.1 *Rate of higher education graduates and rate of women among higher education graduates*

AT: Austria; BG: Bulgaria; CN: China; CY: Cyprus; DE: Germany; DK: Denmark; EE: Estonia; FR: France; IS: Iceland; JP: Japan; KR: South Korea; LV: Latvia; NO: Norway; NZ: New Zealand; PH: Philippines; PT: Portugal; RU: Russia; SE: Sweden; SI: Slovenia; SK: Slovak Republic; TR: Turkey; TW: Taiwan; US: United States; ZA: South Africa.

Note: Other countries (Australia, Belgium, Switzerland, Chile, Czech Republic, Spain, Finland, Great Britain and/or United Kingdom, Croatia, Hungary, Israel, Poland, Ukraine) are classified by welfare regime and regions.

SOURCE: ISSP 2009

China, and Taiwan are all high, showing that the male labor force participation rate is high. The combined male and female labor force participation rates in East Asia are at a relatively high position (results not shown), but the labor force participation rate of women is not as high as that of men. In Figure 1.2, the straight line, which passes through the origin, indicates where the male and female labor force rates are equal. The closer a point is to the line, the lower the disparity in male and female labor force participation. Japan, Korea, and Taiwan are farther from the line than other societies, showing that gender differences in labor force participation are relatively large. The 2007 ILO data show the same results for Korea and Japan (results not shown).

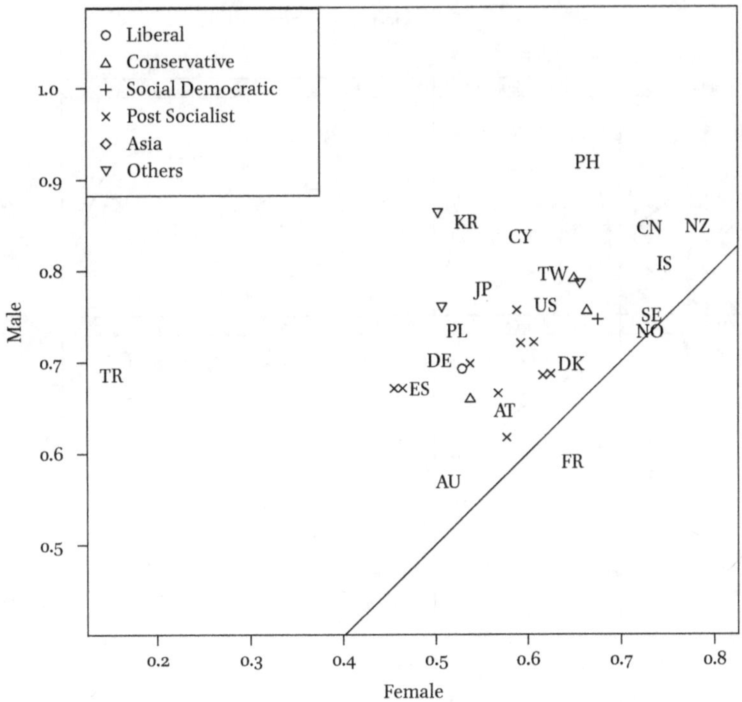

FIGURE 1.2 *Labor force participation rate, 2009*
AT: Austria; AU: Australia; CN: China; CY: Cyprus; DE: Germany; DK: Denmark; ES: Spain; FR: France; IS: Iceland; JP: Japan; KR: South Korea; NO: Norway; NZ: New Zealand; PH: Philippines; PL: Poland; TR: Turkey; TW: Taiwan; US: United States; SE: Sweden.
SOURCE: ISSP 2009. AGED 18–64 YEARS

Figure 1.3 shows the male and female labor force participation rates by age for various countries, including Japan, Korea and Taiwan. Here we see that it is rare for female labor force participation rates to map out into a clear M-shape in societies other than in Korea and Japan. The United States, Germany, and the Czech Republic show a distribution that slightly resembles an M, but the decline in the labor force participation rate of women in their thirties is much smaller in these countries than in Korea and Japan. China and Taiwan's data come from EASS, so while the comparison may be imperfect, we see that no M-shape curve exists in China or Taiwan.

3.3 *Unemployment*

Next we will examine unemployment rates. Table 1.1 shows combined values for men and women, since male and female unemployment rates are highly correlated. The unemployment rate is particularly low in Korea and at about

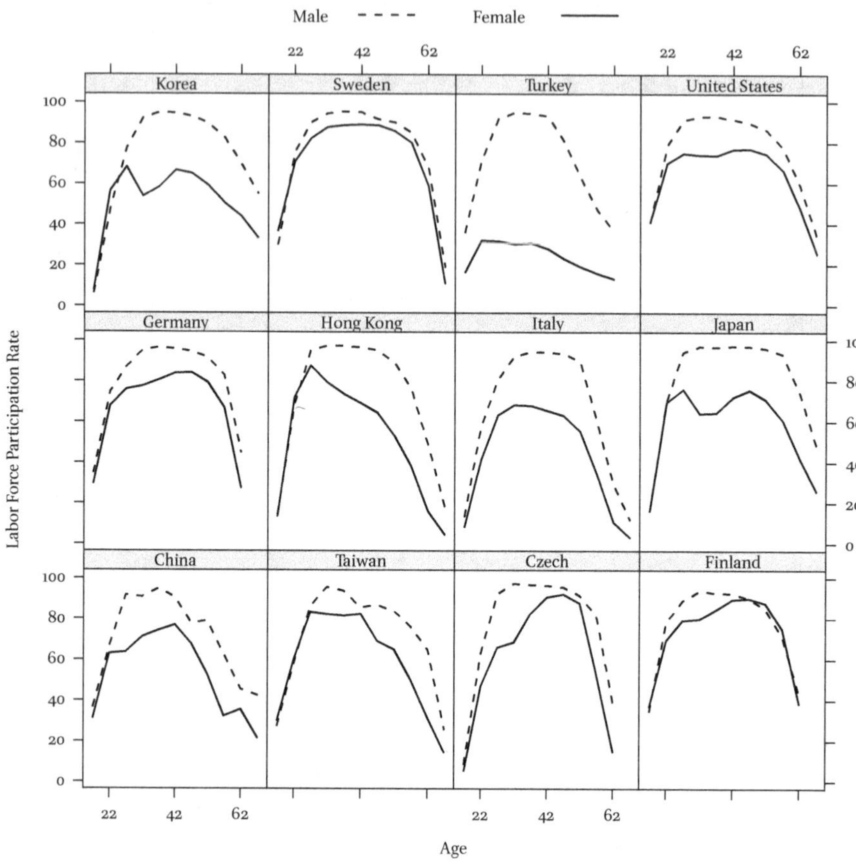

FIGURE 1.3 *Labor force participation rate by age, gender, and society*
Note: The lowest age category is 16–19 years for United States, 18–19 years for China and Taiwan, and 15–19 years for the others.
SOURCE: CHINESE AND TAIWANESE DATA ARE FROM EASS 2008. OTHER DATA ARE FROM ILO LABORSTA 2007

4 percent in Japan, Taiwan, and China. Out of the 114 countries that provided data for the 2007 ILO database, these are among the lowest rates seen. When the economy is steady, the self-employment sector tends to absorb unemployed workers, leading to a reduction in the unemployment rate. This function has been identified in Japan and Korea. Self-employment may play a similar role in Taiwan and China. However, the number of self-employed people in fact shows a downward trend in all these countries with the exception of China, and so the question of whether such rates can be maintained in any future recession remains unclear.

TABLE 1.1 *Perfect unemployment rates in 2007 and ranking (ascending order)*

	Unemployment rate	Ranking among 114 societies
Korea	3.2	16
Japan	3.9	26
Taiwan	3.9	27
China	4.0	29
Mean of 114 societies	7.9	

SOURCE: ILO LABORSTA 2007

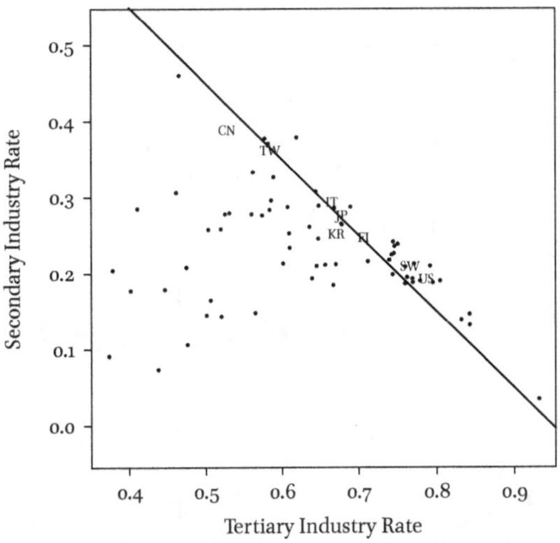

FIGURE 1.4 *Rates of workers employed in secondary and tertiary industries*
CN: China; FI: Finland; IT: Italy; JP: Japan; KR: Korea; SW: Sweden; TW: Taiwan; US: United States.
SOURCE: ILO LABORSTA 2007

3.4 *Industrial Structure*

Next, let us turn to industrial structure. Figure 1.4 plots the percentage of people engaged in secondary and tertiary industries in 74 countries in 2007. A point closer to the bottom left of the graph indicates a smaller number of workers employed in secondary and tertiary industries. In other words, the percentage of people engaged in primary industry is high. The straight line shows the case where the sum of the percentage of workers in the secondary and tertiary industries is 95 percent (with 5 percent in the primary industry). Western countries, Japan, Korea, Taiwan, and China are positioned roughly along this line, with approximately 5 percent of workers engaged in agriculture, forestry, and fishery. As this line climbs to the upper left of the graph, secondary industries decline while tertiary industries grow, that is, post-industrialization occurs. China and Taiwan have not experienced post-industrialization to any great extent, while Japan and Korea show an industrial structure similar to that of Germany and Italy, with the United States, the United Kingdom, and Sweden on one side and Taiwan and China on the other.

Let us now look at the proportion of people working in the public sector and the self-employed sector (the self-employed and those working in family businesses). Figure 1.5 uses data from 39 countries, showing the proportion of

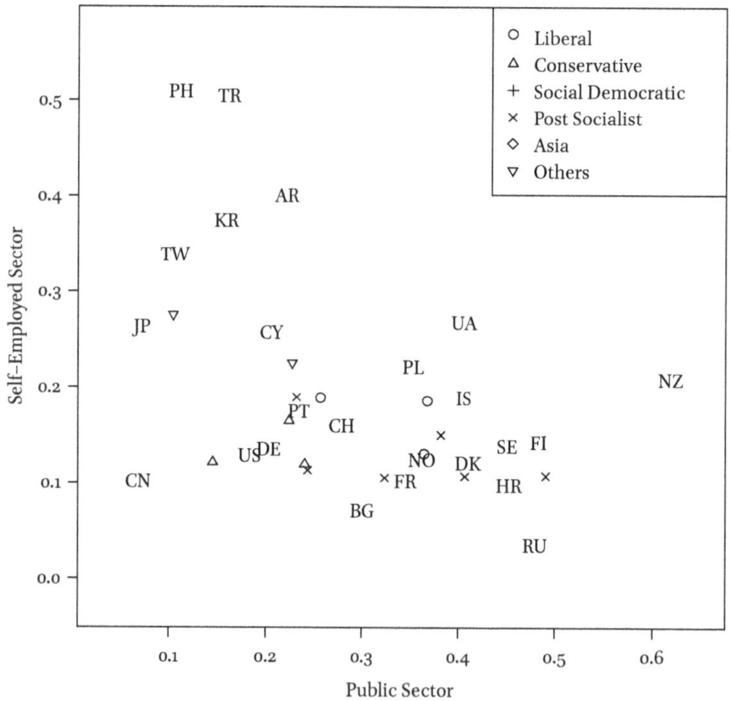

FIGURE 1.5 *Rate of workers employed in public and self-employed sectors*
AR: Argentina; BG: Bulgaria; CH: Switzerland; CN: China; CY: Cyprus; DE: Germany; DK: Denmark; FI: Finland; FR: France; HR: Croatia; IS: Iceland; JP: Japan; KR: South Korea; NO: Norway; NZ: New Zealand; PH: Philippines; PL: Poland; PT: Portugal; RU: Russia; SE: Sweden; TR: Turkey; TW: Taiwan; UA: Ukraine; US: United States.
Note: Public sector: Employed by government, a publicly owned firm, or non-profit organization.
Self-employed sector: Self-employed or family worker.
SOURCE: ISSP 2009, AGED 18–60 YEARS

people working in the public sector on the horizontal axis and the proportion of self-employed or family workers on the vertical axis. The figure shows that the proportion of workers employed in the public sector in Japan, Korea, Taiwan, and China is relatively low. In addition, it shows that the scale of self-employment is rather large in Japan, Korea, and Taiwan, but not in China.

To summarize, East Asian countries generally have low unemployment rates, strong economies, and high labor force participation rates. However, the gender differences in educational attainment and labor force participation are larger than those in other societies, and their industrial structure supports this. Industrialization has progressed to a level comparable with that in the West, but post-industrialization has not. This may have contributed to low female labor force participation rates. There are many women working in the public sector in the West. The smaller public sector in East Asia may be related to the low labor force participation rates for females. Another unique characteristic of East Asia is the relatively large self-employed sector. Further research into the nature of this sector is required.

4 Central Question and Themes of This Book

The central question that this book aims to address is how social or institutional contexts shape the structure of labor markets and social stratification. A variety of topics are discussed—job mobility, unemployment, gender segregation, class identity, and suicide—but they all pertain to the question of how labor markets and social stratification relate to social and institutional contexts. Two of the most important social contexts are gender and family system and they are explored in depth. In some chapters, however, the focus is on other contexts such as labor policy and welfare regimes, and gender is mentioned simply as a control variable. From these somewhat different angles, we analyze the relationship of social stratification with social or institutional contexts in East Asia. We aim to look both at trends in labor markets in East Asia, and to point out commonalities and differences with Western counterparts. I will now give a short summary of the chapters of this book.

4.1 *Transformation of Labor Markets in East Asia*

Chapters 2–4 discuss the features and transformation of labor markets in modern East Asian societies. In Chapter 2, Sakaguchi considers gender differences and the impact that increasing globalization and employment fluidization in Japan and Taiwan have on involuntary unemployment. Blossfield and other researchers have studied employment fluidization through globalization in Europe and the United States, and have shown that just as the effects of globalization vary depending on the welfare regime, its impact also varies depending on gender and age (Mills et al. 2005). However, Sakaguchi's study is the first of its kind for East Asia. According to Sakaguchi, the probability of experiencing involuntary unemployment due to layoffs, insolvency, shutdowns, or contract expiration (hereafter referred to collectively as "unemployment risk") rose in both Taiwan and Japan after World War II. However, this unemployment risk is strongly influenced by the institutions of each society. In Japan, workers have a lower unemployment risk in the internal labor market than in the external labor market, because the internal labor market developed in large firms. In contrast, in Taiwan, despite the privileges enjoyed by state-owned companies, the internal labor market is not as well developed. These different labor market structures give rise to different reactions to the increasing employment fluidization caused by globalization between the two countries. In Japan, unemployment risk is higher in the external labor market. In Taiwan, it increases uniformly in both types of labor markets, with no marked difference—although risk does depend on human capital and occupation. The differences in increasing employment fluidization are also reflected in gender disparities. In Japan women are likely to work in the external labor market, so the unemployment risk for women has continued to grow after World War II. However, unemployment risk has not risen as much for men. In contrast, there is no gender difference in Taiwan, and unemployment risk increased by the same amount for both genders.

In Chapter 3, Phang discusses transformations in the Korean labor market after the 1997 Asian economic crisis. The Korean labor market changed significantly at this time due to intervention by the International Monetary Fund (IMF). However, Phang focuses on mobility barriers between permanent and fixed-term employment and on the differences between the primary and secondary labor markets. In the primary labor market, high levels of human capital are required, wages relatively high, social security well developed, and employment stable; whereas the secondary labor market does not have these protections. Because of this, although the primary labor market overlaps with the concept of an internal labor market to a large extent, they cannot be said to match perfectly.

Requirements in terms of career, skill levels, and skill qualities differ between fixed-term employment[6] and permanent employment, and between the primary

6 Although fixed-term employment is a component of irregular employment, the two concepts are not interchangeable. The concept of irregular employment has been used in Korea in recent years, but because the idea of part-time jobs does not exist in Korea, unlike in Japan, the meaning of the term differs slightly between Japan and Korea.

and secondary labor markets. Hence, mobility for workers between the two markets is relatively low. Labor markets are also considered to be divided into three or more "segments." Chapter 3 shows how this segmentation of the labor market changed after 1997.[7] According to Phang, the proportion of fixed-term employment did not continue to rise in Korea, unlike in Japan. More specifically, although it rose after the 1997 economic crisis, it peaked in 2002, and has been decreasing ever since. In 2010 it fell to approximately the same level as in 1996. Nevertheless, it is worth noting that approximately 40 percent of workers in Korea are still in fixed-term employment, a higher proportion than in Japan.

In general, voluntary employment turnover declines in times of recession. This phenomenon is thought to be particularly evident for good jobs. Thus, because there is less likelihood for employment turnover among permanent employees and those in the primary labor market, no vacancies there are created, leading to greater difficulty in mobility away from temporary employment and the secondary labor market. Phang confirms that this trend existed in Korea after 1998. Of particular interest is that this closed labor market trend has continued even after the economy recovered, suggesting that it is not the result of simple economic fluctuations, but rather that the closed nature of labor markets intensified in the wake of the economic crisis.

In Chapter 4, Yamato analyzes the phenomenon of Japanese women leaving employment at times of marriage and childbirth. In Japan and Korea, the percentage of women who leave the labor force to get married and to have children is high. Because of this, the labor force participation rate among women in their thirties shows a sharp decline. This M-shaped employment pattern has impeded the development of women's careers and their accumulation of human capital.[8] In Japan, this is said to be due to the Japanese employment system, where workers are divided into three types: core workers (mostly male regular employees), marginalized workers (mostly unmarried regular female employees), and irregular workers (both male and female workers). The strong trend for unmarried regular female workers to stop working after marriage or childbirth is the direct cause of the M-shaped employment pattern. However, behind this lies the fact that male core workers accept extremely long working hours and the possibility of geographic relocation ("transfers") in exchange for sufficiently high wages to support a family on a single income. However, this

7 It should be noted that the ambiguity in the term "segmentation of the labor market" leads some to make the argument that the concept is not useful.

8 Human capital refers to accumulated skills and knowledge useful for production, gained and enhanced through education and on-/off-the-job training.

sort of Japanese employment system is not universal, nor is it necessarily evident in small enterprises. The practice of leaving the labor force after marriage or childbirth is most widely seen in clerical employment, and less evident in other occupations. Further, the percentage of women who do continue working, whether because they are provided with additional support by their parents in order to live, or out of the desire to supplement their husband's earning power, is growing.

Yamato shows that increasing employment mobility and the policy of employment growth for women after the 2000s have had certain effects on the Japanese employment system. Specifically, the M-shaped pattern in the labor force has become less marked recently, meaning that even controlling for various related factors, the percentage in the cohort of workers born from 1971 to 1980 who leave the labor force after marriage is smaller than in the previous cohort. The marriage turnover rate in medium to large firms and clerical services has fallen, and there is no longer a difference between small and large firms and between clerical and other jobs. Yamato shows that marriage turnover rates have declined even when parents do not provide support and when husbands earn high income. Regarding childbirth as opposed to marriage turnover however, despite a slight improvement in rates, the usual features of the Japanese employment system can still be seen. In addition, women in irregular employment are more likely to leave the labor force than are women in regular employment, suggesting that an increase in female irregular employees could mean an increase in the number of women who drop out of the labor force after childbirth.

In Chapter 5, Shibata investigates the effect of labor markets and labor policies on suicide rates. Suicide rates in Japan and Korea have increased since the late 1990s. However, while Japan's rate seems to have reached a plateau, Korea's has continued to increase. In 2009, Korea became the country with the highest suicide rate of all the OECD nations. This is thought to relate to the neo-liberal policies imposed by the IMF and the conditions of the labor market. However, according to Shibata, labor market indicators such as unemployment rate do not in themselves affect the suicide rate. More important are active labor policies and marriage—a strong social and family net, in other words—which can provide a strong deterrent. Although unemployment rates do not have a direct effect on suicide rates, they may be mediated through the marriage rates. Further detailed analysis of this issue is necessary.

4.2 *Gender and Social Stratification in East Asia*

While the first half of this book considers the changing labor markets in East Asia, the second half looks at the structure of social stratification in East Asia with a special focus on gender issues.

In Chapter 6, Oda, Yamato, and Tarohmaru analyze the ways in which the strength of occupational gender segregation differs across Japanese prefectures. Occupational segregation generally shows certain similarities across many societies. Women are more likely to get non-manual jobs than men, while men are more likely to get manual jobs. This is referred to as horizontal occupational gender segregation. In addition, there is a trend of vertical occupational gender segregation, whereby women tend to get jobs with lower socioeconomic status than men. These trends can be seen in many economically developed countries, but the degree of occupational segregation varies by society. According to Charles and Grusky (2004), horizontal segregation is strengthened by post-industrialization, whereas vertical segregation is weakened by gender egalitarian ideology. This chapter analyzes these hypotheses using prefectures as the unit of analysis.

When making cross-national comparisons, we often fall into the trap of overlooking regional diversity within countries. Oda et al. state that geographic diversity is significant in regard to gender egalitarianism and post-industrialism, and that it cannot be reduced simply to the difference between urban and rural areas. The strength of gender egalitarian ideology helps women progress in higher education and into professional and managerial occupations. It also weakens vertical segregation in non-manual fields. However, it has no effect on the other forms of occupational gender segregation. This is because horizontal segregation is based on gender essentialism, which suggests that men are suited to physical labor and women to taking care of the weak and to communicating, and as such it does not conflict with gender equality. On the other hand, because post-industrialism encourages women to enter non-manual occupations, horizontal segregation becomes stronger. However, in Japan, where the female labor force participation rate is lower than in the West, vertical segregation within non-manual jobs weakens because there is a large inflow into high-status non-manual jobs. In addition, as post-industrialism progresses, the percentage of women in manual jobs decreases. However, because that tendency is particularly pronounced in skilled manual jobs, vertical segregation within manual jobs strengthens. These trends differ from those seen in research in the west. This is mainly caused by a low female labor force participation rate in Japan and the fact that post-industrialization has generally not progressed as far as it has in the west.

In Chapter 7, Takenoshita focuses on self-employment in East Asia and discusses the nature of the relationship between gender and the labor market. As Marx foresaw, self-employment has shown an overall decline in many countries. However, after the oil shock, in some countries a large number of workers started up their own businesses during the recession, with a resulting increase in self-employment. It is now generally accepted that self-employment will continue to exist to a certain degree because of its flexibility, specialization, and conduciveness to entrepreneurship. In East Asia, while self-employment has continued to decrease overall, the percentage of self-employed workers is still much higher than in the West, and these workers cannot be ignored when considering labor markets and social stratification. It is generally held that discrimination against women still pertains in the labor market, but most research until now has focused on large firms or households. Self-employed women have not been researched in any depth. Self-employment may be a style of work that enables women to more easily maintain a good work-life balance since it offers a relative freedom in terms of time for women who still bear responsibility for childcare and running the household. However, there are also many cases where self-employed people have to work extraordinarily long hours, and women may still suffer discrimination from their business partners, customers, and employees. How such factors affect the duration of female self-employment is analyzed in this chapter.

Comparing Japan, Korea, and Taiwan, Takenoshita makes the following points. In all three countries, self-employed women are more concentrated than men in occupations such as piano teacher, home tutor, hairdresser, and food-service worker, but less in occupations such as real estate agent, driver, and manufacturing/construction workers. Japan has the highest duration rate of self-employment for both men and women, and compared with Korea and Taiwan, fewer new businesses are set up and fewer go out of business. Thus, the self-employed sector has formed a relatively stable labor market in Japan. The percentage of women who quit being self-employed is higher than men in all countries; however, after controlling for related variables, we find that the effect of gender is not actually significant in Japan or Taiwan, but is significant in Korea. It is thought that women are more apt than men to quit self-employment in Japan and Taiwan because women in these countries are concentrated in self-employment with relatively high turnover, such as restaurant work. However, in Korea, self-employed women find it easy to quit for reasons that cannot be reduced to occupation type alone.

In Taiwan and Korea married women are more likely than unmarried women to continue with self-employment, suggesting that this form of employment is easier for married women to maintain. However, this tendency cannot be observed in Japan, illustrating how difficult it must be to find a work-life balance in Japan. In addition, there is a tendency among self-employed men in Japan for their fathers to also be self-employed or for their wives to work in the family business, which makes continuing self-employment easier. However, this is not seen for women, suggesting that the amount of useful assistance that self-employed women receive from their families is limited. In contrast, in Korea this tendency is not seen in either men or women, because few people inherit family businesses from their parents, a factor that is believed to lie behind the many unstable small-scale businesses in Korea. In Taiwan, there is a trend for both men and women to receive some form of family assistance in maintaining their self-employed businesses. However, the details differ between men and women.

In Chapter 8, Chang, Xie, Takamatsu and Kim analyze status identification in Japan, Korea, Taiwan, and China. Previous chapters provided an analysis of the objective aspects of labor markets and social stratification, but including subjective aspects into the analysis and considering them together allows for more comprehensive understanding. The trend for the majority of people to identify as belonging to the middle stratum of society is not limited to East Asia, and has also been observed in the West. However, in general this identification is thought to be affected by economic, cultural, and social capital. Which of these factors has the strongest effect may differ depending on a society's class structure.

According to Chang et al., the average level of status identification is high in Japan and China and low in Taiwan and Korea. This is largely consistent with the hypothesis that there is a tendency for the average level of status identification to be high in countries with high GDP per capita. However, such a hypothesis cannot explain the high level of status identification in China. It may be more convincing to explain the high level through differences in the reference group and in class image, rather than through the absolute level of affluence (Fararo and Kosaka 2003). Regardless of the explanation, this is a problem that must wait for further theoretical development. In the study presented in Chapter 8, musical tastes were introduced into the model as an indicator of cultural capital; however they were found to have no significant impact on status identification. In East Asia, an individual's educational attainment and the level of their household income have the strongest impact on status identification; educational attainment has a relatively high effect in China and Taiwan, but no significant effect in Korea and Japan.[9] On the other hand, levels of household income have a relatively high effect in Korea and Japan. From this we can see that material factors strongly define status identification in East Asia.

9 Since previous research has held that educational attainment increases status identification in Korea and Japan, these results might be unexpected. In this study, English-speaking ability was introduced into the model, with the effect of increasing status identification in all four countries. It may be that this mediates the effect of educational attainment.

References

Acker, Joan. 1973. "Women and Social Stratification: A Case of Intellectual Sexism." *The American Journal of Sociology* 78(4): 936–945.

Alderson, Arthur S. and Francois Nielsen. 2002. "Globalization and the Great U-Turn: Income Inequality Trends in 16 OECD Countries." *American Journal of Sociology* 107(5): 1244–1299.

Arita, Shin. 2009. "A Comparative Study of Social Stratification in East Asian Societies: The Reward Differences between Occupation and Social Inequality." *Japanese Sociological Review* 59(4): 663–681 (in Japanese).

Arum, Richard, Adam Gamoran and Yossi Shavit. 2007. "More Inclusion than Diversion: Expansion, Differentiation, and Market Structure in Higher Education." In Yossi Shavit, Richard Arum and Adam Gamoran, eds., *Stratification in Higher Education: A Comparative Study*, 1–35. Studies in Social Equality. Stanford: Stanford University Press.

Beller, Emily and Michael Hout. 2006. "Welfare States and Social Mobility: How Educational and Social Policy May Affect Cross-national Differences in the Association between Occupational Origins and Destinations." *Research in Social Stratification and Mobility* 24(4): 353–365.

Bian, Yanjie. 2002. "Chinese Social Stratification and Social Mobility." *Annual Review of Sociology* 28(1): 91–116.

Breen, Richard. 2005. "Explaining Cross-national Variation in Youth Unemployment." *European Sociological Review* 21(2): 125–134.

Breen, Richard and Marlis Buchman. 2002. "Institutional Variation and the Position of Young People: A Comparative Perspective." *American Academy of Political & Social Science* 580: 288–305.

Breen, Richard and Ruud Luijkx. 2004. "Conclusions." In Richard Breen, ed., *Social Mobility in Europe*, 383–410. Oxford: Oxford University Press.

Brinton, Mary C. 2001. "Married Women's Labor in East Asian Economies." In Mary C. Brinton, ed., *Women's Working Lives in East Asia*, 1–37. Stanford: Stanford University Press.

Brinton, Mary C., Yean-Ju Lee and William L. Parish. 2001. "Married Women's Employment in Rapidly Industrializing Societies: South Korea and Taiwan." In Mary C. Brinton, ed., *Women's Working Lives in East Asia*, 38–69. Stanford: Stanford University Press.

Cao, Yang and Chiung-Yin Hu. 2007. "Gender and Job Mobility in Post-socialist China: A Longitudinal Study of Job Changes in Six Coastal Cities." *Social Forces* 85(4): 1535–1560.

Castells, Manuel and Alejandro Portes. 1989. "World Underneath: The Origins, Dynamics, and Effects of the Informal Economy." In A. Portes and Manuel Castells, eds., *The Informal Economy: Studies in Advanced and Less Developed Countries*, 11–37. Johns Hopkins University Press.

Chang, Chin-Fen and Paula England. 2011. "Gender Inequality in Earnings in Industrialized East Asia." *Social Science Research* 40(1): 1–14.

Chang, Mariko L. 2012. *Shortchanged: Why Women Have Less Wealth and What Can be Done About It*. Oxford: Oxford University Press.

Chang, Kyung-Sup. 1999. "Compressed Modernity and Its Discontents: South Korean Society in Transition." *Economy and Society* 28(1): 30–55.

Charles, Maria and David Grusky. 2004. *Occupational Ghettos: The Worldwide Segregation of Women and Men*. Stanford: Stanford University Press.

Cheng, Yuan and Jian-Zhong Dai. 1995. "Intergenerational Mobility in Modern China." *European Sociological Review* 11(1): 17–35.

Cohen, Gerald A., 2000. *Karl Marx's Theory of History: A Defence*. Princeton: Princeton University Press.

Coleman, James S. 1982. *The Asymmetric Society*. New York: Syracuse University Press.

Davis-Blake, Alison and Brian Uzzi. 1993. "Determinants of Employment Externalization: A Study of Temporary Workers and Independent Contractors." *Administrative Science Quarterly* 38(2): 195–223.

DiPrete, Thomas A. 2002. "Life Course Risks, Mobility Regimes, and Mobility Consequences: A Comparison of Sweden, Germany, and the United States." *American Journal of Sociology* 108(2): 267–309.

DiPrete, Thomas A., Paul M. Graaf, Ruud Luijkx, Michael Tåhlin and Hans-Peter Blossfeld. 1997. "Collectivist versus Individualist Mobility Regimes? Structural Change and Job Mobility in Four Countries." *American Journal of Sociology* 103(2): 318–358.

Dore, Ronald P. 1974. *British Factory-Japanese Factory: The Origin of National Diversity in Industrial Relations*. London: Allen and Unwin.

England, Paula. 1984. "Wage Appreciation and Depreciation: A Test of Neoclassical Economic Explanations of Occupational Sex Segregation." *Social Forces* 62(3): 726–749.

Erikson, Robert and John H. Goldthorpe. 1992. *The Constant Flux: A Study of Class Mobility in Industrial Societies*. Oxford: Clarendon Press.

Erikson, Robert, John H. Goldthorpe and Lucienne Portocarero. 1982. "Social Fluidity in Industrial Nations: England, France and Sweden." *British Journal of Sociology* 33: 1–34.

Esping-Andersen, Gosta, 1990. *The Three Worlds of Welfare Capitalism*. Princeton: Princeton University Press.

Fararo, Thomas J. and Kenji Kosaka. 2003. *Generating Images of Stratification: A Formal Theory*. Dordrecht: Kluwer Academic Publishers.

Featherman, David L., F. Lancaster Jones and Robert M. Hauser. 1975. "Assumptions of Social Mobility Research in the U.S.: The Case of Occupational Status." *Social Science Research* 4(4): 329–360.

Friedmann, John. 1986. "The World City Hypothesis." *Development and Change* 17(1): 69–83.

Fujihara, Sho. 2012. "Sibling Configuration and Status Attainment in Japan: Multilevel Analyses of Sibling Data." *Soshioroji* 57(1): 41–57 (in Japanese).

Ganzeboom, Harry B.G., Ruud Luijkx and Donald J. Treiman. 1989. "Intergenerational Class Mobility in Comparative Perspective." *Research in Social Stratification and Mobility* 8: 3–84.

Goodman, Roger and Ito Peng. 1996. "Welfare States in East Asia." In Gosta Esping-Andersen, ed., *Welfare States in Transition: National Adaptation in Global Economy*, 192–224. Newbury Park: Sage.

Greenhalgh, Susan. 1994. "De-orientalizing the Chinese Family Firm." *American Ethnologist* 21(4): 746–775.

Grusky, David B. and Robert M. Hauser. 1984. "Comparative Social Mobility Revisited: Models of Convergence and Divergence in 16 Countries." *American Sociological Review* 49(1): 19–38.

Hattori, Tamio. 2005. *Economic Sociology of Development: Economic Development and Social Transformation in Korea*. Bunshindo (in Japanese).

Houseman, Susan N., Arne L. Kalleberg and George A. Erickcek. 2003. "The Role of Temporary Agency Employment in Tight Labor Markets." *Industrial & Labor Relations Review* 57(1): 105–127.

Hout, Michael and Thomas A. DiPrete. 2006. "What We Have Learned: RC28's Contributions to Knowledge about Social Stratification." *Research in Social Stratification and Mobility* 24(1): 1–20.

Ishida, Hiroshi and Satoshi Miwa. 2011. "Comparative Social Mobility and Late Industrialization." Paper presented at the annual meeting of the American Sociological Association, Las Vegas, U.S.A.

Ishida, Hiroshi, Walter Muller and John M. Ridge. 1995. "Class Origin, Class Destination, and Education: A Cross-national Study of Ten Industrial Nations." *American Journal of Sociology* 101(1): 145–193.

Kerckhoff, Alan C. 1995. "Institutional Arrangements and Stratification Processes in Industrial Societies." *Annual Review of Sociology* 21: 323–347.

Kerr, Clark. 1983. *The Future of Industrial Societies: Convergence or Continuing Diversity?* Cambridge: Harvard University Press.

Kerr, Clark, John T. Dunlop, Frederick H. Harbison and Charles A. Myers. 1960. *Industrialism and Industrial Man: The Problem of Labor and Management in Economic Growth*. Cambridge: Harvard University Press.

Kim, Sung-Won. 2009. "Social Changes and Welfare Reform in South Korea: In the Context of the Late-Coming Welfare State." *International Journal of Japanese Sociology* 18(1): 16–32.

Koo, Hagan. 1990. "From Farm to Factory: Proletarianization in Korea." *American Sociological Review* 55(5): 669–681.

Korpi, Tomas and Henrik Levin. 2001. "Precarious Footing: Temporary Employment as a Stepping Stone Out of Unemployment in Sweden." *Work, Employment and Society* 15(1): 127–148.

Kye, Bongoh. 2008. "Internal Labor Markets and the Effects of Structural Change: Job Mobility in Korean Labor Markets between 1998 and 2000." *Research in Social Stratification and Mobility* 26(1): 15–27.

Lee, Yean-Ju and Shuichi Hirata. 2001. "Women, Work, and Marriage in Three East Asian Labor Markets: The Cases of Taiwan, Japan, and South Korea." In Mary C. Brinton, ed., *Women's Working Lives in East Asia*, 96–124. Stanford: Stanford University Press.

Lee, Yih-Jiunn and Yeun-Wen Ku. 2007. "East Asian Welfare Regimes: Testing the Hypothesis of the Developmental Welfare State." *Social Policy and Administration* 41(2): 197–212.

Lipset, Seymour M. and Reinhard Bendix, eds. 1959. *Social Mobility in Industrial Society*. Berkeley: University of California Press.

Lu, Yu-Hsia. 2001. "The 'Boss's Wife' and Taiwanese Small Family Business." In M.C. Brinton, ed., *Women's Working Lives in East Asia*, 263–297. Stanford: Stanford University Press.

Mandel, Hadas and Moshe Semyonov. 2006. "A Welfare State Paradox: State Interventions and Women's Employment Opportunities in 22 Countries." *American Journal of Sociology* 111(6): 1910–1949.

Marshall, Thomas H. and Thomas Bottmore. 1987. *Citizenship and Social Class*. Pluto Press.

Marx, Karl and Freidrich Engels. 1848. *Communist Manifesto*.

Mayer, Karl U. 1997. "Notes on a Comparative Political Economy of Life Courses." *Comparative Social Research* 16: 203–226.

———. 2009. "New Directions in Life Course Research." *Annual Review of Sociology* 35(1): 413–433.

McCall, Leslie and Christine Percheski. 2010. "Income Inequality: New Trends and Research Directions." *Annual Review of Sociology* 36(1): 329–347.

McTague, Tricia, Kevin Stainback and Dondal Tomaskovic-Devey. 2009. "An Organizational Approach to Understanding Sex and Race Segregation in U.S. Workplaces." *Social Forces* 87(3): 1499–1527.

Meyer, Lisa B. 2003. "Economic Globalization and Women's Status in the Labor Market: A Cross-national Investigation of Occupational Sex Segregation and Inequality." *Sociological Quarterly* 44(3): 351–383.

Mills, Melinda and Hans-Peter Blossfeld. 2005. "Globalization, Uncertainty and Early Life Course: A Theoretical Framework." In Hans-Peter Blossfeld, Erik Klijzing, Melinda Mills and Karin Kurz, eds., *Globalization, Uncertainty and Youth in Society*, 1–24. Routledge.

Mills, Melinda, Hans-Peter Blossfeld and Erik Klijzing. 2005. "Becoming an Adult in Uncertain Times: A 14-Country Comparison of the Losers of Globalization." In Hans-Peter Blossfeld, Erik Klijzing, Melinda Mills and Karin Kurz, eds., *Globalization, Uncertainty and Youth in Society*, 423–441. Routledge.

Miyamoto, Taro, Ito Peng and Takafumi Uzuhashi. 2003. "Place and Dynamics in the Japanese Welfare State." In Gosta Esping-Andersen, ed., *Welfare States in Transition: National Adaptations in Global Economies*, 295–336. Waseda University Press (in Japanese).

Müller, Walter and Yossi Shavit. 1998. "The Institutional Embeddedness of the Stratification Process: A Comparative Study of Qualifications and Occupations in Thirteen Countries." In Yossi Shavit and Walter Müller, eds., *From School to Work: A Comparative Study of Educational Qualifications and Occupational Destinations*, 1–48. Oxford: Clarendon Press.

Neckerman, Kathryn M. and Florencia Torche. 2007. "Inequality: Causes and Consequences." *Annual Review of Sociology* 33(1): 335–357.

Ochiai, Emiko. 2010. "Reconstruction of Intimate and Public Spheres in Asian Modernity: Familialism and Beyond." *Journal of Intimate and Public Spheres* (pilot issue): 2–22.

Park, Hyunjoon, 2004. "Intergenerational Social Mobility among Korean Men in Comparative Perspective." *Research in Social Stratification and Mobility* 20: 227–253.

Sakaguchi, Yusuke, 2011. "Trend Analysis of Unemployment Risk: Effects of the Expansion of Non-standard Jobs and Change of Determinants." *Soshioroji* 55(3): 3–18 (in Japanese).

Sassen, Saskia. 1991. *The Global City: New York, London, Tokyo*. Princeton: Princeton University Press.

Sato, Yoshimichi. 2010. "Stability and Increasing Fluidity in the Contemporary Japanese Social Stratification System." *Contemporary Japan* 22(1–2): 7–21.

Sobel, Michael E. 1983. "Structural Mobility, Circulation Mobility and the Analysis of Occupational Mobility: A Conceptual Mismatch." *American Sociological Review* 48(5): 721–727.

Sobel, Michael E., Michael Hout and Otis D. Duncan. 1985. "Exchange, Structure, and Symmetry in Occupational Mobility." *American Journal of Sociology* 91(2): 359–372.

Sørensen, Annemette. 1994. "Women, Family and Class." *Annual Review of Sociology* 20: 27–47.

Stites, Richard. 1982. "Small-Scale Industry in Yingge, Taiwan." *Modern China* 8(2): 247–279.

Takenoshita, Hirohisa. 2007. "Intergenerational Mobility in East Asian Countries: A Comparative Study of Japan, Korea and China." *International Journal of Japanese Sociology* 16(1): 64–79.

———. 2008. "Voluntary and Involuntary Job Mobility in Japan: Resource, Reward and Labor Market Structure." *Sociological Theory and Methods* 23(2): 85–104.

———. 2011. "International Comparison of Labor Market Structure and Mobility to Self-employment." In Hiroshi Ishida, Hiroyuki Kondo and Keiko Nakao, eds., *Structure of Inequality and Mobility: Contemporary Stratified Society* 2, 37–51. University of Tokyo Press (in Japanese).

Tarohmaru, Hiroshi. 2011. "Income Inequality between Standard and Nonstandard Employments in Japan, Korea and Taiwan." In Yoshimichi Sato and Jun Imai, eds., *Japanese Employment under Reforms: Changes in Welfare and Structural Inequality*, 54–70. Melbourne: Trans Pacific Press.

———. 2014. "Factors in the Wage Differential between Standard and Nonstandard Employment: A Comparison of Japan, South Korea, and Taiwan." In Emiko Ochiai and Leo A. Hosoya, eds., *Transformation of the Intimate and the Public in Asian Modernity*, 144–163. Brill.

Wang, Haiyan. 2002. "Class Structures and Social Mobility in Taiwan in the Initial Post-war Period." *The China Journal* (48): 55–85.

Whelan, Christopher T. and Richard Layte. 2002. "Late Industrialization and the Increased Merit Selection Hypothesis. Ireland as a Test Case." *European Sociological Review* 18(1): 35–50.

Yamato, Reiko. 2008. "Is Japanese Mothers' Re-entry into the Labor Market as Part-Timers Associated with Lower Socioeconomic Status? A Comparison of the 1995 and 2005 SSM Surveys." In M. Nakai and I. Sugino, eds., *Social Stratification from a Life Course and Lifestyle Perspective, 121–136: The 2005 SSM Research Series Vol. 9*. 2005 SSM Chosa Kenkyukai (in Japanese).

Yu, Wei-Hsin. 2005. "Changes in Women's Post-marital Employment in Japan and Taiwan." *Demography* 42: 693–717.

Yu, Wei-Hsin and Kuo-Hsien Su. 2006. "Gender, Sibship Structure, and Educational Inequality in Taiwan: Son Preference Revisited." *Journal of Marriage and Family* 68(4): 1057–1068.

CHAPTER 2

Gender Difference in Unemployment Risk in the Face of Globalization: Effects of Institutional Factors in the Case of Japan and Taiwan[1]

Sakaguchi Yusuke

1 Institutional Factors Connected with Gender Difference in Unemployment Risk

The employment environment changed significantly in many advanced countries in the face of globalization in the second half of the 20th century. Employers increasingly found themselves having to deal with the need for employment flexibility and being required to adjust their employment situation accordingly. The increases in unemployment rate and in non-regular employment (which includes employment of part-timers and contract workers) have meant that employees also became more subject to unemployment risk.

Globalization, however, brings risk to different classes of people in different ways. People's occupations and careers are affected through institutional filters such as welfare regime, educational system, and employment system (Mills and Blossfeld 2005). The international comparative analyses on these issues have largely focused on Europe and the United States. They have shown that the classes of people susceptible to unemployment or downward mobility in the face of globalization vary depending on the institutional arrangements of the country in question (Blossfeld et al. 2005; Blossfeld et al. 2006; Blossfeld and Hofmeister 2006; Blossfeld et al. 2011). One comparative analysis (Sakaguchi 2011) focusing on Japan and Taiwan looked at the ways in which differences in unemployment risk changed in the period from 1950 to 2005, by firm size, employment type, education, and occupation. It found that in Japan, the segmental structure of its labor market, where unemployment risk is concentrated on non-regular employees and workers in small firms, remained stable and changed little. In Taiwan, on the other hand, the determinants of unemployment risk changed, as seen in an increase in the difference in risk between those with higher education and those with elementary education (Sakaguchi

1 The author would like to thank the 2005 SSM Survey Research Committee for permission to use the 2005 SSM Survey data, and Tokio Yasuda for use of his program syntax in creating the person-year data set.

DOI 10.1163/9789004262737_003

2011). The difference between the two countries was argued to stem from differences in employment protection regulation and the characteristics of their labor markets.

Whereas the above-mentioned study (Sakaguchi 2011) targeted male employees and (as stated above) analyzed change in differences in unemployment risk by firm size, employment type, education, and occupation, the study presented in this chapter includes women in its analysis and focuses on gender differences. The purpose is to clarify, based on a comparative analysis of Japan and Taiwan, how gender difference in unemployment risk has changed and what institutional factors affect the gender gap. Japan and Taiwan, both late-starting East Asian industrial countries, differ significantly in terms of labor market characteristics and female employment patterns. In Japan, the labor market, which centers on regular employees (*seisha-in*) of large firms, is characterized by segmentation. In Taiwan, small family-run firms have played a central role in the economy. In addition, in Japan, women often quit as regular employees at the time of marriage or childbirth and resume working at a later date as non-regular employees. In Taiwan, many women continue to work after marriage or childbirth.

In this chapter I examine how differences in institutional factors influence the gender difference in unemployment risk under globalization. In the following section, I will summarize institutional differences between Japan and Taiwan, particularly the characteristics of Japan's labor market, and set up a hypothesis as to the institutional factors leading to gender difference in unemployment risk. I will then present a comparative analysis of the situations in Japan and Taiwan. Section 5 summarizes and discusses the results.

2 Institutional Comparison of Japan and Taiwan

2.1 *Japan*

The Japanese employment system is generally characterized by long-term employment, seniority-based wage systems, and enterprise-based labor unions. Length of service in Japan is also generally longer than that in other advanced countries (Sato 1999). Employment is stable on the whole, but this stability also depends on firm size and employment type. Large firms play a central role in the economy, and there is a superordinate-subordinate structure in relationships among firms, where large firms contract work out to small and medium-sized firms (Hamilton and Biggart 1988). Individual large firms each have an internal labor market, and the employment of regular employees therein is stable. It is normal for regular employees to have stable long-term employment and to gain firm-specific skills through work. It is also not customary for firms to fire regular employees. In the external labor market, in contrast, competition is severe, much more so than in the internal labor markets, and employment is unstable. A study by Takenoshita (2008) shows that the rate of voluntary/involuntary job shifts is high for small firms and non-regular employees. As firms face pressure to deal with employment flexibility, it is employees in the external labor market who tend to become the target of employment adjustment.

With regard to the gender composition of the labor market, a large proportion of working women in Japan work outside the internal labor markets. There is still an expectation that women will focus on child rearing, and for this reason employers tend not to offer job training or promotion to women (Brinton 1993). Thus, Japanese women often follow a career path in which they stop working as regular employees at the time of marriage or childbirth and re-enter the labor market for non-regular employment after raising their families. In other words, there is a tendency for them to shift from regular employment to non-regular employment over their life course and to work as non-regular employees in the external labor market. The number of women with such non-regular employment rose through the 1970s and 1980s.

In Japan, one recent change in employment has been that the number of non-regular employees is on the rise, not only among early-middle-aged and middle-aged women, but also among young women—and indeed young people generally. In 2010, one in two early-middle-aged women (aged 35 to 44) worked as a non-regular employee, a situation that has been consistent since the 1990s. Non-regular employment among young people has increased markedly in recent years, and is something of a phenomenon. Between 1990 and 2010, the share of young employees (aged 15 to 24) among non-regular employees increased from 8.0 to 24.9 percent for males and from 13.3 to 37.8 percent for females (Ministry of Internal Affairs and Communications 2012). As these numbers show, the share of non-regular employees has increased significantly among young workers for both genders, but more so for young female workers. Women are now more likely to become non-regular employees not only after marriage or childbirth, but also at the beginning of their occupational career when they transition from school to work.

2.2 *Taiwan*

The internal labor markets in Taiwan are not as rigid as those in Japan. Whereas in Japan large firms comprise the core of the Japanese economy, in Taiwan there are numerous small family-run firms that play a central role in the economy quite separately from the large conglomerates (Hamilton and Biggart

1988). Such small family-run firms provide low wages, drive the country's export-oriented development, and also face severe international competition (Sumiya et al. 1992). Since small and medium-sized firms are the major force, a dual labor market centering on regular employees at large companies like that in Japan has not formed in Taiwan, and the difference between regular employment at large firms and other types of employment is thought to be small. Even so, researchers do point to a dual, public-private enterprise structure that stems from the nationalization of pre-Pacific War Japanese monopoly capital (Sumiya et al. 1992, 129–135). In Taiwan, employment protection regulation is also weaker than it is in Japan (Sumiya et al. 1992, 77–78). For such reasons, the rate of job shifts is higher, and employment is more fluid. The effect of educational attainment on job mobility is strong in such a fluid labor market, and labor market exhibits characteristics of the labor market that human capital is important (Kanbayashi and Takenoshita 2009, 55).

Regarding employment of women, Taiwanese women tend to stay on in their jobs both after marriage and childbirth, which contrasts with the case of Japanese women. The proportion of women staying on their jobs after marriage or childbirth in Taiwan increased during the 1960s and 1970s, and the kind of fall in the labor force participation rate observed for early-middle-aged Japanese women was not apparent (Yu 2009). This increase in the female labor force participation rate in Taiwan is attributed to a number of factors such as the large demand for skilled and highly educated labor, low wage levels for men, and an economy centering on small family-run firms rather than on large firms (Brinton et al. 2001; Yu 2009).

2.3 *Hypothesis*

Based on the institutional differences discussed above, this subsection sets up a hypothesis regarding the gender difference in changes in unemployment risk in Japan and Taiwan in the face of globalization. Blossfeld et al. (2011) compare European countries and reveals the following results in regard to change in employment risk in the face of globalization. In countries where labor market fluidity is low, such as Germany, Spain and Italy, the process of globalization deepens the chasm between a strongly protected male-dominated core group and periphery groups consisting of young people and women. In contrast, in countries with fluid employment, especially under the liberalistic regime in the United Kingdom, this kind of core-periphery chasm is relatively small, and individuals' resources such as skills and education strongly affect employment risk (Blossfeld et a. 2011). This result implies the following. In the globalization process, employers face pressure to deal with employment flexibility and thus a need to freely adjust their employment. In such a situation, in countries with strong employment protection regulation and low employment fluidity, it is not easy for employers to freely adjust the number of their existing employees, and they therefore tend to shift employment risk to peripheral groups. In contrast, in countries with weak employment protection regulation and high employment fluidity, employers face less need to shift employment risk to peripheral groups because it is relatively easy to adjust the number of their existing employees. However, on the downside, due to the ability to adjust employment relatively freely, differences in employment risk readily occur because of varying levels of individuals' resources.

In this context, the analysis described here examines how the gender difference in unemployment risk has changed in Japan and in Taiwan in the face of globalization. As we have seen, Japan has rigid internal labor markets and strong employment protection regulations. In such circumstances, even though globalization requires employers to have employment flexibility, employers cannot easily fire employees in their internal labor market. They therefore make employment adjustments in the external labor market by, for example, increasing the number of non-regular employees. Sato (2009) summarizes recent studies on social stratification in Japan and points out that while the employment of the core group has been stable, among periphery groups employment fluidity has increased. With regard to increased employment fluidity, many studies mention the fact that instability in youth employment increased in the mid-1990s (Genda 2001; Kosugi 2003), an issue that attracted much public interest. My main focus here, however, concerns female employment, not youth employment. There is an employment pattern in Japan where many women find non-regular employment in the external labor market: as employers face pressure for employment flexibility and an increasing need to freely adjust their employment, they try to handle the situation by increasing the number of female non-regular employees. As a result, women have tended to opt for non-regular employment: this entails high employment risk, which consequently has led to increased unemployment risk for women. In other words, the mechanism that is assumed here is not a simple increase in unemployment risk for women, but one in which prevalence of non-regular employment (which entails high employment risk) especially among women has increased the unemployment risk for women and has given rise to a gender difference in such risk.

HYPOTHESIS 1: In Japan, women's unemployment risk has increased by the expanse of non-regular employment among women and the gender difference in unemployment risk has increased in the period from 1950 to 2005.

In Taiwan, internal labor markets with strong employment protection did not develop as they did in Japan, and employment is highly fluid. Also, a large proportion of women stay on in their job after marriage or childbirth, and the employment pattern of women concentrating in non-regular employment observed in Japan is not observed. Notwithstanding the increasing pressure for employment flexibility brought by globalization, therefore, employers in Taiwan have not needed to increase female non-regular employees. This is why the gender difference in unemployment risk does not exist there and is not expected to increase.

HYPOTHESIS 2: In Taiwan, women's non-regular employment has not expanded and the gender difference in unemployment risk has not increased in the period from 1950 to 2005.

3 Data and Variables

3.1 *Data*

The data for Japan and Taiwan used in this analysis are taken from the 2005 National Survey of Social Stratification and Social Mobility (SSM Survey). A person-year data set is created from the data on the respondents' occupational history, which was answered retrospectively. The data describe the job situations of the respondents for each year. Only those under 50 years of age are considered because the number of retired people increases for those aged 50 or more. The analysis excludes self-employees and business owners and targets only employees. Those who engage in agriculture are also excluded. After eliminating observations with missing values, the number of observations is 46,350 for Japanese men (2,283 men, 4,420 jobs), 33,766 for Japanese women (2,624 women, 5,502 jobs), 32,162 for Taiwanese men (2,270 men, 6,158 jobs), and 24,974 for Taiwanese women (2,109 women, 5,359 jobs).

3.2 *Variables*

The dependent variable is the unemployment risk indicator, which is a binary variable indicating whether the individual experienced the event of an involuntary job shift in a given year. For occupational history, the 2005 SSM survey asks the reason for the job shift in the case of a change in a respondent's employer. An involuntary job shift for a given year is defined as separation from a job or a change of job that occurred in that year due to employer bankruptcy, business discontinuation, downsizing, or contract period completion.

Table 2.1 shows the frequency distribution of the variables in the person-year data set. As seen in the table, unemployment risk (the involuntary job shift risk) is 0.6 percent for Japanese men, 0.9 percent for Japanese women, 2.7 percent for Taiwanese men, and 2.7 percent for Taiwanese women. This shows the probability of an employee losing his or her job in each year.

The independent variables are defined as follows.

- *Firm size* has four categories: small firm (29 workers or less), medium-sized firm (30 to 299 workers), large firm (300 workers or more), and government agency.
- *Employment type* has two categories: regular employment and non-regular employment. However, the question regarding the respondent's employment type is different between Japan and Taiwan.[2] Therefore, private-sector employment and non-regular employment (part-time, dispatched, and contract workers) are considered for Japan, whereas regular employment and non-regular employment (part-time and temporary workers) are considered for Taiwan.
- *Occupation* is categorized into professionals or managers, clerical or sales workers, skilled workers, operators or assemblers, and elementary occupations, based on the International Standard Classification of Occupations (ISCO).
- *Educational attainment* has three categories: elementary, secondary, and tertiary education.
- *Experience at other firms* is the number of firms at which the respondent worked prior to the current employment. There are three categories: zero, one, and two or more.
- *Period* has four categories which are slightly different between Japan and Taiwan: for Japan, rapid economic growth period (1950–1970), early stable growth period (1973–1983), late stable growth period (1984–1993), and post-bubble stagnation period (1994–2004); for Taiwan, postwar economic growth period (1950–1973), post-oil-shock unstable growth period (1974–1985), stable growth period (1986–1995), and economic stagnation period (1995–2005).

---

2 For Japan, the choices for responding to the question are: manager or executive; self-employment, family employee, general employee who is constantly employed, temporary worker or part-timer, dispatched or contract worker. For Taiwan, they are: self-employment with employees, self-employment with no employee, family employee, employee (public, public-to-private), employee at a private firm, and temporary employee or part-timer.

TABLE 2.1 *Frequency distribution of variables in the person-year data set (percent)*

	Japan			Taiwan		
		Men	Women		Men	Women
Unemployment risk (involuntary job shift risk)	Other	99.4	99.1		97.3	97.3
	Event	0.6	0.9		2.7	2.7
Firm size	≤29 workers	24.3	34.2		41.4	42.1
	30 to 299 workers	25.3	31.4		18.8	22.1
	≥300 workers	36.4	24.7		16.7	19.8
	Public employment	14.0	9.6	Public employment	23.1	16.0
Employment type				Public employment	23.1	16.0
	Regular employment	96.4	71.9	Private-sector employment	67.9	75.6
	Non-regular employment	3.6	28.1	Non-regular employment	9.0	8.5
Occupation	Professional or managerial	26.2	19.6		30.6	24.1
	Clerical or sales	27.4	53.4		12.9	31.1
	Skilled	18.8	5.8		29.9	11.2
	Operator or assembler	22.2	14.8		19.9	19.9
	Elementary occupation	5.4	6.4		6.7	13.8
Educational attainment	Elementary	19.6	16.8		37.6	39.6
	Secondary	47.2	48.8		29.1	28.3
	Tertiary	33.2	34.4		33.3	32.1
Experience at other firms	0.0	55.6	44.8		28.3	33.6
	1.0	25.2	28.4		26.9	26.7
	≥2	19.2	26.7		44.7	39.7
Period	50–72	20.0	18.0	50–73	11.8	10.9
	73–83	25.8	21.6	74–85	25.3	24.7
	84–93	27.5	27.6	86–94	29.5	29.5
	94–04	26.7	32.8	95–05	33.4	34.9
N		46350	33766		32162	24974

SOURCE: 2005 SSM SURVEY

4 Analysis

4.1 *Comparison of Involuntary Job Shift Risk*

This subsection considers the probability of an employee losing his or her job in the case of Japan and Taiwan. Figure 2.1 shows graphs of the cumulative survival function estimated with the Kaplan-Meier method for men and women in each country. For both countries, as the number of service years increases, more people experience involuntary job shifts. That is, the survival function, which shows the proportion of those who do not experience involuntary job shift, is a decreasing function with respect to the number of service years. A comparison of Japan and Taiwan reveals, however, that the rate of the decrease is higher for Taiwan, which means that employees in Taiwan are more likely to experience an involuntary job shift. For Japan, the survival function declines more slowly as employees are less likely to be exposed to unemployment risk. For men, the probability of an involuntary job shift during 10 years of employment with the same employer is 9 percent for Japan and 27 percent for Taiwan. This shows that employees in Taiwan are three times more likely to experience an involuntary job shift than those in Japan.

4.2 *Japan: Increasing Gender Difference in Unemployment Risk*

This subsection considers whether the gender difference in unemployment risk increased in different periods. For the case of Japan, Figure 2.2 plots the rate of involuntary job shifts (annual average) for four periods for both men and women. For example, the rate for men is 0.8 percent for the 1950–1972 period. This means that men experienced involuntary job shifts with a probability of 0.8 percent on average each year during that time. As seen in the figure,

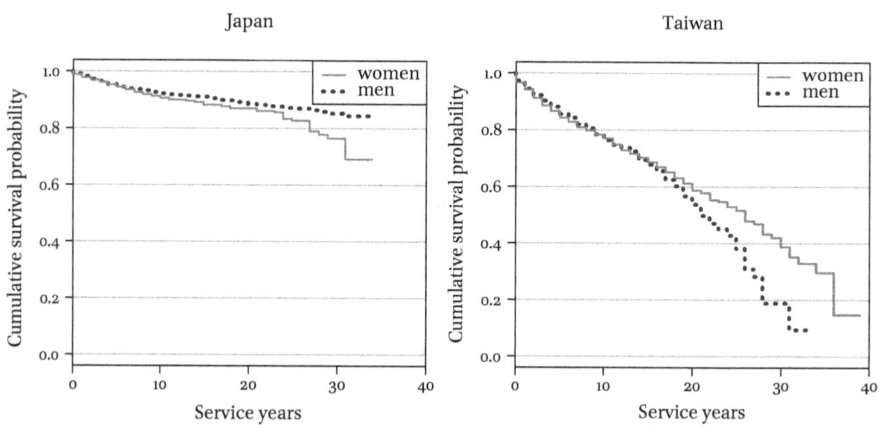

FIGURE 2.1 *Cumulative survival function estimated with the Kaplan-Meier method*
SOURCE: 2005 SSM SURVEY

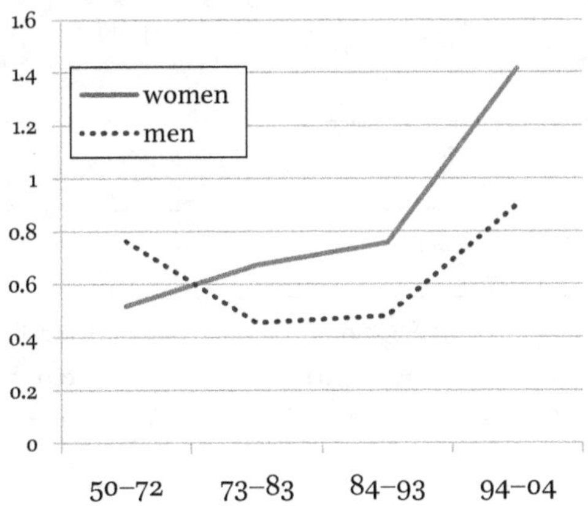

FIGURE 2.2
Rate of involuntary job shifts for different periods (percent, Japan)
SOURCE: 2005 SSM SURVEY

as unemployment risk increased for women, the gender difference in unemployment risk emerged.

We also looked into the question of whether the gender difference identified in the figure increased with time, after controlling for other factors. Table 2.2 shows the effects of independent variables influencing the involuntary job shift hazard, which is estimated using a discrete-time logit model. This model estimates occurrence probability of involuntary job shift at each year with control of another independent variable. The independent variables in Model 1 are age, firm size, educational attainment, occupation, experience at other firms, period, and gender (a dummy variable indicating female employees). In addition to these variables, interaction terms between periods and gender are included in Model 2, and a dummy variable for non-regular employment is also included in Model 3. As seen in Table 2.2, the coefficient of the dummy variable for female employees in Model 1 is 0.23 and is statistically significant, indicating that women are more likely to experience an involuntary job shift. As for the effect of the interaction between different periods and gender in Model 2, the coefficient of the interaction between the 1950–1972 period and female employee is negative (−0.74) and significant. In other words, a tendency for women to be more likely than men to experience an involuntary job shift emerged after 1973 in Japan.

With regard to the hypothesis discussed in Section 2, the gender difference in unemployment risk observed above for recent years appears to be attributed to increasing female non-regular employment. In order to examine this mechanism, a dummy variable for non-regular employment is added in Model 3, and changes in the coefficient of the interaction terms are analyzed. A comparison of Models 2 and 3 in Table 2.2 shows that as a result of adding the

TABLE 2.2 *Discrete-time logit analysis with involuntary shift hazard as dependent variable (Japan)*

	Model 1		Model 2		Model 3	
	Coef.	s.e	Coef.	s.e	Coef.	s.e
Intercept	−3.83	0.26 **	−3.88	0.26**	−4.10	0.26**
Age	−0.02	0.01 **	−0.02	0.01**	−0.02	0.01**
Small firm	0.30	0.10 **	0.30	0.10**	0.20	0.10*
Medium-sized firm (ref)	—		—		—	
Large firm	−0.21	0.12 *	−0.21	0.12*	−0.21	0.12*
Public employment	0.10	0.16	0.08	0.16	0.05	0.16
Elementary	−0.02	0.14	−0.01	0.14	0.00	0.14
Secondarily	−0.26	0.11 *	−0.26	0.11*	−0.24	0.11*
Tertiary (ref)	—		—		—	
Professional or managerial	−0.71	0.18 **	−0.71	0.18**	−0.31	0.18
Clerical or sales	−0.48	0.15 **	−0.47	0.15**	−0.20	0.15
Skilled	−0.49	0.18 **	−0.49	0.18**	−0.24	0.18
Operator or assembler	−0.36	0.16 *	−0.36	0.16*	−0.10	0.16
Elementary occupations (ref)	—		—		—	
No other firm (ref)	—		—		—	
1	0.43	0.11 **	0.41	0.11**	0.27	0.11*
≥2	0.65	0.12 **	0.61	0.12**	0.44	0.12**
50–72	−0.59	0.15 **	−0.30	0.18	−0.27	0.18
73–83	−0.59	0.12 **	−0.54	0.17**	−0.46	0.17**
84–93	−0.53	0.11 **	−0.59	0.17**	−0.52	0.17**
94–04 (ref)	—		—		—	
Female dummy	0.23	0.09 *	0.33	0.14*	−0.15	0.14
50–72 × female			−0.74	0.26**	−0.44	0.26
73–83 × female			−0.11	0.23	0.02	0.23
84–93 × female			0.13	0.22	0.17	0.22
94–04 × female			—		—	
Non-regular employment					1.17	0.11**
N	80116		80116		80116	

$^{*}p < 0.05$
$^{**}p < 0.01$
SOURCE: 2005 SSM SURVEY

dummy variable for non-regular employment, the coefficient of the interaction term that is significant in Model 2 becomes −0.44 (from −0.74) and is no longer significant. The coefficient of the dummy variable for non-regular employment is 1.17, indicating that non-regular employees face higher unemployment risk. This means that the gender difference in unemployment risk observed after 1973 stems from an increase among women in non-regular employment, which entails high unemployment risk.

4.3 *Japan: Effect of Increased Non-regular Employment on Unemployment Risk*

This subsection examines in detail the mechanism by which increased non-regular employment heightened unemployment risk in Japan. The following conjectures can be made regarding this mechanism. First, in Japan, as the proportion of non-regular employment started to rise in the second half of the 1980s, it became easier for people to work as non-regular employees. Second, non-regular employees are more likely to face involuntary job shift risk than regular employees (Takenoshita 2008). It is expected that due to a combination of these two factors, it became more likely for people to be in non-regular employment, which entails high employment risk, in more recent periods, and that this tendency raised the probability of employees experiencing unemployment.

Expressed in the diagram in Figure 2.3, the focus here is the connection from "passing of time" with non-regular employment and then to unemployment risk. This connection is examined first and then the connection from non-regular employment to unemployment risk is examined for men and women separately. Lastly, examination is made of the question of extent to which unemployment risk increased in recent years (the connection from passing of time to unemployment risk) through increased non-regular employment (the connection from passing of time to non-regular employment and then to unemployment risk).

With regard to the connection from passing of time to non-regular employment, Figure 2.4 shows the proportion of non-regular employment for each period. The proportion is on the rise for both men and women, but the increase is more drastic for women. In other words, the connection between passing of time to non-regular employment can be confirmed, and the increase in non-regular employment is greater for women.

As for the connection from non-regular employment to unemployment risk, Figure 2.5 shows the rate of involuntary job shifts (annual average) in each period for different employment types for both men and women. The variability of the rate for men is high as the proportion of non-regular employees

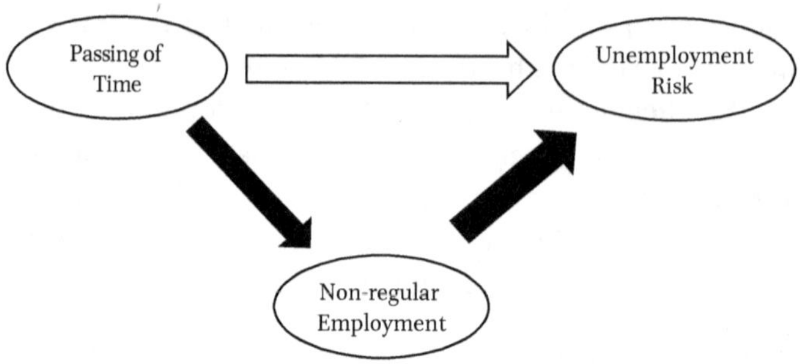

FIGURE 2.3 *Connections between passing of time, non-regular employment, and unemployment risk*

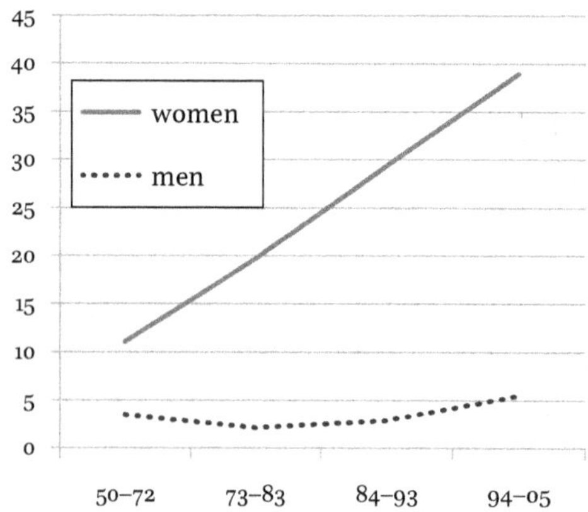

FIGURE 2.4 *Proportion of non-regular employment for different periods (percent, by gender, Japan)*
SOURCE: 2005 SSM SURVEY

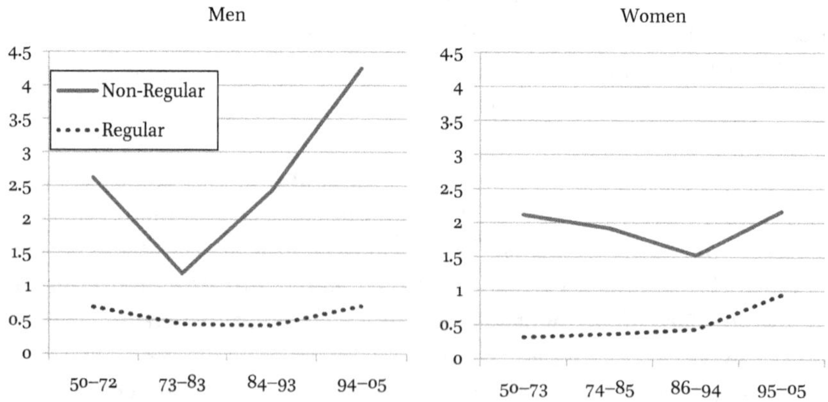

FIGURE 2.5 *Rate of involuntary job shifts for different periods (percent by employment type, Japan)*
SOURCE: 2005 SSM SURVEY

among men is very small. However, as seen in Figure 2.5, the rate is higher for non-regular employment than for regular employment in every period for both men and women.

As to the question of to what extent increased unemployment risk in recent years occurs through increased non-regular employment (the connection from passing of time to non-regular employment and then to unemployment risk), a comparison is made between two models with involuntary job shift hazard as the dependent variable. Examination is made of how much the period effect decreases by including a dummy variable for non-regular employment. Such a decrease in the period effect confirms the existence of a mechanism in which increased non-regular employment in recent years heightens unemployment risk.

Table 2.3 shows the results of estimating the effects of the determinants of the involuntary job shift hazard with discrete-time logit models. The independent variables in Model 1 are age, firm size, occupation, educational attainment, experience at other firms, and period. Besides the independent variables considered in Model 1, a dummy variable for non-regular employment is included in Model 2. The table shows the estimation results for Models 1 and 2 for both genders.

The focus here is on the coefficients for different periods in the two models. For both men and women, these coefficients are negative and significant in Model 1. The result shows that people were less likely to experience unemployment in the periods prior to 1994 than in the 1994–2004 period. Put differently, unemployment risk is higher for the 1994–2004 period. In Model 2 where a dummy variable for non-regular employment is added to the independent variables considered in Model 1, the absolute values of the coefficients for different periods are lower for both men and women. This shows that part of the period effect occurs through non-regular employment. The test of the indirect effect of the connection from passing of time to non-regular employment and then to unemployment risk indicates its statistical significance. Also, the decrease in the absolute values of the coefficients is larger for women. It can thus be confirmed that, for both men and women, increased non-regular employment heightened unemployment risk, and that the effect was stronger for women.

4.4 *Taiwan: Non-increasing Gender Difference in Unemployment Risk*

This subsection describes the situation in Taiwan. As to whether the gender difference in unemployment risk increased with time in Taiwan, Figure 2.6 shows the rate of involuntary job shifts (annual average) for the four periods

TABLE 2.3 *Discrete-time logit analysis with involuntary job shift hazard as the dependent variable (by gender, Japan)*

	Men				Women			
	Model 1		Model 2		Model 1		Model 2	
	Coef.	s.e	Coef.	s.e	Coef.	s.e	Coef.	s.e
Intercept	−3.60	0.36**	−4.27	0.37**	−4.03	0.37**	−4.47	0.38**
Age	−0.02	0.01*	−0.01	0.01	−0.02	0.01*	−0.02	0.01**
Small firm	0.40	0.15**	0.35	0.15*	0.25	0.15	0.11	0.15
Medium-sized firm (ref)	—		—		—		—	
Large firm	−0.36	0.17*	−0.35	0.17*	−0.08	0.18	−0.07	0.18
Public employment	−0.89	0.29**	−0.89	0.29**	0.91	0.20**	0.81	0.20**
Elementary	−0.01	0.21	−0.02	0.21	−0.03	0.20	0.00	0.20
Secondarily	−0.06	0.16	−0.04	0.16	−0.47	0.15**	−0.42	0.15**
Tertiary (ref)	—		—		—		—	
Professional or managerial	−0.64	0.23**	−0.32	0.23	−0.85	0.29**	−0.39	0.29
Clerical or sales	−0.68	0.22**	−0.41	0.22	−0.05	0.23	0.21	0.23
Skilled	−0.92	0.21**	−0.63	0.22**	0.23	0.31	0.33	0.31
Operator or assembler	−0.80	0.21**	−0.53	0.22*	0.30	0.25	0.50	0.25*
Elementary occupations (ref)	—		—		—		—	

No other firm (ref)	—		—		—		—	
1	0.37	0.15*	0.35	0.15*	0.45	0.16**	0.16	0.17
≥2	0.45	0.17**	0.39	0.17*	0.71	0.17**	0.37	0.17*
50–72	−0.26	0.19	−0.11	0.20	−1.04	0.25**	−0.81	0.25**
73–83	−0.50	0.17**	−0.38	0.17*	−0.66	0.18**	−0.49	0.18**
84–93	−0.57	0.17**	−0.49	0.17**	−0.48	0.15**	−0.36	0.15*
94–04 (ref)	—		—		—		–	
Non-regular employment			1.27	0.18**			1.12	0.14**
N	46350		46350		33766		33766	

$^{*}p < 0.05$
$^{**}p < 0.01$
SOURCE: 2005 SSM SURVEY

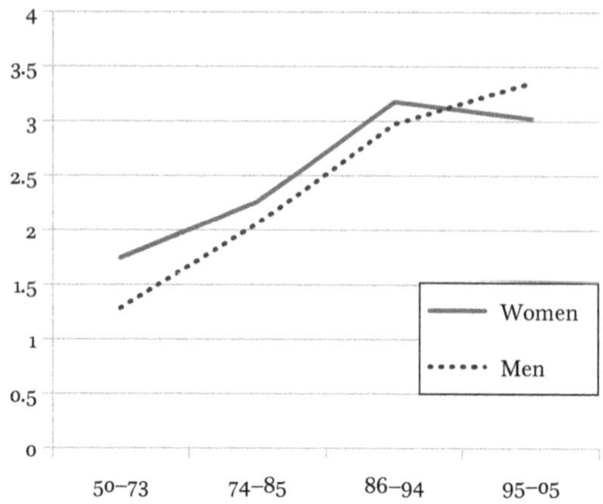

FIGURE 2.6
Rate of involuntary job shifts for different periods (percent, by gender, Taiwan)
SOURCE: 2005 SSM SURVEY

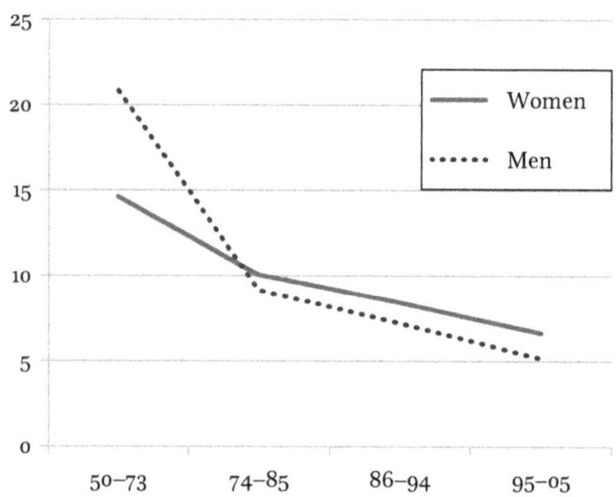

FIGURE 2.7
Proportion of non-regular employment for different periods (percent, by gender, Taiwan)
SOURCE: 2005 SSM SURVEY

for both genders, similarly to the analysis conducted for the case of Japan. As can be seen, unemployment risk increased during the 1970s through the mid-1990s for both men and women, and there is little gender difference. There is no tendency for an increase in the gender difference in recent years either. A discrete-time logit analysis was also conducted to see the effects of gender and interactions between periods and gender, but no significant effect was found (data not shown).

In the case of Japan, female non-regular employment increased. Examination was therefore made of the question of whether non-regular employment increased similarly in Taiwan. Fig 2.7 shows the proportion of non-regular employment for each period. Contrary to the case of Japan, there is no tendency for an increase in the proportion of non-regular employment among women in Taiwan.

5 Discussion: Institutional Factors Affecting Gender Difference in Unemployment Risk

This chapter has focused on Japan and Taiwan, two countries that have different institutional settings, and it has presented a comparative analysis regarding how the gender difference in unemployment risk has changed in the face of globalization. The results show that the gender difference in unemployment risk increased in Japan. Women became more likely to be in non-regular employment, which entails high unemployment risk, and so faced greater job loss risk compared to men. On the contrary, in the case of Taiwan, the gender difference in unemployment risk did not exist and thus could not increase.

These results are thought to stem from factors to do with institutional arrangements in Japan and Taiwan, as discussed earlier along with the hypothesis. Japan has rigid internal labor markets and women tend to work outside these internal labor markets. In the face of globalization, employers face pressure to have employment flexibility—but it is difficult for them to fire employees in their internal labor market. Employers appear to have increased female non-regular employment by taking advantage of the existing employment pattern of women being concentrated in non-regular employment, which has thus led to increased unemployment risk for women.

Taiwan's labor market is more fluid than Japan's, and the internal labor markets have not been formed as rigidly. In Taiwan, women do not concentrate in non-regular employment and they do not operate mainly outside the internal labor markets. The finding for Japan that an increase in female non-regular employment widened the gender difference in unemployment risk is thus not found for Taiwan. It should be pointed out, however, that while unemployment risk is not concentrated for women, it was concentrated for other groups. According to Sakaguchi (2011) who analyzed the same data, the unemployment risk for male employees with low educational attainment has increased in Taiwan, and the gap in terms of unemployment risk widened between them and male employees with high educational attainment over the periods under investigation. This is consistent with the argument made by Blossfeld et al. (2011) that in countries with fluid employment, a gap in unemployment risk scarcely arises between the genders or between different age groups, but easily arises between different groups with different levels of individual resources such as skills and educational attainment.

The results of the analysis conducted here indicate that two institutional factors increase the gender difference in unemployment risk in the face of globalization: a segmented labor market where a significant gap in terms of employment stability exists between the internal labor markets and the external labor market; and a tendency for women to find jobs in the external labor market. These findings are obtained from a comparative analysis of Japan and Taiwan, and further analyses that include other countries are needed for generalization. Additionally, other institutional factors affecting the gender difference in unemployment risk in the face of globalization are expected to include various other macroeconomic factors. Phang shows in Chapter 3 of this book that labor market flexibility may offer new opportunities for workers in Korea, providing yet more demonstration that the results of labor flexibilization differ from country to country. We may find more trends in gender inequality in unemployment risk in Korea. With additional analyses and theoretical refinement based on the present findings, it will be possible to clarify detailed mechanisms regarding what types of institutional factors give rise to the gender difference in unemployment risk in the face of globalization.

References

Blossfeld, Hans-Peter, Erik Klijzing, Melanie Mills, and Karin Kurz, eds. 2005. *Globalization, Uncertainty and Youth in Society.* London and New York: Routledge.

Blossfeld, Hans-Peter, Melanie Mills and Francois Bernardi, eds. 2006. *Globalization, Uncertainty and Men's Careers: An International Comparison.* Cheltenham, UK and Northampton, MA, USA: Edward Elgar.

Blossfeld, Hans-Peter and Heather Hofmeister, eds. 2006. *Globalization, Uncertainty and Women's Careers: An International Comparison.* Cheltenham, UK and Northampton, MA, USA: Edward Elgar.

Blossfeld, Hans-Peter, Sandra Buchholz, Dirk Hofäcker and Kathrin Kolb, eds. 2011. *Globalized Labour Markets and Social Inequality in Europe.* New York: Palgrave Macmillan.

Brinton, Mary C. 1993. *Women and the Economic Miracle: Gender and Work in Postwar Japan.* London: University of California Press.

Brinton, Mary C., ed. 2001. *Women's Working Lives in East Asia.* Stanford, CA: Stanford University Press.

Genda, Yuji. 2001. *Vague Concerns about Work: The Current State of Uncertain Youth.* Tokyo: Chuokoron Shinsha. (in Japanese)

Hamilton, Gary G. and Nicole W. Biggart. 1988. "Market, Culture, and Authority: A Comparative Analysis of Management and Organization in the Far East." *The American Journal of Sociology* 94: 52–94.

Kanbayashi, Hiroshi and Hirohisa Takenoshita, 2009. "Labor Markets in Japan and Taiwan from the Standpoint of Reasons for Job Shifts: Beyond the Dichotomy of Voluntary and Involuntary Transition." *Shakai Kagaku Kenkyu* 86: 33–63. (in Japanese)

Kosugi, Reiko, 2003. *A Life as 'Freeter'.* Tokyo: Keiso Shobo. (in Japanese)

Mills, Melanie and Hans-Peter Blossfeld. 2005. "Globalization, Uncertainty and the Early Life Course: a Theoretical Framework." In Hans-Peter Blossfeld, Erik Klijzing, Melanie Mills and Karin Kurz. eds., *Globalization, Uncertainty and Youth in Society*, 1–24. London and New York: Routledge.

Ministry of Internal Affairs and Communications, 2012. *Labor Force Survey*. http://www.stat.go.jp/data/roudou/longtime/03roudou.htm (accessed January 30, 2012). (in Japanese)

Sakaguchi, Yusuke. 2011. "Japan-Taiwan Comparison of Determinants of Unemployment Risk and Their Changes: Globalization, Institution, and Risk." *The State of Social Class in Contemporary Japan: An Approach Based on the Micro–macro Connection, Vol. 1 Social Class and Social Mobility* (Grant-in-Aid for Scientific Research (A) Research Results Report): 269–289. (in Japanese)

Sato, Hiroki. 1999. "Japanese Employment Systems and the Corporate Community." In Inagami Takeshi and Kawakita Takashi, eds., Labor, *Kozo Shakaigaku Series 6*, 33–73. Tokyo: University of Tokyo Press. (in Japanese)

Sato, Yoshimichi. 2009. "The Class Structure of Contemporary Japan: Fluidity and Gaps." *Japanese Sociological Review* 59(4): 632–47. (in Japanese)

Sumiya, Mikio, Jin-Quing Liu, and Zhao-Yan Tu. 1992. *The Taiwanese Economy: Advantages and Disadvantages of the Typical NIEs Country*. Tokyo: University of Tokyo Press (in Japanese)

Takenoshita, Hirohisa. 2008. "Voluntary and Involuntary Job Mobility in Japan: Resource, Reward and Labor Market Structure." *Sociological Theory and Methods*, 23(2): 85–104.

Yu, Wei-Hsin. 2009. *Gendered Trajectories: Women, Work, and Social Change in Japan and Taiwan*. Stanford, CA: Stanford University Press.

CHAPTER 3

Economic Crisis, Labor Market Restructuring and Job Mobility in Korea: 1998–2008

Phang Hanam

1 Introduction

Until the 1997 Asian economic crisis, Korea was seen as a country with a fast-growing economy that offered expanding opportunities for job mobility and occupational upgrading during an individual's work-life career. However, Korea's rapid economic growth was heavily export-led and heavily large company-centered, and this had given rise to a dual economy and a segmented labor market—a primary sector of modernized industries and large, organized firms, and a secondary sector of traditional industries and small-to-medium sized, unorganized firms. The primary sector largely comprised a company-level internal labor market where workers enjoyed union-protected lifetime employment, good pay and generous fringe benefits (Grubb et al. 2007; Kye 2008). Workers in the secondary sector, in contrast, mostly operated in the external labor market and their employment status was informal, unstable and temporary, with undesirable working conditions (Lee 1992).[1] The 'insider-outsider' problem in employment that is embedded in the dual labor market structure meant that cross-sector labor mobility was very limited (Lindbeck and Snower 1988).

The economic crisis dramatically changed many parts of the Korean economy and labor market. Especially salient were changes in the labor market's employment structure and employment relations at the firm level.[2] Quantitatively, after the economic crisis, economic growth rate rebounded and numerous jobs were created in the labor market. Nevertheless, qualitatively, these jobs were mostly in temporary employment, which saw a rapid increase, and involved other flexible or atypical employment contracts (often referred to as "non-regular" employment). The labor market flexibility that temporary employment allowed was seen as a critical element in employment policy to overcome the economic recession and the growth of joblessness (OECD 2005).

Korean corporations thus opted for irregular and temporary employment when they had any need for additional need workforce (Hwang et al. 2010). One

1 For the Japanese case, see Kenn et al. (2000), and Watanabe and Sato (2000).

2 See Chapter 2 for details on structural change in labor markets in Japan and Taiwan. Chapter 4 deals with changes of women in Japan and Taiwan.

 | DOI 10.1163/9789004262737_004

outcome that might be expected would be that the external duality of the labor market was gradually internalized into the internal labor market in large firms, and more inter-firm job mobility Would be seen in temporary employment.

Table 3.1 shows the long-term trend in the distribution of wage-workers employed on a permanent, fixed-term or daily basis for 1986–2010.

TABLE 3.1 *Distribution of wage workers employed on a permanent, fixed-term, daily basis: 1986–2010*

	Wage workers		
	Employed permanent	Employed fixed-term	Employed daily
1986	53.5	29.3	17.2
1987	54.4	28.9	16.6
1988	55.7	28.8	15.6
1989	54.8	28.6	16.6
1990	54.2	29.0	16.8
1991	55.5	28.7	15.7
1992	57.4	27.7	14.9
1993	58.9	26.7	14.4
1994	57.9	27.8	14.3
1995	58.1	27.9	14.0
1996	56.8	29.6	13.6
1997	54.3	31.6	14.1
1998	53.1	32.9	14.0
1999	48.4	33.6	18.0
2000	47.9	34.5	17.6
2001	49.2	34.6	16.2
2002	48.4	34.5	17.2
2003	50.5	34.7	14.8
2004	51.2	34.1	14.7
2005	52.1	33.3	14.6
2006	52.8	33.1	14.2
2007	54.0	32.4	13.6
2008	55.6	31.3	13.1
2009	57.1	31.0	11.9
2010	59.4	29.9	10.7

SOURCE: LABOR FORCE SURVEY

Fixed term and daily employment increased from roughly 42 percent of total waged employment in 1995 to 52 percent in 2000, and then to 48 percent in 2005. It then decreased to about 40 percent in 2010—the fastest increase and decrease among OECD countries in recent years (KNSO 2011). Women and the low-educated are overrepresented in temporary or atypical employment contracts. The majority of older workers, who remain in the labor market after mandatory retirement, are also in non-regular employment. Lastly, the majority of workers at small firms are in temporary employment (OECD 2005).

In the process of variable-scale structural adjustment and downsizing that a large number of firms adopted to survive the economic crisis and prolonged recession, many regularly employed workers as well as temporary workers were exposed to the risk of job loss and subsequent downgrading into temporary, non-regular forms of employment with lower wages.

Labor force surveys report substantial wage gaps and large differences in access to non-wage benefits between "regular" and "non-regular" workers. The available research suggests— despite some variation in findings, depending on data sources and definition—that a considerable proportion of non-regular workers may be trapped in this type of job. It also suggests that hiring and human resource management practices by Korean firms, aiming to circumvent relatively strict employment protection legislation (EPL) for permanent workers and to profit from labor-cost differentials between different categories of worker, have been the main causes of the growth in temporary employment. As organizational lay-offs and restructuring are now common, it is not surprising that employees today realize that lifelong job security may not be a realistic goal and that many are ready to become more mobile (Arthur and Rousseau 1996).

All this suggests that the Korean labor market and employment structure underwent a significant transformation, from a segmented and protected one to an open and competitive one (Choi 2010; Lee and Yoo 2007). We might expect that, in the process of restructuring, the internal labor market would contract, while the external labor market would expand. As a consequence, overall employment stability would weaken and job mobility increase.

People's work career paths often involve intra-firm mobility as well as inter-firm mobility. Job mobility can occur within a firm or between firms: intra-firm mobility or inter-firm mobility. Intra-firm job mobility usually involves promotions (occupational upgrade or employment status changes), while inter-firm job mobility might or might not involve occupational upgrading. Intra-firm career mobility is subject to the employer's decision, whereas inter-firm mobility is determined by the individuals themselves, who make choices about optimal quitting time to maximize expected lifetime earnings. It is usually argued, along the lines of classical economics, that optimal investment in human capital and optimal quitting time together maximize the individual's expected lifetime income (Sicherman and Galo 1990).

However, such assumptions are only applicable under normal economic and labor market conditions. The process and outcome of job mobility due to involuntary termination may be quite different systemically from job mobility due to voluntary quitting. Job mobility in times of economic recess and downturn is more likely to be forced due to involuntary termination of employment contract. In view of this, there is likely to be a higher risk of unprepared and less desirable transition, especially among disadvantaged groups of workers in the labor market. Unprepared involuntary job transitions are more likely to be made into temporary rather than permanent employment positions. In this study, we will examine temporal changes in employment status through job mobility, and whether temporary employment is a trap or a stepping-stone to permanent employment (Booth et al. 2002).

2 Theoretical Perspectives on Labor Market Restructuring and Job Mobility

First, at the aggregate level, we will examine the ways in which the economic crisis altered the opportunity structure of the labor market in terms of job mobility (Diprete et al. 1997; Diprete and Nonnemarker 1997) for Korea. The following alternative hypotheses are examined.

(1) The trend might have reinforced the persistent duality and segmentation of the labor market of Korea, thus lowered the probability of cross-sector mobility or job upgrading.
(2) The trend might have dismantled or lowered the mobility barriers between sectors/firms and thus raised the probability of cross-sector or inter-firm mobility.

Next, at the individual level, we will explore how and to what extent individuals with different sets of human capital and in different market positions were differentially affected by the structural changes and followed different job transition paths. Was the negative effect of belonging to a minority, disadvantaged class—i.e., being low educated, being female, being old-aged—strengthened or weakened? If the impact of the economic crisis was stronger on the protected or core-sector workers, it might follow, then, that its effect might have been weakened. This is a downward assimilation hypothesis—the weakened duality of labor market. This line of assumption goes closely with the "integration scenario" (see below) as the outcome of increased labor market flexibility (Ng et al. 2007).

Specifically, we will examine:

(1) Who are more likely to be temporarily employed and what are the factors that explain the observed differentials in the probability of being in temporary employment between individuals?
(2) Who are more likely to transit into temporary employment, when do they move jobs, and what are the factors that explain the observed differentials between individuals in the probability of getting temporarily employed?

To address these questions, we investigate the following two scenarios: the integration scenario and the disintegration scenario. The integration scenario predicts that the economic crisis will increase between-sector mobility, and thus integrate the segmented labor market. The disintegration scenario predicts that the economic crisis will raise the mobility barriers between primary and secondary labor market sectors.

Integration Scenario:
If the labor market is restructured along the integration scenario, the restructuring might offer advantages for both employers and employees (Giesecke and Gross 2003). Employers would be more easily able to adjust their personnel in accordance with fluctuations in the demand market and changes in the production process and technology. Increased labor market flexibility might also offer employers stronger leverage for wage adjustment when the productivity gap arises. It might also offer new opportunities, through increased number of job vacancies both in the internal and external job market, for less qualified workers with lower reservation wages.[3]

From this perspective, the entire economy might benefit from increased labor market flexibility. A more flexible labor market, lowered institutional barriers, and increased worker mobility could result in increased productivity and growth, and decreased unemployment. If the integration scenario holds, increased labor market flexibility could lower the barriers between the primary and secondary labor market (i.e., there would be less labor market segmentation). It is observed that the economic crisis in East Asian countries since the 1990s has brought about the demise of the so-called "life-time employment"

3 The reservation wage is the minimum wage at which a job seeker is willing to work.

commonly practiced in the primary labor market (Ahmadjian and Robinson 2001; Grubb et al. 2007; Choi 2010). Thus, one socioeconomic consequence of the integration scenario would be a narrowed gap between workers in the advantaged primary-sector position and workers in the disadvantaged secondary-sector position in terms of career mobility opportunities and outcomes.

Disintegration Scenario:
Increased labor market flexibility might on the other hand lead to a quite different result in terms of employment relations and career mobility of workers. Proponents of the disintegration scenario posit that in times of economic crisis and labor market restructuring, employees lose much of their bargaining power and their employment become more insecure. While there might be new opportunities for career mobility, the new jobs and positions could be less desirable and less secure.

If the disintegration scenario holds, labor market segmentation will strengthen. The reasoning is that economic crisis and structural changes have a much stronger impact on workers in the unprotected secondary labor market, and the closedness of the protected primary labor market tends to tighten with more intense collective bargaining and action. Job mobility between the primary and the secondary labor market decreases, and temporary employment mostly affects the secondary labor market (Giesecke and Gross 2003). Mobility into primary sector jobs becomes more difficult and less frequent, while mobility in and out of the secondary sector jobs becomes easier and more frequent. The socioeconomic consequence of the disintegration scenario is increased inequality in labor market opportunities and outcome: those in the disadvantaged position in the labor market become more disadvantaged and those in the advantaged position become more advantaged in a relative sense.

In sum, if the integration scenario holds and labor market segmentation weakens, job mobility is more likely to occur between the primary and the secondary sector than when the disintegration scenario holds. In contrast, if the disintegration scenario holds, then job mobility would tend to occur more *within* than between sectors of the labor market.

In addition to those aggregate-level expectations, we can further develop expectations for micro-level individual factors that might affect job mobility of workers in general. If increased labor market flexibility increases the sectoral movement of the labor force and opens up new opportunities for the workers in less privileged positions, then, the effect of initial employment status at time t on the subsequent job transition would become more and more weakened over time (i.e., there would be less "state-dependency").

If, on the other hand, the impact of increased labor market flexibility is bounded within the secondary labor market as the disintegration scenario implies, then, state-dependency will become more and more strengthened and workers under temporary employment in the secondary sector at time t will be more likely to be in temporary employment at time t + 1. Further, workers in temporary employment in the primary sector at time t might be more likely to be either unemployed or assimilated into permanent employment depending on the union status and/or firm characteristics. For instance, employers in the public sector tend to be less pressured by profit-maximization motive and more pressured by strong unions than those in private corporations. Thus, workers under temporary employment contract in public sector will be more likely to be promoted to permanent positions than those in private corporations.

An individual worker's human capital and work experiences might exert positive or negative effects on job mobility rate and the direction of mobility taken (upward, downward, lateral). Thus, in this paper I explore and examine the effect of individual workers' characteristics and labor market positions on the incidence of job mobility, and employment status changes through that job mobility.

3 Analytic Strategy

To properly address the research questions raised above we need to look at individual workers' job careers and employment history in longitudinal perspective. They also need to be subject to empirical validation through a dynamic analysis of job transition data. We will thus employ random-effects logit-model analysis using panel data to analyze the effects of (1) individual human capital and labor market experiences, (2) structural position in the labor market (industry, occupation, labor market sector), and (3) type of job termination (voluntary or involuntary exits) on the job transitions made over individuals' work career for a 10-year period after the economic crisis (1997–2008).

One possibility might be that workers try to avoid temporary jobs because such jobs bear significant disadvantages in terms of compensation, job security, and fringe benefits. In reality, however, bargaining power and ability to avoid temporary employment would differ between individuals in different structural positions and with different sets of human capital. The higher the position in the labor market and level of job-specific human capital, the lower the probability would be of being employed in a temporary job.

In the following subsections, I describe the structural and individual factors that might affect the probability of being temporarily rather than permanently employed.

3.1 *Structural Factors* (*Industry, Firm Size, Union Status*)

Industry: The probability of getting a temporary job may be higher in agriculture, construction, personal service, and business service industry than in manufacturing and public service/administration, and can be expected to decrease with firm size. Agriculture and construction industry are characterized by strong seasonal fluctuation in labor demand.

Individual workers' jobs are located in a specific firm (or enterprise) and their union status is largely determined by the firm that employs them. In theory, large firms are required to cut labor costs in order to stay competitive in the globalized economy and it suits them to have as many temporary employment contracts as they can (Giesecke and Gross 2003). However, the opposite is the reality in Korea and other Asian countries where large firms and the public sector are characterized by a tight internal labor market with strong unions.

Firm size: Firm size is a strong indicator of the labor market sector. In Korea, large and clear differences in terms of the quality of jobs and employment contract are observed between large firms (say, >= 300) and small-to-medium sized firms. Public corporations are similar to large firms in many aspects of employment quality.

Union status: This is another strong indicator even though union coverage largely overlaps with firm size. That is, most of the large firms and public sector are unionized, while the opposite is true for the small firms. By combining the two indicator variables (firm size and union status), we can construct another indicator variable that could measure indirectly the labor market sector in which individual workers are employed.

Job type: Workers employed in temporary jobs are expected to face a higher risk of getting into another temporary job when they leave the current job. Moreover, in the disintegration scenario, the barrier between temporary employment in the secondary labor market and unemployment is assumed to lower through economic crisis. In this scenario we can expect to observe more frequent transitions between temporary employment and unemployment or OLF, and vice versa.

3.2 *Individual Factors* (*Age, Gender, Education, Occupation*)

Education: Education can be expected to have a strong impact on the risk of holding a temporary job. Workers with lower education are more likely to be in temporary employment, while firm-specific training and skill would lower this risk. However, it is not clear whether education affects job mobility in a positive or negative way. Employees with higher educational credentials are more likely to be highly paid and more likely to be promoted in the firm, which decreases the incentive to quit the job, while at the same time workers with high education and skills are likely to be in more demand by other firms in the labor market, which increases the probability of job mobility.

More educated workers are likely to face a higher arrival rate of job offers because they face a larger labor market and a larger variety of jobs and because they are more efficient in their searches while employed or unemployed. But since more educated workers will also have a higher reservation wage, the effect of schooling on departure is ambiguous (Sicherman 1990).

Age: Age is an indicator of labor market experience and accumulated specific human capital. In addition, seniority rules prevalent in the primary sector also protect older people in permanent employment. Thus we can expect that the probability of holding a temporary job will decrease with age.

However, this would not hold for older people beyond a certain age. Neither would it hold at the beginning of a job spell. According to human capital theory, employers are reluctant to invest in older people because they have only limited time to pay this investment off. So we can expect that the relationship between age and the probability of getting a temporary job to be non-linear and concave-shaped: decreasing to a certain point and then increasing with age. We can expect that both young workers (=< 29) and older workers (>=50) will face a higher risk of being employed in a temporary job and getting a temporary job when there is a job shift.

In Korea, the majority of firms have a mandatory retirement policy as part of the employment contract, and the average age of retirement is observed to be around 55. Many older workers, after retirement, are eager to find a new job. But most of the jobs available are temporary jobs with a lower wage.

Gender: Women are expected to face a higher risk of getting a temporary job because they are more often found in the secondary labor market. Also, the pattern of female labor force participation in Korea is still strongly subject to family formation stage—getting married, bearing and rearing children—and shows an M-shaped curve. Female work careers are largely discontinuous and intermittent, and women tend to have a hard time finding good regular jobs when they return to the labor market after a career break. Women are thus doubly disadvantaged: firstly due to their minority status in the labor market, and secondly due to their family responsibilities. Thus we expect that female workers will be more likely to be employed in or transit into a temporary job when they enter the labor market.

Occupation: Job mobility may or may not involve occupational mobility. Highly educated persons are able to start their job careers in a high status occupation. Human capital theory predicts that part of the motivation for return to education is the higher probability of occupational upgrading, both within and across firms.

A career path is a series of occupations, and such occupations are related to each other by the transferability of skills and job ability (Sicherman and Galo 1990). We expect that the higher the status of the occupation of the individual, the less likely the individual will be employed in a temporary job. However, it is not clear whether occupational status affects job transition into a temporary employment negatively or positively, since the range of jobs at a higher occupational level is narrower than the range of jobs at a lower occupational level.

4 Data and Models for Analysis

4.1 *Data and Variables*

Data

For the analysis I used data from the Korean Labor and Income Panel Study (KLIPS). The KLIPS is an annually repeated panel survey of households in urban areas in Korea, first conducted in 1998. Currently, 11 "waves" are available (1998–2008). KLIPS data collects a fairly comprehensive set of labor market- and work-related information regarding its panel members, including detailed employment records and job histories of the individuals surveyed. For this analysis, I traced each panel member's work and job change history over the period and identify the type of the job/employment status (temporary, daily, or permanent). Once the current employment is terminated, I then identify the type of termination (voluntary or involuntary) and the direction of transition (to a new job or to unemployment or out of labor force status) and the type of employment (temporary or permanent) with the new job taken.

The units of analysis in this study are job spells and spells not working (unemployed or out of the labor force). Out of the detailed work history of individuals determination can be made of when each job spell started and stopped, employment status, occupation and industry related to the job, and other job characteristics.

Although KLIPS data contain retrospective work histories of the individuals surveyed, only jobs and employment spells captured at the first wave and following waves are included in our analysis. Job shifts and employment transitions that took place after the first wave are analyzed in the transition model.

Variables

(1) *Independent Variables*

The independent (or control) variables included in the analytic model are intended to capture the structural changes of the labor market, the individual worker's position in the labor market, and their human capital that relates to the type and quality of the job occupied and the quality of employment transitions taken after a job shift during their work career.

To capture structural aspects and position of the labor market, industry and occupation variables are included. The *Industry* variable distinguishes between (1) agriculture and forestry, (2) construction, (3) manufacturing, (4) service, and (5) the public sector. In (1) agriculture and (2) construction industry, employment with fixed-term or temporary contract is heavily practiced. *Occupational positions* are divided into (1) upper white-collar (public administrators, high-level managers and professionals), (2) lower white-collar (semi-professionals, clerical and sales), (3) upper blue-collar (operators and skilled workers), and (4) lower blue-collar (lower manual and service) occupations.

To measure the labor market sector to which each individual job spell belongs, I utilize two firm-level variables: size of firm and union status. I combine the two indicator variables (firm size and union status) to construct a categorical variable to capture the labor market sector to which the individual belongs currently: 1 = large (or public) and union; 2 = large (or public) and non-union; 3 = small and union; and 4 = small and non-union. I assume that the first category (large firms unionized) belongs to the primary, the second and third to the periphery, and the last (small firms non-unionized) to the secondary labor market.

There have been some ups and downs in the economy and labor market during the period under observation (1998–2008). I divide the time period into four periods: (1) 1998–2000; (2) 2001–2003; (3) 2004–2006; and (4) 2007–2008. The first period is when the Asian economic crisis began, and the last period is when global financial crisis started.

Individual characteristics are captured by human capital and demographic variables: education, age, gender, marital status, and residence. Education is measured as a categorical variable: (1) less than/equal to middle school; (2) high school; and (3) more than/equal to college-level education. Age at the beginning of the job spell is measured in years; age-squared is used to capture the possible non-linear relationship, if needed. In the model, we include age variable as a categorical variable: (1) 15–29; (2) 30–49; (3) 50 +. Gender is coded 0 for men and 1 for women. To measure individuals' cumulated human capital (skill and job ability) and employability, total work experience by the time surveyed is adopted as a continuous time-varying variable.

(2) *Dependent Variables*

In the first part of analysis, I focus on who are employed temporarily (rather than permanently) and what are the factors that affect the probability of being in temporary employment status. Workers who are employed on a fixed-term or daily contract are treated as "temporarily" and the others are treated as "permanently" employed. The dependent variable is coded 1 if the individual is "temporarily employed" and 0 otherwise.

In the second part of analysis, I examine temporal changes in employment status: (1) permanently employed, (2) temporarily employed, (3) self-employed, (4) not working, on a longitudinal perspective.

Given current employment status at time t, conditional transition probabilities into the other status at time t + 1 will be estimated, focusing on transitions into category (2) "temporary employment" versus "permanent employment" status. Our main interest is on who are more likely to be temporarily employed on job shift and what are the determining factors. I examine, in particular, how and to what extent prior employment status affects the job mover's next employment status. Does "temporary" employment at time t lead to another "temporary" employment at time t+1, or serve as a stepping stone to "permanent employment"?

I follow each individual's employment status from the time the individual enters the KLIPS survey either until he/she drops out, or until the survey stopped (2008).

Probabilities of transition between employment statuses were recorded and analyzed on a discrete time basis, which is equivalent to discrete-time hazard analysis, the hazard being the risk of transiting into "temporary employment status." The status change could result mainly from inter-firm job shift. But it could also result from changes in employment contract with the same employer.

I also compare his/her employment status with the main job at time t with that at time t + 1 on a year base. This may induce some under-estimation of employment instability and/or over-estimation of employment stability by not looking at the process on a continuous-time basis. However, I expect that the bias will not be significant, because this will occur only when multiple job shifts are made between adjacent waves. The advantage is that more permanent status changes can be taken into account in the analysis, leaving out short-term intermittent spells of job search and unemployment.

Table 3.2 provides a summary of the definition of the variables used in the analyses and their descriptive statistics.

TABLE 3.2 *Definition of the variables included and descriptive statistics*

Variables	Measurement	Descriptive statistics (%)
Dependent Variable		
Y1 = Pr (Temporary employment)	1 = if temporarily employed; *0 = otherwise (reference)*	1 = 5,782 (18.24%) 0 = 25,914 (81.76%)
Y2 = Pr (Transition into Temporary Employment Status| Y2 = 1)	*0 = permanent employment* (reference); 1 = temporary employment (fixed term + daily employment); 2 = self-employed; 3 = Out of the labor force	0 = 13,143 (29.3%) 1 = 5, 385 (12.0%) 2 = 7,137 (1.9%) 3 = 19,235 (42.8%)
Independent Variables		
Gender	*0 = male*; 1 = female	(0) 49%; (1) 51%
Age(d)	Age in years grouped (1) 15–29; (2) *30–49*; (3) 50+	(1) 27%; (2) 41%; (3) 32%
Education	(1) ≤ middle school; (2) *high school*; (3) ≥ college education	(1) 37%; (2) 35%; (3) 27%
Labor Market Experience	Log (total work experience measured in years)	6.16 (1.20): mean (s.d.)
Occupation	(1) upper white-collar; (2) *lower white-collar*; (3) upper blue; (4) lower blue-collar	(1) 23%; (2) 24%; (3) 36%; (4) 17%
Industry	(1) agriculture/forestry; (2) manufacturing; (3) construction; (4) public sector; (5) *service industry*	(1) 7.5%; (2) 21.2%; (3) 8.5%; (4) 12.8%; (5) 50.0%
Large Firm	Size of the firm at employment (0, if size <300; 1, if size ≥300)	(0) 67%; (1) 33%
Union Status	0 if in non-union; 1 if in union sector	(0) 79%; (1) 21%
Labor Market Sector	1 if large firm and union (primary sector); *0, otherwise (secondary sector)*	0 = 83.7% 1 = 16.3%
Period	*(1) = 1998–2000*; (2) = 2001–2003; (3) = 2004–2006; (4) = 2007–2008	(1) 28.3%; (2) 26.7%; (3) 23.6%; (4) 23.4%

Note: Italicized categories are referenced categories.
SOURCE: KLIPS

4.2 Analytic Models

Probability of being temporarily employed:

For the analysis of the binary outcome (whether the individual belongs to a "temporary" employment status (1) or "permanent" employment status (0)), a panel probit/logit model is adopted (Baltagi 2008).[4]

The panel probit model for a binary dependent variable can be written as

$$y_{i,t} = \begin{cases} 1, & \text{if } y^*_{i,t} > 0 \\ 0, & \text{if } y^*_{i,t} \le 0 \end{cases}$$

where $y^*_{i,t}$ is a normally/binomially distributed latent variable of belonging to a temporary employment status. If we assume a linear regression model for the latent dependent variable, $y^*_{i,t}$ then, it can be expressed as

$$y^*_{i,t} = \alpha + \beta x_{i,t} + \varepsilon_{i,t}$$

Then, the probability of ($y_{i,t} = 1$) can be solved by the following equation,

$$\Pr(y_{i,t} = 1) = \Pr(y^*_{i,t} > 0) = \Pr(\varepsilon_{i,t} > -\alpha - \beta x_{i,t}) = F(\alpha + \beta x_{i,t})$$

where $F(\cdot)$ is a CDF (cumulative distribution function) of a random variable, $\varepsilon_{i,t}$ with a standard normal distribution (for probit model) or logistic distribution (for logit model).

To fully utilize the panel structure of our data, we can include a term that represents "unobserved individual heterogeneity" (u_i) and a term representing time effects (γ_t) as follows:[5]

$$y^*_{i,t} = \alpha + \beta x_{i,t} + u_i + \gamma_t + \varepsilon_{i,t}$$

The probability function for a probit model can be expressed as follows:

$$\Pr(y_{i,t} = 1) = \Phi(\alpha + \beta x_{i,t} + \gamma_t + u_i)$$

Dynamic analysis of employment status transitions:

The dependent variable in the second part of our analysis is the probability of transition into multiple employment statuses: (1) permanent employment, (2) temporary employment, (3) self-employment, (4) not working (either unemployed or out of labor force), given current employment status.

4 A probit model is a multivariate analysis dealing with a binary response variable. It can be applied to panel data as well as cross sectional data, adding random or fixed effects to the model.

5 u_i could be a random or fixed effect, depending on the assumption on its distribution in the model adopted, while γ_t is normally treated as a fixed time effect.

For the analysis, a multinomial logit model will be adopted. In a multinomial model with M categories, one value (typically the first, the last, or the value with the highest frequency) of the dependent variable is designated as the reference category.

The probability of membership in other categories is compared to the probability of membership in the reference category. For a dependent variable with M categories, this requires the calculation of M-1 equations, one for each category relative to the reference category, to describe the relationship between the dependent variable and the independent variables.

Hence, if the first category is the reference, then, for $m \geq 2$,

$$\ln \frac{P(Y_i = m)}{P(Y_i = 1)} = \alpha_m + \sum_{k=1}^{K} \beta_{mk} x_{ik} = Z_{mi}$$

Hence, for each case, there will be M-1 predicted log odds, one for each category relative to the reference category. (Note that when $m = 1$, we get $\ln(1) = 0 = Z_{1i}$, and $\exp(0) = 1$).

In a multinomial setting, the probabilities of transition into each alternative employment status are computed by the following equations. For $m \geq 2$,

$$P(Y_i = m) = \frac{\exp(Z_{mi})}{1 + \sum_{n=1}^{M} \exp(Z_{ni})}$$

For the reference category, it can be written as follows:

$$P(Y_i = 1) = \frac{1}{1 + \sum_{n=1}^{M} \exp(Z_{ni})}$$

5 Results and Discussions

5.1 *Aggregate Analyses: Labor Market Restructuring and Labor Mobility*

Table 3.3 presents a chart of distribution of employment spell,[6] which is the unit of analysis in this study, out of the panel data constructed on the basis of individuals' work history from KLIPS (1998–2008). Overall, out of the total employment spells observed (=45,069), about 78 percent are permanent employment (including regular, non-fixed term employment contracts), and

6 Here, employment spell is defined as any spell during which a subject is employed without an intervening spell of unemployment or not working. Thus, employment spell could comprise multiple job spells if the job movement were made without a time gap.

TABLE 3.3 *Panel distribution of employment spells by status (permanent versus temporary) (unit: spells; %)*

	Overall (spells)		Between (N = 9,643)		Within
Permanent Employment	35,041	77.75%	7866	81.57%	89.70%
Temporary Employment	10,028	22.25%	3709	38.46%	69.76%
Total	45,069	100.00%	11575	120.04%	83.31%

SOURCE: KLIPS

about 22 percent temporary-employment (including fixed-term, daily, irregular employment contracts) spells. Among the panel subjects extracted (n = 9643), about 20 percent moved between permanent and temporary employment status over the time periods observed.[7] Within-subject rate of stability in employment status is about 90 percent for permanent employment, and about 70 percent for temporary employment. This means that transitions from temporary to permanent employment are more prevalent than the other way around.

Table 3.4 presents employment status-specific transition rates between time points (i.e., t –> t + 1, one year). Transitions from permanent to temporary status occur at the very low yearly rate of 2–3 percent, while transitions from temporary to permanent position occur at the yearly rate of 17.61 percent in the 1998–2000 period and then at the rate about 13 percent thereafter. This is an ironic result given that the labor market situation of massive layoffs and downsizing occurred right after the economic crisis burst in 1998. But it also makes sense if the "disintegration scenario" holds, that is, if a few selected employees under temporary contract were admitted into permanent positions to minimize the probable negative impact of massive layoffs and downsizing. After this time, we can assume that segmentation between regular-permanent and irregular-temporary employment would have been strengthened. This assumption is partly supported by the increased immobility between statuses: 96.92 –> 97.61 percent (permanent); 82.39 –> 86.93 percent (temporary).

Results in Table 3.4 do not distinguish between movers and stayers in terms of job mobility. However, with a more dynamic approach, an individual

7 According to the panel data terminology, within-subject distribution means the distribution of spells occupied by the subjects (i), while between-subject distribution means the distribution of subjects by spells. If there is no movement by the subjects between permanent and temporary employment spells over time, the "between" distribution will exactly match the subject distribution (N = 9,643).

TABLE 3.4 *Employment status transition probabilities between permanent and temporary (spells from both stayers and movers)*

Time periods	Employment status transition rate (%)			
	Permanent→ Permanent	Permanent→ Temporary	Temporary→ Permanent	Temporary→ Temporary
Period 1	96.92	3.08	17.61	82.39
Period 2	97.99	2.01	13.19	86.81
Period 3	97.83	2.17	13.32	86.68
Period 4	97.61	2.39	13.07	86.93

Note: Period 1 = 1998–2000; Period 2 = 2001–2003; Period 3 = 2004–2006; Period 4 = 2007–2008.
SOURCE: KLIPS

employment spell might be divided up into job spells (i.e., intra- and inter-firm mobility).[8] In some employment spells, multiple job spells could be involved. Table 3.5 shows employment status transition rates among job movers, and employment status transitions following job changes. The results indicate that inter-status mobility seems to have considerably weakened over the time periods. Specifically, the transition rate from "permanent" to "temporary" employment has decreased from roughly 51 percent in Period 1 to roughly 18 percent in Period 4, while that from "temporary" to "permanent" decreased from roughly 73 percent to roughly 51 percent during the same period. The flip side of the coin is an increased intra-status immobility for both employment statuses (from about 49 percent to about 82 percent for "permanent status" and from about 27 percent to 49 percent for "temporary" status). Results from Table 3.5 reinforce the observation given by Table 3.4 and also support the "disintegration scenario" over the "integration scenario" with regard to labor market restructuring and its impact on labor mobility at the aggregate level.

As in many East Asian countries, the Korean labor market is characterized by a relatively strong segmentation between the primary and secondary sector, where there exists a large difference in employment security as well as quality. The integration versus disintegration theory proposes a contrasting scenario about the impact of labor market restructuring on labor mobility between

8 In our analysis, 128,678 job spells are observed. Among them, 83,778 (65.11 percent) are stayer spells and 44,990 (34.89 percent) are mover spells.

TABLE 3.5 *Employment status transition probabilities between permanent and temporary (Spells from job movers only)*

Period	Employment status transition rates (%) among job movers			
	Permanent→ Permanent	Permanent→ Temporary	Temporary→ Permanent	Temporary→ Temporary
Period 1	49.14	50.86	72.82	27.18
Period 2	76.35	23.65	66.51	33.49
Period 3	69.93	30.07	61.33	38.67
Period 4	81.64	18.36	51.40	48.60

SOURCE: KLIPS

sectors. In Table 3.6, I present the estimated distribution of job transitions between labor market sectors over the observed periods.[9]

The results indicate that upward labor mobility occurs only rarely (less than 5 percent) between labor market sectors and this infrequency only increased over the periods (4.875 -> 2.16 percent). On the other hand, downward mobility occurs at much higher rates. However, overall, the rate also decreased from about 61 percent in Period 1 to about 46 percent in Period 4. In sum, the results imply that in Korea labor market restructuring initiated by economic crisis both strengthened sector barriers in labor mobility and weakened upward mobility opportunities over the periods that followed.

5.2 *Individual-level Dynamic Analyses*

Analysis of Risk of being in Temporary Employment

In Table 3.7, I present estimation results of the panel data analysis using the random effects logit model. Here the purpose of the analysis is to examine who are more likely to be temporarily rather than permanently employed in the current position. The dependent variable thus is a binary variable logit (1 = being in temporary employment, 0 = otherwise). The estimated effects of the individual-level variables confirm what is normally expected from labor market theory and past studies. Females, the low-educated, and younger or

9 Here, "primary" sector is defined as a combination of firm-size (≥ 300) and union organization (yes). Any other is defined as "secondary." Thus defined, out of the total job spells observed, 16.3 percent belongs to the primary sector and the rest to the secondary sector.

TABLE 3.6 *Panel distribution of labor market sector transition between t and t + 1 (movers only)*

	Labor market sector transition between t and t + 1 (Job movers spell)			
	Primary→ Primary	Primary→ Secondary	Secondary→ Primary	Secondary→ Secondary
Period 1	39.29	60.71	4.87	95.13
Period 2	55.00	45.00	3.69	96.31
Period 3	47.37	52.63	4.88	95.12
Period 4	54.17	45.83	2.16	97.84

SOURCE: KLIPS

TABLE 3.7 *Risk of being in temporary employment: Estimated coefficients of random effects logit model*

Variable	Coefficient	Std.Err.	z-value
Individual variables			
Female	0.555	(0.057)	9.74
Age (15–29)	0.090	(0.066)	1.35
Age (30–49: reference)			
Age (50+)_d3	0.064	(0.075)	0.86
Education (≤ middle school)	0.381	(0.072)	5.31
Education(high school)			
Education(≥ college)	−0.268	(0.070)	−3.85
Emp_status(t − 1) (permanent emp.)			
Emp_status(t − 1) (temporary emp.)	4.871	(0.071)	68.81
Emp_status(t − 1) (self-employed)	2.805	(0.108)	25.86
Emp_status(t − 1) (out of labor force)	3.173	(0.067)	47.65
No. of prev. jobs	0.024	(0.014)	1.74
Labor-market variables			
Large firm	0.243	(0.067)	3.60
Union	−0.501	(0.086)	−5.82
Industry (Agriculture+)	1.146	(0.252)	4.55
Industry (Manufacturing)	−0.634	(0.069)	−9.20
Industry (Construction)	1.293	(0.092)	14.04

Variable	Coefficient	Std.Err.	z-value
Industry (Public Sector)	0.241	(0.081)	2.97
Industry (Service)			
Occupation (upper white)	-0.571	(0.087)	-6.55
Occupation (lower white)			
Occupation (upper blue)	0.674	(0.075)	9.01
Occupation (lower blue)	1.202	(0.093)	12.88
Period variables			
(Year 1999)			
Year 2000	0.409	(0.098)	4.15
Year 2001	-0.058	(0.103)	-0.56
Year 2002	-0.107	(0.101)	-1.06
Year 2003	-0.146	(0.103)	-1.42
Year 2004	-0.154	(0.102)	-1.51
Year 2005	0.042	(0.1)	0.42
Year 2006	-0.001	(0.1)	-0.01
Year 2007	0.065	(0.098)	0.66
constant	-4.671	(0.135)	-34.7
ln σ_u^2	-0.494	(0.172)	
Sigma_u*	0.781	(0.067)	
Rho**	0.156	(0.023)	

Likelihood-ratio test of rho=0: chi squared (01) = 54.44 Prob ≥ chi squared = 0.000
* Sigma_u refers to square root of (σ_u^2), which is the variance of (u_i) in the panel model specified, $y^*_{i,t} = \alpha + \beta x_{i,t} + u_i + \gamma_t + \varepsilon_{i,t}$. ** 'Rho' refers to the the fraction of total variance due to u_i.
SOURCE: KLIPS

older people are more likely to be employed in temporary positions than males, the high-educated, and middle-aged people. But a more important result is the strong and dominating effect of state dependency observed in employment status. In other words, previous status strongly affects current employment status. If a person's previous employment status was temporary, self-employed, or out of the labor force, then, his/her risk of being in temporary employment now is much higher than when permanently employed in the previous position, even when other individual characteristics and labor market positions are statistically controlled.

Individuals' labor market positions also significantly affect the risk of being temporarily employed currently. Belonging to a large firm significantly raises the risk of temporary employment, while being in an organized workplace significantly lowers the risk. The union effect is much larger than the effect of belonging to a large firm, indicating a significant deterring effect of the labor union on employment flexibility in large firms. In agriculture, construction, and service industries, workers are more likely to be employed temporarily, as is often observed in other labor surveys, than in manufacturing or public service industries. Belonging to a lower or upper blue-collar occupational class also significantly raises the risk of being in a temporary position relative to lower or upper white-collar class.

In sum, the results closely follow those normally expected from a theoretical perspective and past labor force surveys, which implies that our panel data well represents the labor market reality in Korea. Further, the large and significant $\sigma_u = 0.78$ indicates that there exists a significant individual heterogeneity latent in the process and that our random effects panel model is more efficient than a pooled OLS model.

Analysis of risk of transition into temporary employment:
Next, I analyze the risk of getting into a temporary employment position when a job move occurs. Regardless of origin status, an individual worker's job move must end up belonging to one of the four alternative destinations: (1) permanent wage employment, (2) temporary wage employment, (3) self-employment, (4) getting out of the labor force. My interest in this analysis is in the question of who are more likely to end up belonging to (2) temporary wage employment rather than to (1) permanent wage employment. But (3) self-employment or (4) getting out of the labor force are two competing alternatives. In view of this, we adopt a multinomial logit model to analyze the multiple paths of transition in one model. In this setting where (1) permanent wage employment status is referenced, three sets of coefficients are estimated, but here I present only two sets belonging to (2) temporary employment and (3) self-employment.

Table 3.8 present the results of the analysis. According to these results, individuals with different characteristics and work experience are faced with significantly different risk of transiting into a temporary rather than permanent employment status when they move their jobs. In general, the results show that the vulnerable groups in the labor market (females, the elderly, the low-educated) are significantly more likely to transit into temporary employment than their counterparts.

TABLE 3.8 *Risk of transiting into temporary or self-employment status: Estimated coefficients of multinomial logit model (job movers)*

Variable	Employed fixed term or daily		Self-employed	
	β (Std. Err.)	z	β (Std. Err.)	z
Individual variables				
Female	0.39(0.05)	7.82	-0.019(0.053)	-0.36
Age (15–29)	-0.034(0.069)	-0.49	-0.781(0.083)	-9.4
Age (30–49)(reference)				
Age (≥ 50)	0.224(0.068)	3.31	0.038(0.067)	0.58
Education (< Middle Sch.)	0.303(0.063)	4.79	-0.084(0.067)	-1.25
Education (High School)				
Education (≥ College)	-0.178(0.062)	-2.88	0.036(0.062)	0.57
Emp_status (t–1) (Permanent emp.)				
Emp_status (t–1) (Temporary emp.)	3.631(0.063)	57.48	1.482(0.083)	17.86
Emp_status (t–1) (Self-employed.)	2.063(0.086)	24.1	4.259(0.061)	69.73
Emp_status (t–1) (out of labor force)	2.568(0.066)	38.88	1.746(0.073)	23.98
No. of rev. jobs	0.067(0.013)	5.32	-0.031(0.013)	-2.44
ln (total work experience)	-0.187(0.026)	-7.15	0.275(0.033)	8.24
Labor-market variables				
Industry (Agriculture+)	0.749(0.189)	3.95	2.975(0.174)	17.07
Industry (Manufacturing)	-0.492(0.063)	-7.82	-1.26(0.068)	-18.51
Industry (Construction)	1.332(0.081)	16.43	-0.738(0.102)	-7.24
Industry (Public Sector)	0.394(0.077)	5.12	-1.061(0.092)	-11.48
Industry (Service: reference)				
Occupation (upper white-)	-0.432(0.08)	-5.39	-0.169(0.072)	-2.34
Occupation (lower white-)				
Occupation (upper blue-)	0.577(0.066)	8.71	0.141(0.064)	2.2
Occupation (lower blue-)	1.117(0.081)	13.78	-0.958(0.101)	-9.47
Period variables				
(Year 1998: reference)				
Year 1999	0.736(0.088)	8.4	0.443(0.09)	4.9
Year 2000	0.095(0.093)	1.02	0.097(0.097)	1

TABLE 3.8 *Risk of transiting into temporary or self-employment status: Estimated coefficients of multinomial logit model (job movers)* (cont.)

Variable	Employed fixed term or daily		Self-employed	
	β (Std. Err.)	z	β (Std. Err.)	z
Year 2001	0.137(0.095)	1.45	−0.002(0.097)	−0.02
Year 2002	0.166(0.093)	1.79	0.295(0.094)	3.14
Year 2003	0.138(0.09)	1.52	0.08(0.094)	0.85
Year 2004	0.417(0.09)	4.63	0.081(0.095)	0.86
Year 2005	0.343(0.096)	3.58	0.411(0.097)	4.24
Year 2006	0.299(0.093)	3.22	−0.11(0.099)	−1.11
Year 2007	0.291(0.093)	3.12	0.035(0.097)	0.36
constant	−2.71(0.189)	−14.34	−3.586(0.231)	−15.56

Note: χ^2 (df = 52)=21912.87, p < 0.000, Pseudo R^2=0.4631.
SOURCE: KLIPS

In a similar manner to the previous analysis, past employment status again strongly affects the path of transition taken on job moves. That is, being in other than permanent employment status in the previous position raises the risk of transiting into a temporary position to a great extent even when the effect of labor market variables is controlled. We observe a strong status-dependency in labor mobility. We also observe that those with unstable employment history (i.e., many job changes and less work experience) are more likely to get into a temporary employment when they move jobs. But the opposite is true for the risk of transition into self-employment.

The effects of the industry and occupation to which the job mover belongs show a similar pattern with the analysis results presented in Table 3.7. That is, relative to service industry, the risk of transiting into temporary employment is much lower when in the manufacturing industry. If working in agriculture, the job mover's risk of transiting into self-employment is much higher than working in other industries. In terms of occupational effect, the results also show a pattern similar to that in Table 3.7: upper or lower blue-collar workers are much more likely to get into a temporary position than white-collar workers when they move jobs. In contrast, low blue-collar workers are much less likely to transit into self-employment than low white-collar workers, which is understandable considering the limited financial resources available to the low-income manual workers.

6 Conclusions

The economic crisis that started in 1998 resulted in dramatic changes taking place in many parts of the Korean economy and labor market. The most noticeable were increased labor market flexibility and instability of employment relations. To remain competitive and survive the crisis, firms in many industries laid off large numbers of workers and now opted for irregular or temporary employment contract when they had any need to supplement their workforce. As an outcome, the proportion of temporary employment for wage-workers greatly increased.

In this paper, we addressed the following issues: How and to what extent did the increased flexibility and restructuring affect the opportunity structure of the labor market, i.e., job mobility for workers in Korea for the 10-year period that followed the crisis? Were old inequalities reinforced, or did new windows of opportunity open? Classical labor theories tell us to expect that increased labor market flexibility might offer new opportunities, through increased number of vacancies both in the internal and external labor market, for less qualified, disadvantaged workers with lower reservation wages.

With regard to the relation between labor market restructuring and mobility at the aggregate level, two contrasting scenarios are proposed by past studies: the integration and disintegration scenarios. The integration scenario posits that, as a consequence of increased flexibility in the labor market, extant mobility barriers between labor market sectors (primary versus secondary) and firms (large firms versus SMEs) should be lowered and "new opportunities" opened for cross-sector or inter-firm mobility. In contrast, the disintegration scenario posits that the persistent and duality and segmentation of the labor market, that is to say "old inequalities," will be reinforced.

To address this issue, we analyzed the rate and the pattern of job mobility among Korean workers using individual work history data from the Korean Labor and Income Panel Study, or KLIPS (1988–2008). Analyses were made at the aggregate and the individual level, focusing on changes in employment status (permanent versus temporary) as a consequence of job mobility. At the aggregate level, we also examined the extent to which job mobility occurred across labor market sectors (primary versus secondary) and how the extent changed over the time period observed.

We found that, over the 10-year period after the economic crisis, within-status (temporary to temporary or permanent to permanent) job mobility increased, while between-status job mobility decreased. We also found that between-sector barriers were strengthened as most job mobility was taking place within an individual sector. Specifically, the mobility of workers in the secondary sector took place within the secondary sector, and a substantial amount of job mobility from the primary sector took place downwardly, to the secondary sector.

On the basis of these results, we can conclude that, at the aggregate level, labor market flexibility initiated by the economic crisis has strengthened between-sector barriers in labor mobility, and weakened the upward-mobility opportunities of the secondary-sector workers over the years that followed the economic crisis.

At the individual level, the panel data (random effects/multinomial logit) model was adopted to estimate the effects of the individual's characteristics, prior employment and labor market position on the probability of being or getting into temporary rather than permanent employment when job mobility takes place. The focus of interest was whether temporary employment at time (t) is a trap or a stepping-stone to a permanent employment at time (t + 1).

The analytic results showed that there exists a strong employment status-dependency in labor mobility as the individual's prior employment status strongly affects the path of transition taken on job moves. That is, being in a temporary position raises the risk of transiting into another temporary position in job mobility to a great extent even when the effect of labor market variables is controlled. Thus the results at the individual level analysis also seem to support the "disintegration" scenario.

The significant effect of working in a "large firm" on the risk of being employed in a temporary position seems to support our initial proposition that the external duality of labor market would gradually be internalized into the internal labor market in large firms. However, further studies are needed on intra-firm job mobility to determine how and to what extent within-firm barriers between temporary (irregular) and permanent (regular) employment have been strengthened.

Another important finding from our panel data model analysis is that union effect exercises a powerful role in deterring the negative impact of increased labor market flexibility even when other structural variables are controlled. This means that, even though employers at large firms are more likely to opt for cheap temporary employment as a substitute for costly permanent employment, the negative effect of the "large firm" is offset to an extent by the existence of the labor union. It also implies that strong labor unions in large firms and in the public sector were able to play a role by raising workforce entry barriers, and strengthening internal labor markets and job security, while workers in SMEs who were not in unions do not have this option. This suggests that the internal labor market in the primary sector contracted but tightened, while external labor market in the secondary sector expanded and loosened.

In sum, we find that those in a disadvantaged position in the labor market in Korea are more likely to be employed with fixed-term contracts, and that there is a concomitant likelihood for a pattern of "chains of temporary employment" over individuals' career mobility (Booth et al. 2002).

In this study we focused only on changes in employment status (temporary versus permanent) as an outcome of individuals' job mobility in Korea. However, it should be recognized that the type of formal employment contract only partly reflects the quality of the job taken. Large differences in compensation, working hours (part-time versus full-time) and working conditions are commonly observed even among workers in permanent employment. Thus more in-depth studies are needed to take the substantive quality of jobs into account in analyzing job mobility outcomes (see Kim et al 2008; Lee and Lee 2007).

References

Ahmadjian, Christina. L. and Patricia Robinson. 2001. "Safety in Numbers: Downsizing and the Deinstitutionalization of Permanent Employment in Japan." *Administrative Science Quarterly*, 46(4): 622–654.

Arthur, Michael B., and Denise M. Rousseau. 1996. "Introduction: The Boundaryless Career as a New Employment Principle." In Michale B. Arthur & Denise M. Rousseau, eds., *The Boundaryless Career: A New Employment Principle for a New Organizational Era*, 3–20. New York: Oxford University Press.

Baltagi, Badi. H. 2008. *Econometric Analysis of Panel Data*. John Wiley & Sons, Ltd.

Booth, Alison, Marco Francesconi, and Jeff Frank. 2002. "Temporary Jobs: Stepping Stones or Dead Ends?" *Economic Journal* 112: 198–213.

Choi, Seongsoo. 2010. "Occupational Mobility in the Economic Crisis: The Example of South Korea." Paper presented at the American Sociological Association Annual Meeting, 2010.

DiPrete, Thomas, A. and K. Lynn Nonnemarker. 1997. "Structural Change, Labor Market Turbulence and Labor Market Outcomes." *American Sociological Review* 62(3): 386–404.

DiPrete, Thomas A., Paul M. de Graaf, Ruud Luijkx, MichaeL Tahlin and Hans-Peter Blossfeld. 1997. "Collectivist Versus Individualist Mobility Regimes? Structural Change and Job Mobility in Four Countries." *American Journal of Sociology* 103(2): 318–358.

Giesecke, Jobannes and Martin Gross. 2003. "Temporary Employment: Chance or Risk?" *European Sociological Review* 19(2): 161–177.

Grubb, David, JaeKap Lee, and Peter Tergeist. 2007. "Addressing Labour Market Duality in Korea." *OECD Social Employment and Migration Working Papers*, 61. OECD Publishing.

Hwang, Soo-Kyung. 2010. "Global Financial Crisis and Labor Market Changes." In Hwang et al., ed., *Economic Crisis and Employment*. Korea Labor Institute. (in Korean).

Kenn, Agisa, Giorgio Brunello and Yasushi Ohkusa. 2000. *Internal Labor Markets in Japan.* Cambridge: Cambridge University Press.

Kim, Hye-Won, Sung-Hoon Kim and Min-Sik Choi. 2008. *Labor Market Effects of Job Mobility*. Seoul: Korea Labor Institute.

KNSO. 2011. *A Survey of the Economically Active Population.* Korea National Statistics Office.

Kye, Bongoh. 2008. "Internal Labor Markets and the Effects of Structural Change: Job Mobility in Korean Labor Markets between 1998 and 2000," *Research in Social Stratification and Mobility* 26(1): 15–27.

Lee, Byung-Hee and S. Lee. 2007. *Minding the Gaps: Non-Regular Employment and Labour Market Segmentation in Korea.* International Working Party on Labour Market Segmentation.

Lee, Byung-Hee and Bum-Sang Yoo. 2007. "From Flexibility to Segmentation: Changes in Employment Patterns in Korea." Paper presented at the Workshop on Globalization and Changes in Employment Conditions in Asia and the Pacific. Seoul: Korea Labor Institute and ILO.

Lee, Ju-Ho. 1992. *An Empirical Analysis of the Dual Labor Market in Korea.* Korea Development Institute. (in Korean).

Lindbeck, Assar and Dennis J. Snower. 1988. *The Insider-Outsider Theory of Employment and Unemployment*. Cambridge and London: MIT Press.

Ng, Thomas W., Kelly L. Sorensen, Lillian T. Eby and Daniel C. Feldman. 2007. "Determinants of Job Mobility: A Theoretical Integration and Extension." *Journal of Occupational and Organizational Psychology* 80: 363–386.

OECD. 2005. *The Labor Market in Korea: Enhancing Flexibility and Raising Participation.* Economics Department Working Papers, 469. Paris: OECD.

Sicherman, Nachum. 1990. "Education and Occupational Mobility." *Economics of Education Review* 9 (2): 163–179.

Sicherman, Nachum and Oded Galor. 1990. "A Theory of Career Mobility." *Journal of Political Economy* 98 (1): 169–192.

Watanabe, Tsutomu and Sato Yoshimichi. 2000. "Analysis of Labor Markets in Postwar Japan." *International Journal of Sociology* 30(2): 3–33.

CHAPTER 4

The Impact of a Changing Employment System on Women's Employment upon Marriage and after Childbirth in Japan[1]

Yamato Reiko

1 Employment Flexibility and Women's Employment

The latter half of the 1980s saw a growing trend toward employment flexibility in many countries developing amid intensifying international competition caused by economic globalization (Blossfeld and Hofmeister 2006). In Japan the issue of men who became unemployed in their middle to early old age became an object of focus in the 1990s (Nakatani 1987; Nomura 1994), followed in the 2000s by the rise of non-standard employment among the young (Genda 2001; Jo 2006). However, the trend toward employment flexibility in fact developed earlier for women than men in Japan, and had broader and deeper reach. The rate of non-standard employment among women in the labor force started rising as early as the 1970s and the proportion of women among non-standard employees has been consistently far higher than that of men (Otobe 2006).

Nevertheless, in Japan, it was the trend toward employment flexibility among men (young, middle-aged, or old) that aroused public concern. After World War II, systems of family, employment, and social security developed based on the model of the male breadwinner, namely that men earn the income while women carry out domestic chores and provide child and elderly care (Osawa 1993). The trend toward men's employment flexibility thus shook established institutions to their core. In contrast, the trend toward women's employment flexibility drew much less public attention. The reason for this was that women were not regarded as the main breadwinners in the above-mentioned systems and their employment insecurity was therefore not considered as problematic as men's. However, with the male breadwinner model under question, changes in women's employment have been recognized as having a crucial impact not only on employment and social security systems but also on family and individual security.

1 This study uses, with permission, data for Japan from the 2005 SSM survey. The author refers to the syntax used by Yasuda Tokio regarding data analysis. The author would like to express her appreciation for the helpful comments made on this study by other contributors of this book.

 DOI 10.1163/9789004262737_005

This chapter analyzes data provided by the Social Stratification and Mobility (SSM) Survey of 2005 to clarify the ways in which the trend toward employment flexibility has transformed Japan's employment system and how this transformation has impacted women's employment at marriage and childbirth. On the basis of these results we will discuss how the life course of women is changing in Japan today.

2 Research in Europe and the United States on Impacts of Economic Globalization on Women's Employment

According to research from Europe and the United States, economic globalization has had the following effects on the employment of women. Firstly, on the quantitative side, there was an increase both in terms of the rates of labor participation among women and in the length of service. Formerly the main causes for women to interrupt employment were marriage and childbirth, but from the 1990s onward the trend for marriage as a cause of employment interruption declined considerably. In the United States and Sweden, with their liberal and social democratic welfare regimes, childbirth also declined as a reason for employment interruption (Esping-Andersen 1990). Further, the extent to which women decided to re-enter the labor market after an interruption rose. Two factors lay behind this quantitative expansion of women's labor participation. The first was that an increase in flexible employment opportunities caused by global economic competition made it easier for women to reconcile work and family. The second was that flexible employment also sometimes resulted in insecurity. The rising insecurity in male employment increased the need for women to have gainful work, which further increased because of the expanding risks of divorce or relationship dissolution associated with men's rising employment insecurity (Blossfeld and Hofmeister 2006). These changes are sometimes understood as the transformation from "male-breadwinner model family" to "adult worker model family" (Lewis and Giullari 2005), or as a change from the "Fordist model" to the "post-Fordist model" (Mayer 2004).

Secondly, on the qualitative side, women's employment has become more insecure. The risk of unemployment increased in comparison with the past, and re-employment became more difficult. Moreover, downward mobility (moving to a lower level of employment according to socio-economic indices) has increased, while upward mobility (moving to a higher level of employment) has decreased (Blossfeld and Hofmeister 2006; Glover and Kirton 2006).

Thirdly, not all women are exposed to the risk of employment insecurity to the same extent. Depending on the resources that individual women possess (human capital, position in the labor market, domestic environment), a polarization of women's employment can be seen. Women whose human capital (work experience, skills, academic background) is not so high are easily exposed to the risks of increasingly insecure employment, as are women who are in a disadvantageous position in the labor market (non-standard employment, employment in the private sector) and women who carry heavy family responsibilities (those who have small children, for example). Other women not in these circumstances are protected from such risks and can easily continue working under good labor conditions, which brings their life course in terms of employment closer to that of men. Thus, while diversification caused by the individuals' resources is seen among women, a trend toward convergence between men and women is also observed (Blossfeld and Hakim 1997; Blossfeld and Hofmeister 2006; Glover and Kirton 2006; McRae 2003). This situation is referred to as "converging divergence" (Moen 2006; Moen and Spencer 2006).

Lastly, economic globalization exerts an influence on individuals through the intermediary of country-specific institutions. Some institutions foster societies where the individual is easily exposed to the risk of increasingly insecure employment while other institutions foster societies where this is not the case. According to research that compared five types of Western countries identified on the basis of Esping-Andersen's (1990) classification (social democracy, liberalism, conservatism, southern Europe-style familism, and post-communism), in northern Europe with its social democratic welfare regimes, the trends toward both employment insecurity and polarization are not as serious as in countries with other types of regimes. The reason for this is thought to be the various institutions that are in place in social democratic regimes that protect individuals from global risks (Blossfeld and Hakim 1997; Blossfeld and Hofmeister 2006).

3 Comparative Research on East Asian Capitalist Societies

3.1 *Similarities and Differences between Japan, Taiwan, and South Korea*

Next we will look at research on the three East Asian capitalist societies of Japan, Taiwan, and South Korea, whose cultures differ from those of Western countries, and where capitalism has developed over a different timespan. These three East Asian societies belong to the same cultural sphere of Confucianism and they share similar cultural ideas on how human relations work, including on family and gender relations. All three of them also saw a delayed development of capitalism in comparison to the West, and have an export-oriented economy. Moreover, due to Japan's colonial rule over Taiwan and Korea in the past, many of their institutions, such as educational systems, show common features. They have all been influenced by the recent economic globalization and the trend toward employment flexibility is observed in all three societies (Hayashi 2009; Kanbayashi and Takenoshita, 2009; Sakaguchi 2011b; Tarohmaru 2014; Yokota 2003; Wo 2006).

Comparisons of the extent and pattern of increasing flexibility show considerable differences between the three societies themselves, however. The first difference is that the increase in flexibility as a whole is more advanced in Taiwan and South Korea, while it is relatively restrained in Japan (Hayashi 2009; Kanbayashi and Takenoshita 2009; Sakaguchi 2011b; Tarohmaru 2014). The reason for restrained flexibility in Japan is that, while workers at the periphery of the labor market (e.g., women, non-standard employees, young people newly entering the labor market, and employees of small firms) are exposed to the risks of increasing flexibility, workers at the core (men, standard employees, and employees of large firms) are comparatively protected (Kagawa 2011; Nakazawa 2011; Sakaguchi 2011a; Takenoshita 2008; Watanabe 2011; Yoshida 2011). When viewed as a whole, the extent of increase in flexibility in Japan is not so large compared to that in the other two societies. Sato (2009) refers to this situation in Japan as the coexistence of stabilization and increasing flexibility (see also Sato and Hayashi 2011).

The second difference is related to a comparison of the effect between workers' human capital and workers' position in the labor market on the extent of their employment insecurity. Human capital includes work experience, skills, and academic background. Position in the labor market (which indicates how close workers are located to the core of the internal labor market) includes employment status and size of the firm. In Taiwan and South Korea, workers' human capital strongly influences the extent to which they are exposed to the risks of employment flexibility, whereas in Japan their position in the labor market also exerts an influence as large as that of human capital (Brinton 2001; Hayashi 2009; Kanbayashi and Takenoshita 2009; Sakaguchi 2011b; Tarohmaru 2014). In other words, in Taiwan and South Korea, human capital is the most important factor in the segmentation of workers; in Japan, in contrast, the position in the labor market is also important. This was also confirmed by research comparing factors regulating income and class identification in the three societies (Arita 2009).

3.2 *Differences in the Three Societies' Employment Systems*

The differences in the employment systems are the main factor in the abovementioned differences between Taiwan, South Korea, and Japan. In the Taiwanese and South Korean labor markets, market mechanisms are comparatively strong (and the influence of human capital is therefore large). In Japan, on the other hand, market mechanisms are restrained because the variety of Fordist employment system (Mayer 2004) established during the period of rapid economic growth in the late 1950s and 1960s has continued to work to a certain degree even under a globalized economy. Therefore, the influence of position in the labor market is greater than that of human capital in Japan.

The Fordist employment system is based on the gendered division of labor—"the man works, the woman takes care of the household"—and it segments workers on the basis of gender and marital status. The Japanese employment system, a subtype of the Fordist employment system, is characterized below

TABLE 4.1 *Differences in employment systems in Japan and Taiwan*

	Japanese employment system			**Taiwan**
Employment status	(A) Standard		(B) Non-standard	Standard
Position in internal labor market	(A1) Core	(A2) Peripheral	Peripheral	[Less rigidly defined]
Career track	Long-term & manager	Pre-marital & non-manager	Short-term & non-manager	[Less rigidly defined]
Recruit	New graduates	New graduates	Re-entrees	[Less rigidly defined]
Gender and marital status	Male	Female & unmarried	Female & married	[Less rigidly defined]
Employment security and other work conditions[a]	High	Low	Low	Medium
Required loyalty to firm[b]	High	Low	Low	Medium
Effects of changes in the Japanese employment system				
For male youth	● - - - - - -	- - - - - - - -	- - →	
For female youth	←————	———●————	———→	

a Promotion, pay rise, training, etc.
b Longer working hours, overtime work, jobs transfer with geographical relocation, etc.

(Inagami 1999; Nomura 1994. See also the panel "Japanese Employment System" in the center of Table 4.1). According to this system, workers can be divided first into standard (A) and non-standard (B) employment. Standard employment recruits new graduates, while non-standard employees are recruited mid-career. A very important point is a further division within standard employment into core employees (A1) and peripheral employees (A2): the former are expected to be promoted to management in long-term employment while the latter are expected to be employed only short term until marriage (or childbirth) and are not expected to be promoted to management. Normally, standard core employment (A1) is assigned to men, standard peripheral employment (A2) to unmarried (or pre-childbirth) women, and non-standard employment (B) is peripheral employment assigned to reemployed married women. Loyalty toward the firm (including long work hours and job transfers with geographical relocations) is demanded of standard core employees (A1), but in return they receive better work conditions such as long-term employment, promotion, salary raises, and the firm's internal training. Standard peripheral (A2) and non-standard (B) employment do not demand the abovementioned loyalty (which is why such employment is often chosen by married women with domestic responsibilities or unmarried women who are expected to undertake such responsibilities in the near future) but have unfavorable and insecure work conditions.

Such an employment system is more easily applicable to larger firms and to white-collar occupations. The reason for the former is that the larger firms can guarantee the employment of standard core employees even during a recession, and can more easily recruit new young female workers when their existing female employees retire upon marriage or childbirth. The reason for the latter is that white-collar jobs are the kind of occupations where continued long-term employment and subsequent promotion to management are expected (Nomura 1994).

Segmentation within standard employment based on gender or marital status in Japan was made illegal with the Equal Employment Opportunity Act for Men and Women (effective 1986). However, such segmentation continues to be in effect even after the legislation: openly labeled distinction by gender is no longer the norm, but continues under the superficially different rubric of "*sōgō shoku* (comprehensive job)" (A1) and "*ippan shoku* (ordinary job)" (A2) (Otobe 2010).

In the Japanese employment system, standard core employment is difficult to terminate as it is protected by a variety of laws and customary practice (Nomura 1994). With the intensification of international competition under economic globalization and the increased necessity to cut labor costs, most firms react by keeping their already employed standard core employees (A1), reducing the number of newly recruited standard employees, and increasing the number of non-standard employees (B). In the 1970s and 1980s, increases were made in the labor force without increasing labor costs by employing married women in non-standard employment (B) (Otobe 2010). This adjustment ran alongside the male-breadwinner model and was not seen as a serious threat to the Japanese employment system. From the 1990s onward, however, new graduates who would have previously been employed in standard employment were being employed in a non-standard way; and this applied not just to women but also to men (Genda 2001). In other words, the tracks that were previously assigned to young men (i.e., standard core employment (A1)) and to women (i.e., standard peripheral employment (A2)), were reduced; and instead the risk increased for young men and women to enter non-standard employment (B), which used to be mainly for married women.

Consequently, employment opportunities for standard core employment (A1) decreased in Japan, but workers who were already in this type of employment were protected. At the same time, employment opportunities for non-standard employment (B) rose and both male and female workers in this type of employment were exposed to the risks of unemployment. A situation therefore arose in which stabilization and increasing flexibility in employment coexisted.

3.3 *Analyzing Women: The Necessary Perspectives*

As stated above, most sociological research on the Japanese employment system has focused mainly on men. Since the Japanese employment system revolved mainly around male employment, it made sense to focus on men in the analysis of its fluctuations. However, since the Japanese employment system treats men and women very differently, the influence of such fluctuations may well be different for men and women. The following points need to be taken into account when analyzing women's position.

First, despite the tendency in research involving male–female comparisons to treat all women as peripheral workers, there are in fact wide variations among women in regard to human capital, position in the labor market, and family situation, among other things. Research carried out in western countries (Blossfeld and Hakim 1997; Blossfeld and Hofmeister 2006; Glover and Kirton 2006; McRae 2003) actually reported both diversification among women and convergence between men and women proceeding. It is thus surely reasonable and right that heterogeneity among women should be taken into account.

Second, while previous research focusing on male employment has placed great concern on human capital and position in the labor market as factors influencing employment security, little attention has been paid to family events such as marriage and childbirth. Marriage and childbirth exert a strong influence on women's employment. The employment interruption brought about by these events is one of the major causes of women's peripheral positioning in the labor market and their employment insecurity. We should surely pay attention to family circumstances such as marriage and childbirth as well.

As a third point, especially in regard to Japan, support systems for female employment have developed alongside the increases in the employment flexibility. Although these systems began to develop in the latter 1980s, they have shown a previously unseen qualitative development since the 2000s. It is necessary to take the influence of these support system into account as well. These support systems can be largely divided into two types: legislative policy to promote equal opportunities for men and women in the workplace, and support measures for childcare (childcare leave, child care services, etc.) (Siaroff 1994).

With regard to the first type, equal opportunity legislation in the workplace, the Convention on the Elimination of All Forms of Discrimination against Women (adopted by the UN in 1979) was ratified by Japan in 1985 and as a consequence the Equal Employment Opportunity Act for Men and Women (effective 1986) was enacted to maintain consistency with the UN convention. However, although gender discrimination in regard to retirement and discharge was prohibited, discrimination in recruitment, employment, deployment, and promotion was not legally prohibited at this point. For the latter categories of discrimination, the only provision was one that asked employers to make efforts to avoid such discriminations. Thus, the power of the Act to push equal opportunities forward was weak. However, with the 1997 revision (effective 1999), gender discrimination in recruitment, employment, deployment, promotion, and even education and training was prohibited. The revision also made it possible for the state to publicize the names of firms that were not abiding by the state's leadership and guidance. Regulations that made it possible for the state to provide advice and support for positive action were also included. This revision made for stronger support for equal opportunities in the workplace by public authority (Otobe 2010).

The second type of support, childcare support, began to develop in the 1990s with the Childcare Leave Law (1992) and the Angel Plan (1994), among others. Public concern over the declining birth rate lay behind these developments, and the declining birth rate itself was, according to Kato (2011), caused by increasing employment insecurity among the youth. These childcare support measures introduced in the early 1990s were, however, mostly measures that targeted only "working mothers" and were constructed in a way that implied women using the measures were, in a way, receiving an "exceptional" service in the workplace. They did nothing to stop the tendency to view working mothers as exceptions and such support measures were difficult to use. In the 2000s, a qualitative overhaul of these support systems was planned, when it became clear that the trend of declining marriage and birth rates could not be halted. Policies were introduced that aimed at promoting work-life balance not only for working mothers but also for single women and men (including those with wives who did not work). The new measures included Measures to Cope with a Fewer Number of Children: Plus One in 2002, the Basic Act for Measures to Cope with Society with Declining Birthrate in 2003, and Plans for Supporting Children and Childcare in 2004 (Takeishi 2006). Such qualitative changes weakened the tendency to view the use of support measures as an "exception" and made it easier for working mothers to use them (NHK 2011).

It is possible that fostering employment support systems in this way, coupled with the aforementioned increase in non-standard employment among young people, has changed employment patterns for young women in Japan. Moreover, the changes that have taken place could well have different effects for young women to the effects for young men. According to previous research (Hayashi 2009; Nakazawa 2011; Sakaguchi 2011a), for young men the reduction in the standard core employment track (A1) coupled with the widening of non-standard employment (B) has resulted in a one-way downward mobility. For young women, on the other hand, while the downward mobility risk of entering non-standard employment (B) has increased, the upward mobility possibility of entering the standard long-term employment track (A1) has also increased when they are in a position to use the abovementioned support systems. This means that, for young women, two contrary possibilities of descending and ascending have opened up (see bottom row of Table 4.1).

It should be noted that the employment support systems for women do not cover all employers or employees equally. In Japan, equal opportunity legislation and childcare support measures are mainly used by standard employees (A). Moreover, strong legal compliance is only required by, and official supervision directed at, the larger-scale firms, as a rule. Such differences in employment status and scale of work place should thus also be taken into account.

3.4 *Comparative East Asian Research on Women's Employment at the Times of Marriage and Childbirth*

We will next look at some of the results derived from comparative research that targets women in the East Asian societies of Japan and Taiwan and that does take the heterogeneity among women and the influence of marriage and childbirth into account (see Section 3.3).

If we look at labor force participation rate by age and birth cohort in Japan and Taiwan, we see that the rates for women born before the war peaked in their early 20s; and that in this period no large difference existed between the two societies. However, for women born after the war, a gap between the two societies does emerge. The younger the women in Taiwan, the more they continue to work during periods of marriage and childbirth. In Japan, in contrast, an M-shaped life course emerges as women leave the workplace after marriage or childbirth and later get re-employed. In other words, in Taiwan after the war women increasingly continued employment during marriage and childbirth, whereas this did not happen in Japan. Why was this?

Possible reasons might be expected to include Japanese women having more conservative gender role attitudes, less human capital, heavier domestic responsibilities, and husbands with a higher household-finance-support power, as well as Japan having weaker public welfare systems and laws supporting women's employment. The data, however, does not support any of these hypotheses (Yu 2009). Focus then is placed on the differences in the two countries' employment systems.[2] Research carried out by Yu (2009) has shown how it is the differences in the employment system and labor demand in the two countries that have led to a difference in employment at marriage and childbirth, and the following explanation is based on her findings.

It is generally thought in the field of sociology that modernization brings about an increase in white-collar work, larger firms, higher household-finance-support power for men, and a trend toward nuclear families. However, it is possible that these social changes exert a different influence on women's employment in differing institutions.

Japan after World War II saw no serious labor insufficiency due to the development of capital-intensive industries.[3] Employers were thus not incentivized to employ women in the core labor force, and the Japanese employment system presented in Table 4.1 emerged at this period. As it was difficult to reconcile work and family in the standard core employment track in this employment system, women were mostly assigned to the standard pre-marriage employment track, in which there was a trend toward choosing to exit the labor force at marriage or childbirth. Since the Japanese employment system was more likely to be applied to clerical work or larger-scale firms, women in such employment were more likely to retire. However, despite this pressure to retire, women whose husbands' household-finance-support power was low, or who had support in childcare from grandparents, could be expected to resume employment easily. The hypothesis can thus be made that, in the Japanese context, the progress of modernization in the form of increased white-collar work,

2 See Chapters 1 and 2 for differences of women's status in Japanese and Taiwanese labor markets.

3 Capital-intensive industry is industry that requires a large amount of capital compared to labor costs: for example, steel, automobile, and heavy-chemical industries.

larger firms, higher household-finance-support power for men, and a trend toward nuclear families all acted to make women interrupt employment.

In Taiwan, by contrast, incentives for employers to employ women, especially those with high human capital, were strong due to a labor force insufficiency, particularly from the 1980s onward. As can be seen in the "Taiwan" section on the right side of Table 4.1, an employment system with strict worker segmentation by gender and marital status did not develop; rather, the influence of market mechanisms based on human capital was strong. Contrary to Japan, there were incentives for women with advantageous work (white-collar, large firm, etc.) to continue employment in Taiwan. Moreover, because small-scale firms were predominant in Taiwan, individual negotiations regarding work conditions were easy due to an informal work culture, and thus reconciling work and family was also easy. Therefore, regardless of the husbands' household-finance-support power and support by grandparents, Taiwanese women could be predicted to continue employment if they had advantageous work. In other words, the hypothesis can be made that social change caused by modernization in the form of an increase in white-collar work, larger firms, higher household-finance-support power for men, and a trend toward nuclear families had, in the Taiwanese context, the opposite effect to that in the Japanese context, namely acting to make women continue employment (or at least not promoting retirement).

Table 4.2 shows the results of an analysis using life history data up to 1995 conducted by Yu (2009). These results support the abovementioned hypotheses. In Japan, the attributes of white-collar work, employment at a large firm, husband with high household-finance-support power, and nuclear family all promoted women's exit of the workforce at marriage or childbirth; in Taiwan,

TABLE 4.2 *Determinants of women's exit from the labor force or staying on at work upon marriage or first childbirth for Japanese and Taiwanese women, as summarized from the results in Yu (2009)*

		Japan	Taiwan
Employment	White-collar job (vs. blue-collar job)	Exit	Stay
	Larger firms (vs. smaller firms)	Exit	Stay
Family	Husband's longer years of education[a]	Exit	n.s.[b]
	Nuclear family (vs. extended family)	Exit	n.s.[b]

[a] Proxy of the husband's earning ability.
[b] Not statistically significant.

the same attributes promoted continued employment or at least did not promote exit. In other words, the changes due to modernization led to women's exit at marriage or childbirth in Japan and the contrary, continued employment, in Taiwan.

4 Research Questions and Hypothesis: How have Changes in the Japanese Employment System Influenced Women's Employment?

The research done by Yu (2009) outlined in the above section covers only the period until 1995. Since then, the Japanese labor market and employment system have undergone substantive change. One such change is the increase in non-standard employment among young unmarried women; another, the quantitative and qualitative improvement in women's employment support systems (see Section 3.3). The research outlined below analyzes how these two changes in the Japanese employment system have influenced women's employment at marriage and childbirth.

With regard to the first change, young women's increasing non-standard employment, there are two hypotheses possible. The first posits that in addition to non-standard employment being insecure in itself, employment support systems for women are often not being applied to it and thus young women exit the workforce even more because of increasing non-standard employment (the "retirement through increased non-standard employment" hypothesis). The second hypothesis, on the contrary, posits that because non-standard employment is more time-flexible and makes it easier to reconcile work and family than standard employment, non-standard employment at marriage and childcare leads to continued employment (the "continued employment through increased non-standard employment" hypothesis), which is also possible.

With regard to the second change, the development of support systems for women's employment, another two hypotheses are possible to explain its effect. The first posits that support systems make continued employment easier (the "continued employment through support systems" hypothesis), whereas the second posits that because support systems are nothing more than pretense and are difficult to use in reality, their effect in promoting continued employment is very weak (the "support systems are ineffective" hypothesis), which is also possible.

Which of these hypotheses will the actual data support? Will the supported hypothesis differ for marriage and childbirth? Moreover, will one hypothesis be correct for a certain group of women but incorrect for a different group of women?

5 Data and Methods

Our research uses data on Japan from the SSM Survey 2005, a Japanese survey that was administered nationally from November 2005 to April 2006 and targeted people aged 20 to 69 years (as of September 30, 2005), yielding 5,742 valid samples (valid return rate 44.1 percent).

In this research the discrete-time event history analysis is used (Yamaguchi 1991).[4] The unit of time is a year. The sample below is the analysis target. In the analysis of retirement upon marriage, we target women aged between 25 and 59 years who have experience of marriage and who have been employed at the point in time one year before marriage. There were 1,323 results from the survey for these cases. For these, we created person-year data for the four years from the year of marriage to the third year after marriage and analyzed this period until the year of retirement (i.e., the years after retirement are exempted from the analysis target). However, the number of person-year observations where agriculture is listed as the previous year's occupation is small and may therefore distort the estimate. To avoid such distortion, these person-year observations were omitted. Person-year observations with missing values were also omitted as well. Once these omissions were made, a total of 2,905 person-year observations were obtained as the target for the analysis upon marriage.[5]

Next, for the analysis of retirement before and after childbirth, we focused on the birth of the first child. We targeted women between 25 and 59 years who have experience of marriage, have one child or more, and have been employed at the point in time two years before the birth of their first child (thus before

4 Event history model is a statistical model predicting the occurrence probability of an event such as death, marriage and job change. If time is measured as a discrete variable, a logit or probit model is appropriate to predict the occurrence probability. This logit or probit model applied for event data with a discrete time variable is called discrete-time event history model.

5 Two additional sets of data were generated for the analysis upon marriage and for the analysis upon childbirth: the first is a data set in which person-year observations with agriculture listed as the previous year's occupation are *not* exempted; and the second is a data set in which the person-year observations with agriculture or the self-employed sector listed as a previous year's occupation or employment status, respectively, are exempted. The reason for the exemptions is that the Japanese employment system and women's employment support measures are mainly associated with employees, but not with agriculture or the self-employment sector. For each of the additional data sets, the same analyses as those in the present study were conducted. The results of these additional analyses were almost the same as the analyses shown in this study.

the pregnancy). The results from the survey in these cases are 1,078. For these cases we created person-year data for the five years from the year before childbirth to the third year after childbirth and analyzed this period until the year of retirement (i.e., the years after retirement were exempted from the analysis target). As in the previous analysis, the person-year observations where agriculture is given as the previous year's occupation were omitted to avoid distortion of the estimate due to low sample size. Person-year observations with missing values were omitted as well. From these procedures, 2,834 person-year observations were obtained as the target for the analysis around childbirth.

The dependent variables are retirement (1) and continued employment (0) in the year in focus. The independent variables are, first, variables reflecting direct influence of the Japanese employment system, namely the woman's occupation, the scale of the employer organization, and the employment status, all of which are those in the year before the year in focus. For occupation, we used manual labor occupations as the base category and managerial/professional, semi-professional, clerical and sales/service occupations as dummy variables. For scale of the firm, we used 1 to 9 employees as the base category and 10 to 99, 100 to 499, more than 500 employees, public sector, and unknown, as dummy variables. For employment status, we used standard employment as the base category and non-standard employment as well as the self-employed sector (employer/self-employed/family-employed) as dummy variables.

For variables expressing indirect influence of the Japanese employment system, we focused on the family situation and used husband's household-finance-support power and family structure. For husband's household-finance-support power, there is no data on the income at marriage or childbirth, and so we used husband's years of education as a proxy variable. In general, men's years of education correlate with their income, and this tendency is confirmed for Japanese men (Arita 2009). For family structure, we used nuclear family (1) and extended family (0) meaning a family with at least one parent of either the husband or wife in co-residence.

With regard to women's employment support systems in Japan, we use the birth cohort as a proxy variable reflecting its development. We used 55- to 59-year-old women (the oldest cohort) as the base category and 25- to 34-, 35- to 44-, 45- to 54-year-old women as dummy variables. The younger cohort of 25- to 34- and 35- to 44-year-old women, who were in their twenties in the year 2000 and 1990 respectively, when support systems began to develop in Japan, are the first two generations to spend their period of first employment and family formation under the new systems. We therefore paid special attention to the differences between these two generations and older generations.

As control variables, we first used two variables common to both the analysis upon marriage and the analysis around the childbirth, namely the woman's years of education and her present residence. Present residence is a proxy variable for residence at the times of marriage and childbirth and is classified into either urban residence (1) or other (0). In addition to these two common variables, we used for the analysis at the time of marriage variables expressing the timing (with the marriage year as the base category and first year, second year, and third year after marriage as dummy variables), and the variable of whether the year in focus coincides with the year of the birth of the first child (1), or not (0). For the analysis at the time of childbirth, in addition to the two common variables above we used two other variables: one expressing the timing (with one year before childbirth as the base category and the year of birth and the first, second, and third year after birth as dummy variables), and the other expressing married (1), or not (0), in the year in focus.

In this analysis, we predicted the following three models at the two points in time: marriage and childbirth. Model 1 as the baseline model is the same as the model in Yu (2009), namely the model containing all independent variables except employment status. The next model, Model 2, adds the employment status to Model 1. The last model, Model 3, adds to Model 2 the three kinds of interaction terms of (a) woman's occupation and cohort, (b) scale of employers' organization and cohort, and (c) family structure and cohort, with the aim of seeing how the Japanese employment system has changed through the historical development of women's employment support systems.

6 Results of Analyses

6.1 *Changes in the Distribution of Employment Status for Young Japanese Women: Increase in non-Standard Employment and Decrease in the Self-Employed Sector*

Figure 4.1 shows the distribution of employment status by cohort in two life stages for the Japanese women analyzed in this study: (a) one year before marriage and (b) two years before first childbirth. For both life stages, non-standard employment, which can be thought of as insecure, accounts for a larger percentage in younger cohorts than in older ones. The percentage of the self-employed sector, where reconciling work and family is thought to be easier, decreases for younger cohorts. Looking only at these changes in employment status, we could expect that the younger the cohort, the less likely that women continue employment at the time of marriage or childbirth. However, the actual picture obtained from the multivariable analysis below was different from our expectation.

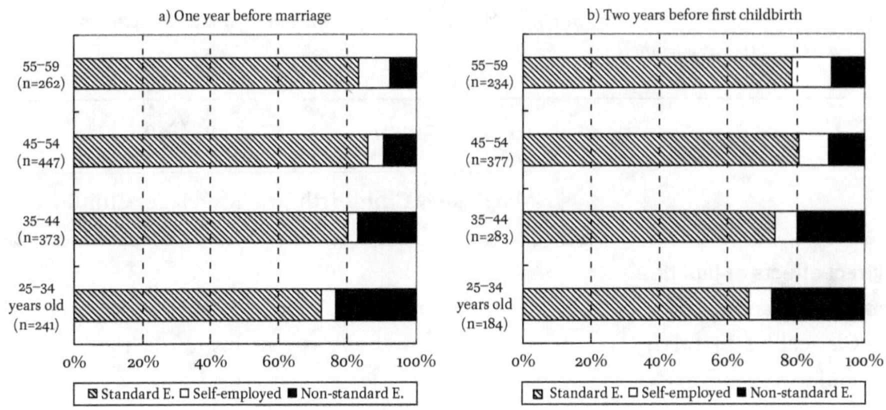

FIGURE 4.1 *Employment status of Japanese women by cohort at two life stages. (Women in the labor force) (a) One year before marriage (b) Two years before first childbirth*
Note: women employed in agriculture are not included.
SOURCE: SSM 2005

6.2 *Comparing 1995 and 2005 According to the Baseline Model*

Detailed results for the event history analysis are shown in Appendix 4.1 (upon marriage) and Appendix 4.2 (around first childbirth), and major findings are summarized in Tables 4.3 to 4.5.

To start with, comparing the results of Yu (2009) for the 1995 data with the results of the present research for the 2005 data, we can understand how influences exerted by the Japanese employment system have changed.

The results of the comparison are summarized in Table 4.3 (see Model 1 in Appendices 4.1 and 4.2 for detailed information). First, examining the direct influence (expressed as the effects of occupation and scale of the firm) and indirect influence (expressed as effects of husband's household-finance-support power and family structure) of the Japanese employment system, these factors had significant impact and the influencing patterns were almost the same at marriage and childbirth for the 1995 data. In the 2005 data, however, the influences of these factors have mostly disappeared for the time of marriage, and remain only for the time of childbirth in a weaker manner. Let us look at this in detail.

With regard to the direct influence of the Japanese employment system, as this system is more prevalent in clerical work and larger-scale firms, these women can be thought to retire more easily. We can clearly saw this effect in the 1995 analysis, but in 2005 this effect has disappeared for the time of marriage and remains only for the time of childbirth. Next, in the case of indirect influence of the Japanese employment system, as this system makes it difficult to reconcile work and family duties, women whose husbands have a high

TABLE 4.3 *Determinants of exiting the labor force at marriage and at first childbirth for Japanese women*

	1995 (Yu 2009)		2005 (Model 1)	
	Marriage≒Childbirth		Marriage≠Childbirth	
Direct effects of Japanese employment system				
Clerical (vs. Manual)	+	+	n.s.	+
Mid to larger firms (vs. Smaller firms)	+	+	n.s.	+
Indirect effects of Japanese employment system (Family situations)				
Husband's year of education	+	+	n.s.	n.s.
Nuclear family (vs. Extended family)	+	+	+	+
Woman's year of education	–	n.s.	n.s.	n.s.

Note: Promoting (+), restraining (–), or having no significant effect (n.s.) on exiting the labor force.

TABLE 4.4 *Effects of non-standard employment on exiting the labor force at marriage and at first childbirth for Japanese women*

	Model 2 (2005)	
	At marriage	At childbirth
Non-standard (vs. Standard) employment	n.s.	+
Younger cohort (vs. Older cohort)	–	n.s.
Mid to larger firms (vs. Smaller firms)	n.s.	n.s.

Note: Promoting (+), restraining (–), or having no significant effect (n.s.) on exiting the labor force.

TABLE 4.5 *Effects of women-friendly employment measures on exiting the labor force at marriage and at first childbirth for Japanese women*

	Model 3 (2005)	
	At marriage	**At childbirth**
Mid-size firms (vs. Smaller firms)	+	+
× Younger cohorts	−	−
Nuclear family (vs. Extended family)	+	+
× Younger cohorts	−	n.s.[a]

Note: Promoting (+), restraining (−), or having no significant effect (n.s.) on exiting the labor force.
[a] Not statistically significant at the 5% level, but significant at the 10% level.

household-finance-support power and women in a nuclear family can be expected to retire much more easily. In the 1995 analysis, we could see this effect clearly, but for 2005 the effect of the husband's high household-finance-support power has disappeared both at marriage and childbirth. To summarize, in 2005 both the direct and indirect influences of the Japanese employment system have almost disappeared for the time of marriage, remaining only for the time of childbirth, although in a weaker manner.

As a second point, women's high academic background had a restraining effect on retirement at marriage in 1995 but has no such effect on marriage or childbirth in 2005. In other words, the situation has changed to one where human capital (academic background) has less influence on women's employment at marriage and childbirth than institutional position in the labor market (employment status, scale of firm, etc.) does. This means the mechanisms regulating women's employment in Japan have become similar to those regulating men's, as mentioned in sections 3.1 and 3.2.

6.3 *Effects of Non-standard Employment*

We next examine what kinds of effects the employment status has on women's retirement and how the effects of other variables change when employment status is added in Model 2. The results are summarized in Table 4.4 (see Model 2 in Appendices 4.1 and 4.2 for detailed information). Looking at the effect of non-standard employment in Table 4.4, we can see that non-standard employment has no effect for the time of marriage but increases the risk of retirement for the time of childbirth.

In addition, by controlling employment status in Model 2, the effects of certain variables change from those in Model 1 where employment status was not controlled. Firstly, in Model 2, the birth cohort comes to have a significant effect at the time of marriage in that women in younger cohorts are more likely than those in older cohorts to continue employment (see Table 4.4). The interpretation of this change is as follows. Working in the self-employed sector has a *positive* effect on continued employment, but there are *fewer* self-employees in younger cohorts than in older ones (see Figure 4.1), which possibly counteracts the positive effect of being in younger cohorts on continued employment (see the effects of age in Model 1 in Appendix 4.1). However, once this effect of employment status is controlled and exempted from Model 2 (in other words, if the employment status is the same), it is found that being in younger cohorts has a positive effect itself on continued employment.

Secondly, again when employment status is controlled, the effect of firm size is no longer significant at marriage and childbirth (see Table 4.4). In other words, if the employment status is the same, we can no longer observe the "usual" characteristics of the Japanese employment system, namely that "the larger firm, the more female retirement at marriage or childbirth".

6.4 *Effect of Women's Employment Support Systems*

Finally, the interactions between cohort and both scale of firm and family structure are added in Model 3. Focusing on these interactions, we now examine how the effects of the Japanese employment system change between different generations of women. In the "conventional" Japanese employment system, women employed in larger-scale firms or in the nuclear family more easily retire than their counterparts in smaller-scale firms or in extended families. As summarized in Table 4.5, however, such tendencies are weaker in younger cohorts. These results indicate that it is mainly in younger cohorts that the influence of the Japanese employment system weakens. The development of women's employment support systems seems to lie behind this change (see Model 3 in Appendices 4.1 and 4.2 for detailed information).

7 Conclusion and Implications

7.1 *Conclusion*

The Japanese employment system has changed since the 1990s and the change has brought about (1) an increase in non-standard employment among young women, (2) an improvement in women's employment support measures.

In this study, using data covering years up to 2005, we analyzed how changes in the Japanese employment system have influenced women's employment at the times of marriage and childbirth.

With regard to the effects of the increase in non-standard employment, women's non-standard employment does not influence retirement at the time of marriage but promotes retirement at the time of childbirth (in this point, there was no difference between the cohorts). Therefore, if the increase in young women's non-standard employment continues, the number of women retiring at childbirth will rise, even if they continue to work after marrying. This supports the "retirement through increased non-standard employment" hypothesis.

Next, if we look at the effect of women's employment support systems, up to 1995 women working in clerical positions, at large firms, having a husband with high breadwinning ability, or in the nuclear family, tended to retire easily after marriage or childbirth as an influence of the Japanese employment system. In the 2005 data, however, these tendencies, except for that associated with the nuclear family, disappeared for time of marriage and weakened for time of childbirth. For the young cohorts, even the tendency associated with the nuclear family also disappeared or weakened. These results indicate that the influence of the Japanese employment system weakened (especially for time of marriage and for younger cohorts). This can be considered as related to the development of the employment support system for women. This supports the "continued employment through support systems" hypothesis.

7.2 *Implications for Women's Life Course in Japan*

Here we will discuss the implications of the findings for Japanese women's life course. First, the polarization of women's employment proceeds in Japan just as it does in the west. As seen above, women in non-standard employment easily interrupt their employment. Once interrupted, return to standard employment is difficult, as suggested by other studies (Yamato 2011; Yu 2009). However, women who can use employment support systems have a higher chance of continuing employment: such women are mostly in standard employment. In other words, between women in standard employment and women in non-standard employment, there is the possibility for polarization between secure, continued employment and insecure, interrupted employment.

Second, if the abovementioned trend continues, there is a possibility that the social class implication of a continued-employment life course and an interrupted-employment life course will be reversed for Japanese women. As is clear from Yu (2009), for Taiwanese women *continuing* employment at marriage and childbirth was the life course of women who had a "fortunate" class status (because continuation occurred more easily for women who worked at a large firm or in professional or white-collar work). In the Japanese employment system, in contrast, *interrupted* employment was the life course of women with a "fortunate" class status (because interruption occurred more easily for women working at a large firm or in white-collar work or for women with a husband having high breadwinning ability). However, the 2005 analysis makes clear that in the changed Japanese employment system, *continuation* occurs more easily for women with a "fortunate" social status—women in standard employment, for example; and having a husband with high breadwinning ability does not necessarily restrain women's continuous employment. If this trend continues, in the near future, continued employment will be the life course of "fortunate" women in Japan too.

Third, with regard to the main factors regulating Japanese women's life course, there is a possibility that the influence of the woman's own social status will be stronger than that of her husband. For example, this study reveals that the influence of the husband's breadwinning ability on the wife's employment at marriage or childbirth weakens on the one hand, while on the other hand the influence of the woman's own status (especially employment status) strengthens. In the analysis of Taiwanese women in 1995, such a trend was already visible, but the situation for Japanese women is possibly now approaching theirs. Moreover, research on marriage in recent times in Japan has also shown that women in standard employment can marry more easily than women in non-standard employment (Nagase 2002; Tarohmaru 2011). If this trend continues, the time will come, even in Japan, when a woman's own resourcefulness is more important for her life course than the resourcefulness of her husband.

Appendices

APPENDIX 4.1 *Discrete-time event history models predicting labor force exit upon marriage for Japanese women*

	Model 1			Model 2			Model 3		
	B	*SE*	*Exp(B)*	*B*	*SE*	*Exp(B)*	*B*	*SE*	*Exp(B)*
Age (years): 55–60 (ref.)									
25–34	−0.233	(0.157)	0.792	−0.387*	(0.161)	0.679	1.152	(0.607)	3.166
35–44	−0.060	(0.137)	0.941	−0.163	(0.140)	0.850	0.565	(0.527)	1.760
45–54	−0.138	(0.132)	0.871	−0.208	(0.133)	0.812	−0.379	(0.510)	0.684
Urban residence	0.330**	(0.105)	1.391	0.303**	(0.106)	1.354	0.313**	(0.108)	1.367
Timing: Year of marriage (ref.)									
1 year after marriage	−0.864**	(0.114)	0.421	−0.815**	(0.115)	0.443	−0.793**	(0.117)	0.452
2 years after marriage	−1.353**	(0.151)	0.258	−1.330**	(0.152)	0.265	−1.330**	(0.154)	0.264
3 years after marriage	−1.473**	(0.173)	0.229	−1.436**	(0.176)	0.238	−1.419**	(0.178)	0.242
First child's birth	0.735**	(0.123)	2.085	0.773**	(0.125)	2.165	0.794**	(0.127)	2.213
Husband's education (years)	0.040†	(0.024)	1.041	0.044†	(0.024)	1.045	0.050*	(0.025)	1.051
Nuclear family	0.331**	(0.105)	1.393	0.356**	(0.106)	1.427	0.802**	(0.263)	2.229
Education (years)	−0.023	(0.034)	0.977	−0.003	(0.035)	0.997	−0.010	(0.036)	0.990
Occupation: Manual (ref.)									
Managerial, Professional	−0.551**	(0.206)	0.576	−0.597**	(0.210)	0.551	−0.446	(0.643)	0.640
Semi-professional	−0.187	(0.193)	0.829	−0.254	(0.197)	0.776	−1.208**	(0.461)	0.299

APPENDIX 4.1 *Discrete-time event history models predicting labor force exit upon marriage for Japanese women* (cont.)

	Model 1			Model 2			Model 3		
	B	*SE*	*Exp(B)*	*B*	*SE*	*Exp(B)*	*B*	*SE*	*Exp(B)*
Clerical	0.258†	(0.141)	1.294	0.229	(0.143)	1.257	0.210	(0.280)	1.234
Sales, Service	0.192	(0.161)	1.212	0.214	(0.163)	1.238	-0.363	(0.353)	0.696
Firm size: 1–9 (ref.)									
10–99	0.183	(0.138)	1.201	-0.182	(0.149)	0.833	-0.053	(0.339)	0.948
100–499	0.292†	(0.163)	1.339	-0.065	(0.172)	0.937	0.908*	(0.395)	2.478
500 and over	0.136	(0.146)	1.146	-0.235	(0.159)	0.791	-0.024	(0.360)	0.977
Public sector	-0.675**	(0.232)	0.509	-1.076**	(0.239)	0.341	-0.891	(0.587)	0.410
Don't know	0.472*	(0.186)	1.604	0.084	(0.195)	1.087	0.537	(0.435)	1.711
Employment status:									
Standard (ref.)									
Non-standard				0.209†	(0.127)	1.233	0.229†	(0.130)	1.257
Self-employment sector				-1.484**	(0.276)	0.227	-1.489**	(0.279)	0.226
*Manual * 55–60 years old (ref.)*									
Manag., Profes. * 25–34							-0.537	(0.835)	0.585
* 35–44							-0.301	(0.713)	0.740
* 45–54							0.347	(0.710)	1.415
Semi-professional * 25–34							0.207	(0.690)	1.230
* 35–44							0.795	(0.569)	2.215
* 45–54							2.214**	(0.575)	9.149

	Model 1			Model 2			Model 3		
	B	*SE*	*Exp(B)*	*B*	*SE*	*Exp(B)*	*B*	*SE*	*Exp(B)*
Clerical * 25–34							−0.219	(0.483)	0.803
* 35–44							−0.142	(0.381)	0.868
* 45–54							0.405	(0.365)	1.500
Sales, Service * 25–34							0.690	(0.545)	1.994
* 35–44							0.475	(0.473)	1.608
* 45–54							0.952 *	(0.463)	2.591
*Firm size: 1–9 * 55–60 years (ref.)*									
10–99 * 25–34							−0.649	(0.472)	0.522
* 35–44							−0.095	(0.422)	0.909
* 45–54							−0.021	(0.421)	0.979
100–499 * 25–34							−1.863 **	(0.536)	0.155
* 35–44							−1.223 *	(0.496)	0.294
* 45–54							−0.630	(0.498)	0.533
500 + * 25–34							−0.629	(0.513)	0.533
* 35–44							−0.120	(0.443)	0.887
* 45–54							−0.176	(0.443)	0.839
Public sector * 25–34							−0.275	(0.802)	0.759
* 35–44							−0.119	(0.710)	0.888
* 45–54							−0.275	(0.717)	0.760

APPENDIX 4.1 *Discrete-time event history models predicting labor force exit upon marriage for Japanese women* (cont.)

	Model 1			Model 2			Model 3		
	B	*SE*	*Exp(B)*	*B*	*SE*	*Exp(B)*	*B*	*SE*	*Exp(B)*
Don't know * 25–34							−1.224*	(0.617)	0.294
* 35–44							−0.403	(0.570)	0.668
* 45–54							−0.359	(0.542)	0.698
Nuclear family * *55–60 years (ref.)*									
* 25–34							−0.964*	(0.400)	0.381
* 35–44							−0.671*	(0.323)	0.511
* 45–54							−0.271	(0.314)	0.762
Constant	−1.435**	(0.394)	0.238	−1.315**	(0.396)	0.268	−1.761**	(0.539)	0.172
$\chi 2$	291.752**			42.940**			55.249**		
−2 Log likelihood	2992.334			2949.394			2894.145		
Nagelkerke R2	0.141			0.161			0.186		
Person-year spells, n	2905			2905			2905		
Events, n	734			734			734		

Note: **p<.01; *p<.05; †p<.1.

SOURCE: SSM 2005

APPENDIX 4.2 *Discrete-time event history models predicting labor force exit around the first childbirth for Japanese women*

	Model 1			Model 2			Model 3		
	B	*SE*	*Exp(B)*	*B*	*SE*	*Exp(B)*	*B*	*SE*	*Exp(B)*
Age (years): 55–60 (ref.)									
25–34	0.189	(0.172)	1.208	−0.001	(0.176)	0.999	1.595*	(0.690)	4.929
35–44	0.215	(0.156)	1.240	0.110	(0.158)	1.117	0.787	(0.613)	2.198
45–54	−0.048	(0.147)	0.953	−0.095	(0.149)	0.909	0.305	(0.569)	1.357
Urban residence	0.415**	(0.116)	1.514	0.376**	(0.117)	1.456	0.395**	(0.121)	1.485
Timing:									
Pre-childbirth year (ref.)									
Year of childbirth	−0.279*	(0.119)	0.757	−0.217†	(0.120)	0.805	−0.199	(0.122)	0.819
1 year after childbirth	−1.152**	(0.162)	0.316	−1.065**	(0.164)	0.345	−1.020**	(0.165)	0.361
2 years after childbirth	−1.944**	(0.222)	0.143	−1.850**	(0.224)	0.157	−1.821**	(0.225)	0.162
3 years after childbirth	−2.467**	(0.275)	0.085	−2.413**	(0.278)	0.090	−2.389**	(0.279)	0.092
Married	0.803**	(0.179)	2.232	0.822**	(0.181)	2.274	0.851**	(0.184)	2.341
Husband's education (years)	0.040	(0.027)	1.041	0.058*	(0.028)	1.059	0.057*	(0.029)	1.059
Nuclear family	0.324**	(0.113)	1.382	0.366**	(0.115)	1.441	0.732**	(0.279)	2.080
Education (years)	−0.024	(0.039)	0.976	−0.016	(0.040)	0.984	−0.016	(0.041)	0.984
Occupation: Manual (ref.)									
Managerial, Professional	−0.266	(0.222)	0.766	−0.263	(0.228)	0.769	−0.885	(0.833)	0.413
Semi-professional	0.086	(0.215)	1.089	0.068	(0.218)	1.070	−0.649	(0.512)	0.522

APPENDIX 4.2 *Discrete-time event history models predicting labor force exit around the first childbirth for Japanese women* (cont.)

	Model 1			**Model 2**			**Model 3**		
	B	*SE*	*Exp(B)*	*B*	*SE*	*Exp(B)*	*B*	*SE*	*Exp(B)*
Clerical	0.529**	(0.159)	1.697	0.538**	(0.162)	1.713	0.558†	(0.319)	1.748
Sales, Service	0.447*	(0.184)	1.564	0.518**	(0.187)	1.678	0.305	(0.421)	1.357
Firm size: 1–9 (ref.)									
10–99	0.506**	(0.152)	1.658	0.042	(0.163)	1.043	0.248	(0.398)	1.282
100–499	0.497**	(0.183)	1.644	0.046	(0.193)	1.047	1.030*	(0.461)	2.801
500 and over	0.446**	(0.164)	1.561	−0.033	(0.179)	0.968	0.623	(0.435)	1.865
Public sector	−0.450†	(0.244)	0.638	−0.975**	(0.252)	0.377	−0.525	(0.657)	0.591
Don't know	0.900**	(0.215)	2.460	0.414†	(0.224)	1.513	1.152*	(0.507)	3.166
Employment status:									
Standard (ref.)									
Non-standard				0.393**	(0.140)	1.482	0.381**	(0.144)	1.463
Self-employment sector				−1.843**	(0.310)	0.158	−1.905**	(0.312)	0.149
*Manual * 55–60 years old (ref.)*									
Manag., Profes. * 25–34							−0.494	(1.029)	0.610
* 35–44							0.964	(0.904)	2.621
* 45–54							0.847	(0.890)	2.331
Semi-professional * 25–34							−0.084	(0.739)	0.920
* 35–44							0.871	(0.640)	2.389
* 45–54							1.448*	(0.647)	4.255

	Model 1			Model 2			Model 3		
	B	*SE*	*Exp(B)*	*B*	*SE*	*Exp(B)*	*B*	*SE*	*Exp(B)*
Clerical * 25–34							−0.634	(0.549)	0.530
* 35–44							0.052	(0.446)	1.054
* 45–54							0.207	(0.409)	1.230
Sales, Service * 25–34							−0.084	(0.634)	0.919
* 35–44							0.215	(0.564)	1.240
* 45–54							0.326	(0.533)	1.386
*Firm size: 1–9 * 55–60 years (ref.)*									
10–99 * 25–34							−0.544	(0.536)	0.581
* 35–44							−0.085	(0.492)	0.918
* 45–54							−0.340	(0.482)	0.712
100–499 * 25–34							−1.428 *	(0.605)	0.240
* 3544							−1.078 †	(0.576)	0.340
* 45–54							−1.155 *	(0.573)	0.315
500 + * 25–34							−0.866	(0.605)	0.420
* 35–44							−0.520	(0.533)	0.594
* 45–54							−0.993 †	(0.518)	0.370
Public sector * 25–34							0.123	(0.903)	1.131
* 35–44							−0.770	(0.786)	0.463
* 45–54							−0.572	(0.776)	0.565

APPENDIX 4.2 *Discrete-time event history models predicting labor force exit around the first childbirth for Japanese women* (cont.)

	Model 1			Model 2			Model 3		
	B	*SE*	*Exp(B)*	*B*	*SE*	*Exp(B)*	*B*	*SE*	*Exp(B)*
Don't know * 25–34							−0.752	(0.693)	0.471
* 35–44							−1.120	(0.691)	0.326
* 45–54							−0.997	(0.632)	0.369
*Nuclear family * 55–60 years (ref.)*									
* 25–34							−0.712†	(0.416)	0.491
* 35–44							−0.663†	(0.350)	0.515
* 45–54							−0.131	(0.336)	0.877
Constant	−2.861 **	(0.485)	0.057	−2.764**	(0.488)	0.063	−3.385**	(0.643)	0.034
χ^2	417.753**			65.398**			34.514		
−2 Log likelihood	2454.744			2389.345			2354.831		
Nagelkerke R2	0.215			0.246			0.262		
Person-year spells, n	2834			2834			2834		
Events, n	580			580			580		

** p<.01; * p<.05; † p<.1.

SOURCE: SSM 2005

References

Arita, Shin. 2009. "A Comparative Study of Social Stratification in East Asian Societies: The Reward Differences Between Occupation and Social Inequality." *Japanese Sociological Review* 59(4): 663–680. (in Japanese).

Blossfeld, Hans-Peter and Catherine Hakim, eds. 1997. *Between Equalization and Marginalization: Women Working Part-Time in Europe and the United States of America*. Oxford: Oxford University Press.

——— and Heather Hofmeister, eds. 2006. *Globalization, Uncertainty and Women's Careers: An International Comparison*. Cheltenham: Edward Elgar.

Brinton, Mary C. 2001. *Women's Working Lives in East Asia*. Stanford, California: Stanford University Press.

Esping-Andersen, Gosta. 1990. *The Three Worlds of Welfare Capitalism*. Cambridge: Polity Press.

Genda, Yuj. 2001. *A Nagging Sense of Job Insecurity: The New Reality Facing Japanese Youth*. Tokyo: I-House Press.

Glover, Judith and Gill Kirton, eds. 2006. *Women, Employment and Organizations*. Milton Park: Routledge.

Hayashi, Yusuke. 2009. "Fluidity and Disparity in the Japanese and Korean Labor Markets: A Comparative Study on Job Turnover and Changes in Income." *The Study of Sociology, 86*: 7–31. Tohoku Sociological Association. (in Japanese).

Inagami, Tsuyoshi. 1999. "Introduction: Industrial Society and labor in Japan." In Tsuyoshi Inagami and T. Kawakita, eds., *Lecture Series of Sociology: 6: Labor*, 1–31. University of Tokyo Press. (in Japanese).

Jo, Shigeyuki. 2006. *Why Do Japanese Youth Quit Their First Job After Just Three Years of Working?* Tokyo: Kobunsha. (in Japanese).

Kagawa, Mei, 2011. "Transformation of the Transition System from School to Work and Early Career in Japan." In Hiroshi Ishida, H. Kondo, and K. Nakao, eds., *Social Stratification in Contemporary Japan: 2: Structure of Social Stratification and Mobility*, 189–203. Tokyo: University of Tokyo Press. (in Japanese).

Kanbayashi, Hiroshi and Takenoshita Hirohisa. 2009. "Resignation Reasons and Labor Markets in Japan and Taiwan: Beyond a Dichotomy of Voluntary and Involuntary Mobility." *The Study of Sociology* 86: 33–63. Tohoku Sociological Association. (in Japanese).

Kato, Akihiko. 2011. "Two Major factors Behind the Marriage Decline in Japan: The Deterioration in Macroeconomic Performance and the Diffusion of Individualism Ideology." *Journal of Population Problems* 67(2): 3–39. (in Japanese).

Lewis, Jane and Susy Giullari. 2005. "The Adult Worker Model Family, Gender Equality and Care: the Search for New Policy Principles and the Possibilities and Problems of a Capabilities Approach." *Economy and Society* 34(1): 76–104.

Mayer, Karl Ulrich. 2004. "Whose lives? How History, Societies, and Institutions Define and Shape Life Courses." *Research in Human Development* 1(3): 161–187.

McRae, Susan. 2003. "Constraints and Choices in Mothers' Employment Careers: A Consideration of Hakim's Preference Theory." *British Journal of Sociology* 54(3): 317–338.

Moen, Phyllis. 2006. "Foreword," in H-P. Blossfeld and H. Hofmeister, eds., *Globalization, Uncertainty and Women's Careers: An International Comparison*, xvi–xx. Cheltenham: Edward Elgar.

——— and Donna Spencer. 2006. "Conversing Divergences in Age, Gender, Health, and Well-Being: Strategic Selection in the Third Age." In R.H. Binstock and L.K. George eds., *Handbook of Aging and the Social Sciences* (6th edition), 127–144. San Diego: Academic Press.

Nagase, Nobuko. 2002. "Marriage Timing and the Effect of Increase in Non-Standard Employment among the Youth in Japan", *Journal of Population Problems* 58(2): 22–35. (in Japanese).

Nakatani, Iwao. 1987. *Japanese Companies in Transformation*, Tokyo: Kodansha. (in Japanese).

Nakazawa, Wataru. 2011. "Increasing Segregation of the Youth Labor Market in Japan." In Y. Sato and F. Ojima eds., *Social Stratification in Contemporary Japan: 1: Disparity and Diversity*, 51–64. Tokyo: University of Tokyo Press. (in Japanese).

NHK [Japan Broadcasting Association]. 2011. "Womanomics Changes Society." A *Close-Up of Today*. Broadcast January 11, 2011. (in Japanese)

Nomura, Masami, 1994. *Life-long Employment System in Japan*. Tokyo: Iwanami. (in Japanese).

Osawa, Mari. 1993. *Overcoming the Company-Centered Society of Japan*. Tokyo: Jiji Tsushin. (in Japanese).

Otobe, Yuko. 2006. *The Life Cycle of Middle-aged Women and Part-time Employment in Japan*. Minerva Shobo. (in Japanese).

——— 2010. *Continued Careers for Women*. Keiso Shobo (in Japanese).

Sakaguchi, Yusuke. 2011a. "Trend Analysis of Unemployment Risk: Effects of the Expansion of Non-Standard Jobs and Changes of Determinants." *Sociology*, 55(3): 3–18. (in Japanese).

——— 2011b. "Japan-Taiwan Comparison of Determinants of Unemployment Risk and Their Changes: Globalization, Institution, and Risk." In Y. Sato, ed., *Studies of Social Stratification in Contemporary Japan: From the Perspective of Micro–macro Linkages, Vol. 1. Social Class and Social Mobility* (Report of Research Results funded by the 2008–2010 Grant-in-Aid for Scientific Research, Japan Society of the Promotion of Social Science), 269–289. (In Japanese).

Sato, Yoshimichi. 2009. "Inequality and Fluidization of the Social Stratification System in Contemporary Japan." *Japanese Sociological Review* 59(4): 632–647. (in Japanese).

——— and Hayashi, Yusuke. 2011. "Various Aspects of Disparity in Social Status in Contemporary Japan." In Y. Sato and F. Ojima eds., *Social Stratification in Contemporary Japan: 1: Disparity and Diversity*, 3–17. [PUBLISHING INFO.] (in Japanese).

Siaroff, Alan. 1994. "Work, Welfare and Gender Equality: A New Typology." In Diana Sainsbury ed., *Gendering Welfare States*, 82–100. London: Sage.

Takeishi, Emiko. 2006. *Employment System and Women's Career in Japan*. Tokyo: Keiso Shobo. (in Japanese).

Takenoshita, Hirohisa. 2008. "Voluntary and Involuntary Job Mobility in Japan: Resources, Rewards and Labor Market Structure." *Sociological Theory and Methods* 23(2): 85–104. (in Japanese).

Tarohmaru, Hiroshi. 2011. "Non-standard Employment and Marriage for the Youth in Japan." In Y. Sato and F. Ojima, eds., *Social Stratification in Contemporary Japan: 1: Disparity and Diversity*, 131–142. Tokyo: University of Tokyo Press. (in Japanese).

———. 2014. "Factors in the Wage Differential between Standard and Nonstandard Employment: A comparison of Japan, South Korea, and Taiwan." In E. Ochiai and L. A. Hosoya, eds., *Transformation of the Intimate and the Public in Asian Modernity*, 144-163. Leiden: Brill.

Watanabe, Tsutomu. 2011. "Employment Flexibility and Employment Immobilization from the Viewpoint of Job History in Japan." In H. Ishida, H. Kondo, and K. Nakao eds., *Social Stratification in Contemporary Japan: 2: Structure of Social Stratification and Mobility*, 173–187. Tokyo: University of Tokyo Press. (in Japanese).

Wo, Hak-soo. 2006. "Problem of Non-standard Employment in Korea." *DIO* (*Monthly Report of Rengo Research Institute for Advancement of Living Standards*) 206, 17–23. (in Japanese).

Yamaguchi, Kazuo. 1991. *Event History Analysis*, Newbury Park: Sage.

Yamato, Reiko. 2011. "A Comparison between Japan and Korea of Women's M-shaped Life Course: Focusing on Re-entry into the Labor Market after Childbirth." In Y. Sato and F. Ojima, eds., *Social Stratification in Contemporary Japan: 1: Disparity and Diversity*, 161–175. Tokyo: University of Tokyo Press. (in Japanese).

Yokota, Nobuko. 2003. "Increase in Labor Market Flexibility and Non-Standard Employment in Korea," *Journal of Ohara Institution of Research for Social Problem* 535: 36–54 (in Japanese).

Yoshida, Takashi. 2011. "Increasing Flexibility in Early Career and its Impact on Workers' Income in Japan," in Y. Sato and F. Ojima (eds.), *Social Stratification in Contemporary Japan: 1: Disparity and Diversity*, 19–34. Tokyo: University of Tokyo Press. (in Japanese).

Yu, Wei-Hsin. 2009. *Gendered Trajectories*. Stanford, California: Stanford University Press.

CHAPTER 5

Can Active Labor Market Policies Enhance the Suicide-Preventive Effect of Intimacy? A Dynamic Panel Analysis of 27 OECD Countries Including Japan and Korea, 1980–2007

Shibata Haruka

Introduction

Since the late 1980s, suicide rates have shown a decrease in most Organisation for Economic Co-operation and Development (OECD) countries. In Japan and South Korea, however, the rates increased sharply during the late 1990s and have remained high ever since (Figure 5.1). In this chapter, we examine the following questions, with the aim of contributing to the development of suicide prevention policies. Question 1 (Q1): Why did the suicide rate increase in Japan and Korea? Question 2 (Q2): What are the main factors in suicide rate change? Question 3 (Q3): What social policies can prevent suicide attempts and reduce national suicide rates, and how do such social policies prevent suicide?

International comparison of suicide rates in previous studies suggest that the main factors that affect suicide rates include change in unemployment rate, (crude) divorce rate, (crude) marriage rate (Neumayer 2003), and public expenditure on active labor market policies (ALMPs), which include labor market training, subsidized employment, employment services, administration (Stucker et al. 2009). Unemployment rate and divorce rate are suggested to increase suicide rate, whereas marriage rate and public expenditure on ALMPs are suggested to decrease suicide rate. The backgrounds of these effects are that unemployed persons and divorced persons are thought to tend to suffer severe stress from social isolation, whereas marriage and ALMPs are thought to tend to reintegrate divorced persons or unemployed persons into new intimate or social relationships through new marital life or public job training and other assistive services. However, these previous studies neither focused on Japan and Korea nor investigated how ALMPs can prevent suicide.

In this study, we conducted dynamic first-difference generalized method of moments (FD-GMM) estimation on the determinants of country-level suicide rate, using the most comprehensive panel data available today that covers 27 OECD countries including Japan and Korea during the period 1980 to 2007. In the estimation, we controlled for suicide rates in the previous year, country-specific

 | DOI 10.1163/9789004262737_006

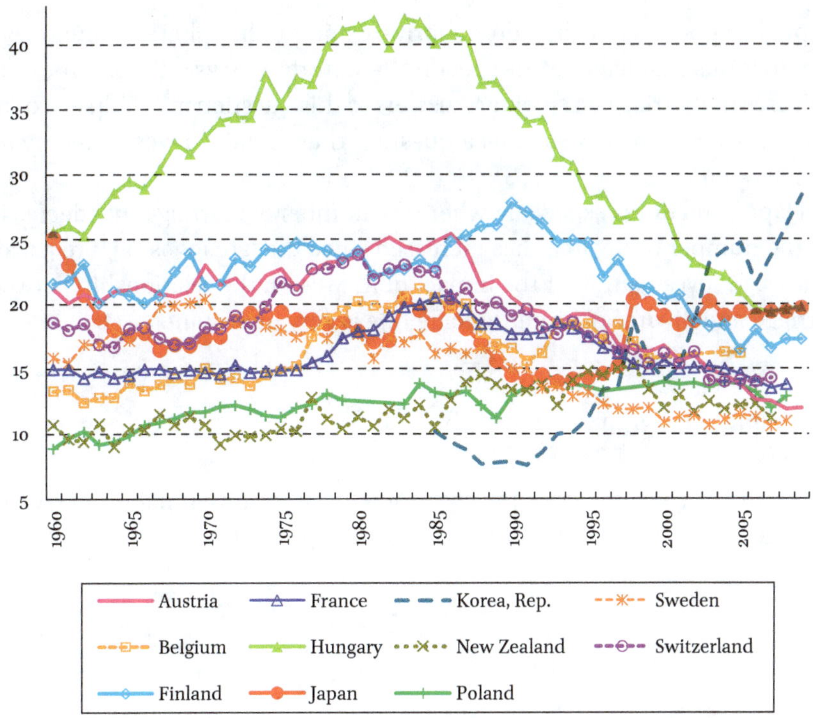

FIGURE 5.1 *Suicides per 100,000 persons (age-standardized)*[1]
Notes: data are from OECD (2012) *health data 2011*. The 11 countries with the highest average suicide rate during the period 2005 to 2009 are shown (except for czech republic, estonia, slovak republic, and slovenia, which have been excluded from our analysis). The suicide rates of the four excluded countries have been decreasing since the late 1990s, and have been lower than the rate in korea since 2004, and lower than the rate in japan since 2007.

linear time trends, year-specific fixed effects, changes in unemployment, divorce rate, marriage rate, general-government (or public) social expenditure in each policy area, and other variables that could be thought to relate both to suicide rate and the above independent variables. In the estimation, we focused especially on Japan and Korea, using the country-dummy variables of these two countries.

Additionally, we pursued a new theoretical inquiry. Divorce rate and marriage rate are thought to belong to the private sphere, whereas ALMPs are in

1 "Age-standardised death rates per 100,000 population for selected causes are calculated by the OECD Secretariat, using the total OECD population for 1980 as the reference population. The age-standardised death rates are necessary for comparing the level of mortality across countries and over time since they take into account the differences in age structure of the populations" (cited from *Definitions, Sources and Methods* in OECD (2012). *Health Data 2011*).

the public sphere. How then do the private and public spheres relate to each other in terms of suicide? More specifically, how do ALMPs influence the effect of divorce or marriage on suicide? Answers to this question may help to explain how ALMPs can prevent suicide, a question that remains investigated by any previous studies.

In Japan and Korea especially, where the number of marriages has decreased and the number of divorces has increased since the late 1990s (Figure 5.2 and Figure 5.3), investigation of the impact of ALMPs on the relationship between marriage and divorce rates and suicide rate is very important.

Previous Studies

Since Émile Durkheim's (1897) study on suicide, it is a given that intimacy (e.g., marriage, family) can reduce social isolation, promote meaning in life, and

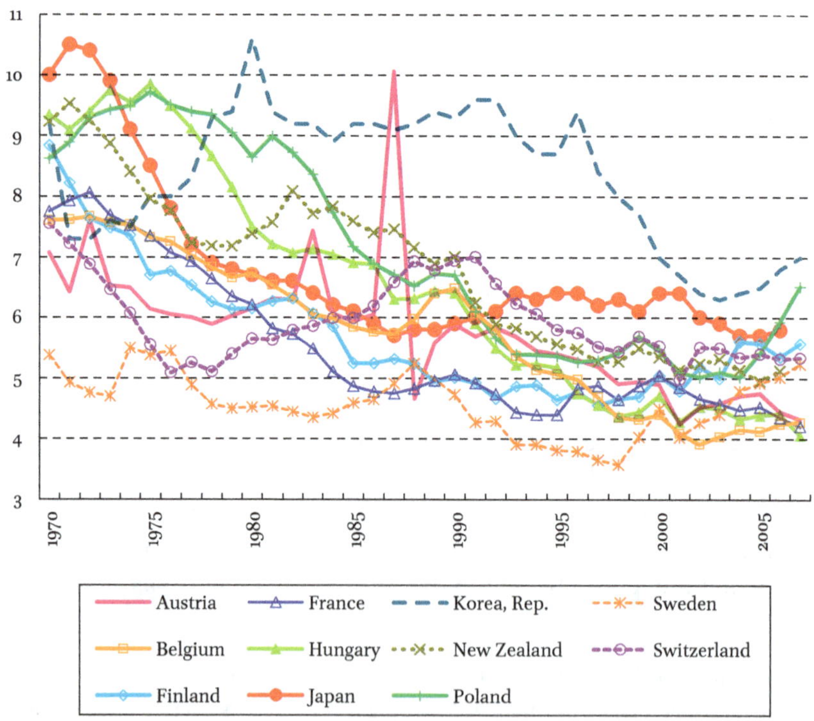

FIGURE 5.2 *Crude marriage rate (number of new marriages per 1,000 persons)*
Notes: data are from OECD (2010) *society at a glance 2009*. The 11 countries with the highest suicide rates are shown (see the notes for figure 5.1 For additional detail).

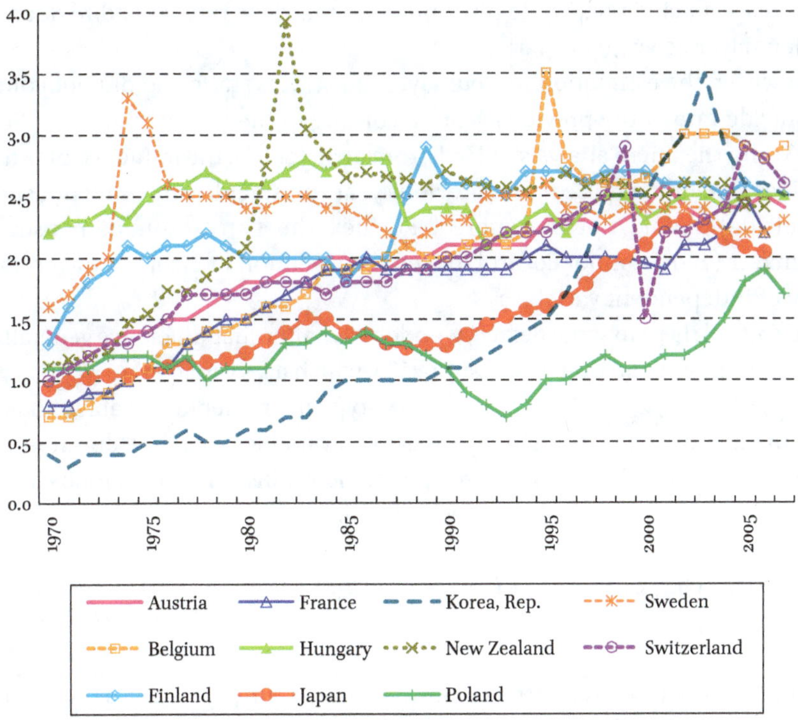

FIGURE 5.3 *Crude divorce rate (number of divorces per 1,000 persons)*
Notes: Data are from OECD (2010) *Society at a Glance 2009*. The 11 countries with the highest suicide rates are shown (see the notes for Figure 5.1 for additional detail).

thereby prevent suicide. Data from the late 20th and early 21st century on the United States, Italy, Australia, and Japan show that the suicide rate is higher in divorced persons than in married persons (Stack 1990; Masocco et al. 2008; Wyder et al. 2009; Japan Ministry of Health, Labour and Welfare 2010).

For the purposes of more detailed caution in analyzing the factors affecting national suicide rates than Durkheimian descriptive approach, previous quantitative studies have used nation-level panel analysis controlling for county and year using dummy variables. Among such studies, the broadest was Neumayer (2003), which analyzed the suicide rate in 68 countries around the world (including Japan and Korea) during the period from 1980 to 1999 using the static least-squares-dummy-variable (LSDV) estimation. This included (1) control dummies for country in order to control spatial correlation of errors and (2) control dummies for period. The results showed that unemployment, female labor force participation, divorce rate, and alcohol consumption tended to increase suicide rate, while birth rate and marriage rate tended to decrease it (Neumayer 2003: 318–9, 321).

However, the estimation in Neumayer (2003) was static and did not control for suicide rate of the previous year. According to the macro analysis of Stack (1996) and the micro analysis of Hedström et al. (2008), the influence of others' suicides (including those in the previous year) on suicide (the "infectiousness" of suicide) should not be ignored. Further, the LSDV estimation used by Neumayer (2003) cannot control for serial correlation of errors or the endogeneity of independent variables.

To control these to some degree, we adopt dynamic first-difference generalized method of moments (FD-GMM) estimation, which uses variables $w_{i,t} = (y_{i,1},\ldots,y_{i,t-2})$ and $z_{k,i,t} = (x_{k,i,1},\ldots, x_{k,i,t-2})$, $t = 3,\ldots, T$, as GMM-type instrumental variables and also uses the first differences of strictly exogenous variables (*i.e.*, time dummies and individual-specific linear time trends) as standard instrumental variables.[2] The equation is as follows (Wooldridge 2010: 213–6, 372):

$$y_{i,t} = \alpha_0 + \alpha_1 y_{i,t-1} + \beta_1 x_{1,i,t} + \beta_2 x_{2,i,t} + \ldots + \beta_k x_{k,i,t} + \mu_t + \eta_i + \delta_i (t - 1960) + \varepsilon_{i,t}$$
$$(i = 1,\ldots, N;\ t = 3,\ldots, T),$$

where i is individuals (countries), t is observation time (year), N is the number of individuals, T is the largest number of observation years for the same individual, k is the number of independent (endogenous) variables, $y_{i,t}$ is the value of the dependent variable for an individual i at the time point t, $x_{k,i,t}$ is the value of an independent (endogenous) variable x_k for an individual i at the time point t, α_0 is a constant, α_1 and β_1-β_k are coefficients, μ_t is year-specific fixed effects with a mean of 0 (year-specific global condition), η_i is country-specific fixed effects with a mean of 0 (country-specific time-invariant condition), δ_i is county-specific linear time trends, and $\varepsilon_{i,t}$ is errors independent and identically distributed with a mean of 0 and variance σ^2_ε.[3] We should note that the first differences of the dependent variable, independent variables, and errors are taken before the estimation, and thus we can consider only the time-series differences in each country when we interpret the estimation results.

Among recent studies on suicide rates, Neumayer (2004) used dynamic FD-GMM estimation. However, the equation included only unemployment as an independent variable and the data set was limited to the states of Germany. Stuckler

2 The limitation of the total number of instrumental variables is "Number of observations + 1" when a constant is included in the equation.

3 Note, however, that we need to modify heteroscedasticity of errors by using robust standard errors.

et al. (2009), using dynamic first-difference fixed-effects within-group (FD-FE-WG) estimation, found that ALMPs tend to decrease the suicide-stimulatory effect of increases in unemployment in 17 European countries during the period from 1980 to 2003. ALMPs were therefore thought to prevent suicide among unemployed people because ALMPs reintegrate them into new social relationships through public job training and other assistive services. However, the estimation in Stuckler et al. (2009) did not use instrumental variables and thus could not control for the endogeneity of independent variables. In addition, the equation included change in unemployment but did not include other independent (control) variables whose effects were significant in Neumayer (2003), such as divorce rate, marriage rate, birth rate, female labor force participation, and alcohol consumption.

Among previous quantitative studies on suicide rate that consider the effects of social policies, we have not found any previous study that has used dynamic FD-GMM estimation and controlled Neumayer's (2003) key variables (Andrés 2005; Chen et al. 2009; Fishback et al. 2007; Flavin and Radcliff 2009; Gerdtham and Ruhm 2006; Helliwell 2007; Hooijdonk et al. 2008; Kelly et al. 2009; Maimon and Kuhl 2008; Ruhm 2000; West 2003; Yoon and Bruckner 2009; Zimmerman 1992, 1993, 1995, 2002).

Hypotheses

To investigate the impact of ALMPs, we created and tested two new hypotheses. The first hypothesis (H1) is "The interaction between public expenditure on ALMPs and marriage rate is negatively associated with suicide rate." That is, public expenditure on ALMPs enhances the suppressive effect of marriage rate on suicide rate. The theoretical reason for this hypothesis is that ALMPs provide free-of-charge job training and the chance to change workplaces, which frees people from their dependence on their present workplaces, enhances work-life balance, enables them to feel more happiness in their marital relationships during leisure time, and enhances the suicide-preventive function of the marital relationship.

The second hypothesis (H2) is "The interaction between public expenditure on ALMPs and divorce rate is negatively associated with suicide rate." That is, public expenditure on ALMPs decreases the stimulatory effect of divorce rate on suicide rate. The theoretical reason for this hypothesis is that ALMPs can enhance work-life balance, promote social relationships (e.g., friendships) outside their marital relationships during leisure time, and prevent isolation and suicide after divorce.

Data and Methods

To test these two hypotheses, we estimated the impact on suicide rate of the interaction between ALMPs and divorce/marriage rate. We used the panel data of 27 OECD countries including Japan and Korea from 1980 to 2007 (Table 5.1).[4] The estimation method is dynamic FD-GMM estimation.[5]

When we estimated the interaction effects, the independent variables that construct the interaction terms were centered at their in-country means (group-mean centering) to decrease the correlations between the interaction term and the independent variables, and to help avoid multi-collinearity. After conducting the group-mean centering, we compared the above-mentioned correlations with the correlations before group-mean centering.

TABLE 5.1 *Definitions and sources of variables*

Variables	Definitions	Sources
Suicide rate	Suicides per 100,000 population (age-standardized[6])	OECD (2012) *Health Data 2011* (with the data for the year 2000 of United Kingdom supplemented by OECD (2010) *Society at a Glance 2009*)
GDP per capita	GDP per capita, PPP (constant 2005 international $)	World Bank (2010) *World Development Indicators 2010*

4 We excluded data of the Czech Republic, Estonia, Slovak Republic, and Slovenia from our panel data, because the time that these four countries have spent as independent nation-states with their own social policies is too short to be compared with other OECD countries. We also did not use the Germany's data during the period 1980 to 1990, because this was a time when data from Germany only covered West Germany, making it unsuitable to compare with data covering the period 1991 to 2007 (when Germany was unified).

5 We used Stata 12.1 and its commands of "xtabond" for dynamic FD-GMM estimation, "estat sargan" for Sargan test of overidentifying restrictions, "r" for robust standard errors, and "estat abond" for Arellano-Bond test for zero autocorrelation in first-differenced errors.

6 Age-standardized suicide rate is ideal for use in estimation models because the national and over-time differences in age structure are controlled (Neumayer 2003: 316). See Note 2 for further information.

Variables	Definitions	Sources
Unemployment	Unemployment, total (% of total labor force)	OECD (2010) *Factbook 2010*
Annual change rate of unemployment	In %	
Working hours	Average hours actually worked (hours per year per person in employment)	
Union density	Union density (%)	OECD (2010) *Employment Database 2010*
Female labor participation rate	Labor participation rate, female (% of female population ages 15+)	World Bank (2010) *World Development Indicators 2010*
Male population rate	Male population (% of total)	
Child population rate	Population ages 0–14 (% of total)	
Elderly population rate	Population ages 65 and above (% of total)	
Marriage rate	Crude marriage rate (number of new marriages per 1,000 population)	OECD (2010) *Society at a Glance 2009*
Fertility rate	Fertility rate, total (births per woman)	World Bank (2010) *World Development Indicators 2010*
Divorce rate	Crude divorce rate (number of divorces per 1,000 population)	OECD (2010) *Society at a Glance 2009*
Alcohol consumption	Alcohol consumption, liters per population aged 15 and over	OECD (2012) *Health Data 2011*
Total tax revenue	Compulsory, unrequited payments to general government (including social security contributions) (% of GDP)	OECD (2010) *Factbook 2010*
Rate of value added tax	General sales tax, %	OECD (2010) *Tax Database*
Rate of basic (non-targeted) corporate income tax	%	
Public non-social expenditure	General government expenditure minus public social expenditure (% of GDP)	OECD (2010) *Factbook 2010*, OECD (2012) *Social Expenditure Database*

TABLE 5.1 *Definitions and sources of variables* (cont.)

Variables	Definitions	Sources
Public expenditure on old age	As % of GDP	OECD (2012) *Social*
Public expenditure on health	As % of GDP	*Expenditure Database*
Public expenditure on incapacity	As % of GDP	
Public expenditure on family	As % of GDP	
Public expenditure on ALMPs	As % of GDP	
Public expenditure on unemployment	As % of GDP	
Public expenditure on survivors	As % of GDP	
Public expenditure on housing	As % of GDP	
Public expenditure on public assistance and other social policy areas	As % of GDP	

Results

The descriptive statistics are shown in Table 5.2. The correlations between the interaction terms and the independent variables from which they are constructed are shown in Table 5.3. The correlations after group-mean centering were all smaller than those before group-mean centering. Thus, we adopted group-mean centering in our analyses.

The results of our analyses are shown in Table 5.4. The final model for the estimation of the impact of ALMPs on suicide rate is Model 7, which captures the suicide-stimulatory effects of rise in unemployment and of divorce rate, and the suicide-preventive effect of marriage rate.[7] In this model, multicollinearity does not seem to occur to a considerable degree for any variable whose coefficient is significant (change in unemployment, child population rate, marriage rate, marriage rate * ALMPs, divorce rate, divorce rate * ALMPs, ALMPs,

7 Regarding the significant coefficients for child population rate and expenditure on survivors in Model 7, we can interpret these as follows. An increase in child population rate, after controlling for increases in the elderly population rate, decreases the working-age population rate and may increase the economic burden on workers or bread-winners and thus their suicide rate. An increase in the number of deaths, from any cause, will increase the number of survivors and may increase the number of suicides following the death of the bread winner of the household.

and expenditure on survivors), because no sign for the coefficients of these variables reversed from Models 1 through 6 to this Model 7. In this final model (Model 7), the interaction effect between ALMPs and marriage rate on suicide rate was estimated to be significantly negative ($p < 0.01$), which supports hypothesis H1. The interaction effect between ALMPs and divorce rate on suicide rate was also estimated to be significantly negative ($p < 0.001$), which supports hypothesis H2.

We further carefully checked the reliability of our findings by conducting other additional analyses. First, to check the robustness of the negative interaction effect between ALMPs with marriage rate and divorce rate on suicide rate, we estimated these interaction effects on suicide rate for the next year by using dynamic fixed-effects within-group (FE-WG) estimation.[8] This is because this estimation results in smaller biases in the coefficients of lagged dependent variables than dynamic FD-GMM estimation when $T > N$, as in the case of our panel data (27 countries during the period 1980 to 2007) (Alvarez and Arellano 2003). Models 8 and 9 show the result of this estimation, with the final model being Model 9.[9] In this model, the interaction between ALMPs and marriage rate was significantly negative on suicide rate in the next year.[10] However, the interaction between ALMPs and divorce rate was not significant. These results suggests that the suicide-preventive effects of marriage, ALMPs, and ALMPs at the time of marriage last for at least one year,[11] but that the suicide-stimulatory effect of divorce and the suicide-preventive effect of ALMPs at the time of divorce do not seem to last for a whole year.

8 FE-WG estimation uses group-mean centering for all the variables in order to eliminate country-specific fixed effects.

9 Regarding the significant coefficients for corporate income tax and expenditure on incapacity and public assistance in Model 9, we can interpret them as follows. A rise in corporate income tax may promote corporate downsizing and increase the number of unemployed persons and thus their suicide rate in the next year. An increase in the number of seriously injured and disabled workers may increase both expenditure on incapacity and their suicide rate in the next year. An increase in public assistance may indicate a greater number of poor people, which could increase suicides in the next year.

10 Even if we consider multicollinearity and exclude the independent variables whose coefficients were significant in Model 9 but not significant in Model 7 (i.e., fertility rate, corporate income tax, expenditure on incapacity, and expenditure on public assistance and other areas), the coefficients for marriage rate and its interaction with ALMPs are still significantly negative and those of divorce rate and its interaction with ALMPs are still not significant.

11 We also estimated the coefficients of all the independent variables in Model 9 on suicide rate of *the year after the next*. As a result, the coefficient of the interaction between marriage rate and ALMPs was still significantly negative. The coefficients of lagged suicide rate and the interaction between change in unemployment and ALMPs were still significantly positive. However, the effects of the other independent variables (including marriage rate, divorce rate, and their interaction with ALMPs) were not significant.

TABLE 5.2 *Descriptive statistics (averages before group-mean centering, 1980–2007)*

Country	Suicide rate	GDP per capita	Unemployment	Annual change rate of unemployment	Working hours	Union density	Female labor participation rate	Male population rate	Child population rate	Elderly population rate	Marriage rate	Fertility rate
Australia	12.5	27366	6.1	3.3	1783	39.7	51.8	50.0	24.6	10.4	5.6	2.2
Austria	20.1	27679	4.2	0.2	1653	50.9	45.8	47.6	19.8	14.7	5.8	1.8
Belgium	16.5	26650	7.7	4.0	1601	49.7	39.8	48.9	20.1	14.7	5.8	1.9
Canada	12.0	28795	7.5	0.4	1792	31.5	57.2	49.8	24.0	10.2	6.6	2.1
Denmark	19.1	27761	6.0	−2.4	1601	70.3	59.9	49.4	20.3	14.0	6.3	1.9
Finland	22.4	24206	6.8	6.7	1807	64.1	57.5	48.5	21.3	12.1	5.7	1.9
France	16.2	25320	9.0	1.9	1735	14.7	47.3	48.7	21.8	14.1	5.5	2.1
Germany[a]	11.7	29774	8.3	4.3	1486	25.9	49.4	48.8	15.4	16.9	5.0	1.3
Greece	3.2	19601	8.7	0.6	2117	28.8	37.6	49.1	20.7	13.3	6.2	1.8
Hungary	31.7	13033	8.1	−1.0	2032	24.4	44.4	48.1	20.1	13.0	6.5	1.8
Iceland	12.2	27366	3.3	4.1	1883	78.3	73.1	50.4	27.6	10.1	5.9	2.5
Ireland	7.3	23839	10.6	−2.1	1830	46.3	40.7	50.1	27.6	11.1	5.6	2.8
Italy	6.0	24475	8.6	0.9	1856	37.6	34.7	48.5	19.6	14.3	5.5	1.7
Japan	18.1	25959	2.6	0.7	1997	28.3	49.2	49.1	20.7	11.4	6.8	1.7
Korea, Rep.	13.7	14612	3.4	5.8	2643	13.2	47.1	50.0	31.0	5.1	8.3	2.4
Luxembourg	14.1	48601	3.0	3.5	1687	45.8	38.0	49.1	19.4	13.2	5.5	1.7
Mexico	3.1	11031	3.5	1.9	1872	18.3	36.8	49.7	40.6	4.3	6.8	4.5
Netherlands	8.7	28736	5.1	5.3	1377	30.2	47.6	49.6	22.2	11.9	6.1	2.0
New Zealand	11.8	20650	3.7	29.4	1818	43.5	55.9	49.7	26.6	10.2	6.8	2.4
Norway	10.8	37256	3.4	3.2	1546	56.4	58.3	49.6	21.7	14.3	5.4	2.1
Poland	12.3	11206	14.4	−3.0	1981	33.1	52.4	48.6	24.3	9.9	7.1	2.0
Portugal	8.4	16748	6.4	0.9	1832	32.6	50.5	48.0	23.0	12.3	7.3	2.1
Spain	5.7	21374	13.2	3.0	1812	13.9	36.4	48.9	22.1	12.6	5.8	2.0
Sweden	15.6	26011	4.5	6.3	1596	76.1	60.2	49.6	19.2	15.9	4.6	1.9
Switzerland	18.6	32633	3.6	1.8	1674	26.0	57.5	48.8	19.7	13.5	5.9	1.7
United Kingdom	7.6	25767	6.8	2.7	1766	38.7	51.2	48.6	20.8	14.6	6.5	2.0
United States	11.5	34146	5.8	1.1	1833	19.9	56.9	49.1	24.1	11.3	9.4	2.2
Average	13.2	24704	6.3	3.9	1807	39.5	48.8	49.2	23.6	11.8	6.3	2.2

Notes:
[a] Germany is unified Germany covering only 1991–2007.

SOURCE: SEE TABLE 5.1

Divorce rate	Alcohol consumption	Total tax revenue	Rate of value added tax	Rate of basic corporate income tax	Public non-social expenditure	Public expenditure on old age	Public expenditure on health	Public expenditure on incapacity	Public expenditure on family	Public expenditure on ALMPs	Public expenditure on unemployment	Public expenditure on survivors	Public expenditure on housing	Public expenditure on public assistance and other social policy areas
2.7	10.9	26.8	1.8	37.3	21.3	3.7	4.8	1.8	2.0	0.4	1.0	0.3	0.2	0.2
2.0	13.7	39.4	13.1	38.0	25.9	10.2	5.9	2.7	2.8	0.5	1.1	2.2	0.1	0.3
2.0	11.5	41.0	13.1	40.3	27.4	6.8	6.5	3.0	2.6	1.1	3.1	2.5	0.0	0.4
2.4	8.6	32.6	2.4	42.0	27.2	3.8	6.4	1.1	0.8	0.5	1.4	0.4	0.6	2.6
2.7	10.7	43.7	15.3	36.3	28.6	7.3	5.2	3.7	3.2	1.4	3.9	0.0	0.6	1.0
2.3	7.5	39.6	6.7	38.5	23.8	7.6	5.8	4.2	3.0	1.0	2.1	1.0	0.3	0.5
1.7	16.8	40.2	12.9	40.1	24.8	9.7	6.8	2.2	2.8	1.0	1.4	1.8	0.8	0.2
2.2	10.7	36.3	15.8	47.5	21.2	8.4	8.0	2.2	2.1	1.2	1.6	2.5	0.4	0.2
0.8	10.7	25.7	7.7	39.4	25.0	8.7	4.5	1.2	0.7	0.2	0.4	1.0	0.4	0.2
2.5	12.4	39.9	10.4	24.9	27.4	7.5	5.8	2.7	3.3	0.4	0.9	1.2	0.5	0.2
0.7	4.7	32.7	9.3	20.3	26.5	3.6	6.1	2.0	2.6	0.1	0.4	0.0	0.1	0.5
1.8	9.8	30.9	14.8	33.7	27.6	3.5	5.3	1.8	1.8	1.0	1.7	1.0	0.5	0.2
0.5	13.6	34.4	12.0	42.5	25.9	9.9	5.8	1.9	1.0	0.5	0.7	2.3	0.0	0.0
1.5	7.5	24.8	1.6	44.6	20.6	5.5	5.3	0.7	0.6	0.3	0.5	1.1	0.0	0.2
1.4	8.7	18.5	5.9	29.0	18.5	1.2	2.2	0.4	0.1	0.1	0.1	0.2	0.0	0.3
1.7	14.1	34.7	8.8	31.7	18.7	6.4	5.3	3.4	2.5	0.3	0.6	1.9	0.1	0.3
0.5	4.7	16.2	8.1	35.8	.	0.6	2.0	0.0	0.4	0.0	0.0	0.2	0.7	0.5
1.9	9.5	40.0	12.3	36.7	28.0	5.8	5.5	5.0	1.8	1.2	2.3	0.6	0.4	0.9
2.3	10.0	31.9	5.3	35.9	25.2	5.9	5.7	2.4	2.4	0.7	1.1	0.2	0.5	0.2
1.9	5.0	40.2	14.6	37.0	26.3	6.8	4.9	4.6	3.0	0.8	0.7	0.4	0.2	0.7
1.2	8.8	34.7	6.7	30.4	22.7	8.1	4.3	4.3	1.4	0.4	1.0	2.0	0.1	0.3
1.1	15.7	26.1	7.5	39.8	26.5	5.5	4.6	2.3	0.8	0.5	0.6	1.1	0.0	0.1
0.8	15.0	26.5	6.4	34.5	21.2	7.0	5.1	2.5	0.6	0.6	2.6	1.2	0.1	0.1
2.4	6.4	45.5	15.9	38.6	29.3	9.1	7.1	5.1	3.8	1.9	1.3	0.7	0.8	0.7
1.9	12.7	25.2	2.2	27.8	16.6	6.2	4.7	2.5	1.1	0.5	0.6	0.4	0.1	0.7
2.6	9.3	34.7	10.4	34.7	25.7	5.1	5.5	2.1	2.5	0.5	1.0	0.7	1.3	0.4
4.5	9.1	26.7	.	41.7	21.7	5.3	5.5	1.1	0.6	0.2	0.5	0.9	0.0	0.5
1.8	9.9	32.3	9.0	36.9	24.8	6.1	5.3	2.4	1.8	0.6	1.2	1.0	0.3	0.5

TABLE 5.3 *Correlations between the interaction term and the independent variables*

	Before group-mean centering			**After group-mean centering**		
	Public expenditure on ALMPS	Marriage rate	Divorce rate	Public expenditure on ALMPS	Marriage rate	Divorce rate
Marriage rate[c] * Public expenditure on ALMPS	0.9542	−0.1870		−0.4883	0.0030	
Divorce rate[c] * Public expenditure on ALMPS	0.9548		0.4474	0.4320		0.1943

Notes: 'X * Y' represents the interaction term of X and Y.
SOURCE: SEE TABLE 5.1

Second, to examine the specific tendency in Japan for the effects of the main independent variables (change in unemployment, marriage rate, divorce rate, and ALMPS), we estimated the interaction effects between a Japan country dummy and the main variables on suicide rate. To avoid multicollinearity, we added the interaction terms separately, as shown in Models 10 through 14. The final model is Model 14, because no sign of significant coefficients reversed from Models 1 through 7, or Models 10 through 13 to Model 14. The final model (Model 14) shows that Japan is not an exception to the significant effects of the main independent variables, as all the signs of the significant coefficients for the interactions with the Japan dummy match the signs of the significant coefficients of the main independent variables.

Third, to examine the specific tendency in Korea for the effects of the main independent variables, we estimated the interaction effect between a Korea country dummy and the main variables on suicide rate. To avoid multicollinearity, we added the interaction terms separately, as shown in Models 15 through 19. As it turned out, Model 19 was not the final model because the sign of the significant coefficient for the interaction between the Korea country dummy and divorce rate reversed from Model 17 to Model 19 (from positive to negative) and the sign of significant coefficient for the interaction between Korea's dummy and ALMPS reversed from Model 18 to Model 19 (from negative to positive), both of which suggest the existence of considerable multicollinearity in Model 19. Thus, we adopted not Model 19 but Model 7 (the final model before adding interactions with the Korea dummy variable) as the final model for Korea. On the other hand, the interaction effects with the Korea country dummy in Models 15 through 18 show that Korea is not an exception to the significant effects of the main independent variables, as all the signs of the significant coefficients for the interaction terms matched the signs of the significant coefficients for the main independent variables.

Lastly, we estimated the predicted values of suicide rate in Japan and Korea. Using the estimates of the final models for Japan (Model 14) and Korea (Model 7), we created equations for the estimation of each country's predicted values of suicide rate. For Japan, the equation based on Model 14 is as follows:[12]

$$\text{Predicted suicide}_t = \text{Suicide}_{t\text{-}1} + (0.0123 + 0.0564) * \Delta\text{Change in unemployment}^c_t + 0.638 * \Delta\text{Child}_t - (1.038 + 1.973) * \Delta\text{Marriage}^c_t - 1.549 * \Delta(\text{Marriage}^c_t * \text{ALMPS}^c_t) + (1.575 + 7.990) * \Delta\text{Divorce}^c_t - 3.155 * \Delta(\text{Divorce}^c_t * \text{ALMPS}^c_t) - (1.254 + 19.73) * \Delta\text{ALMPS}^c_t + 1.874 * \Delta\text{Expenditure on survivors}_t + \text{Year-specific fixed effect}_t - \text{Year-specific fixed effect}_{t\text{-}1}.$$

For Korea, the equation based on Model 7 is as follows:

$$\text{Predicted suicide}_t = \text{Suicide}_{t\text{-}1} + 0.214 * \Delta\text{Suicide}_{t\text{-}1} + 0.0128 * \Delta\text{Change in unemployment}^c_t + 0.561 * \Delta\text{Child}_t - 0.933 * \Delta\text{Marriage}^c_t - 1.550 * \Delta(\text{Marriage}^c_t * \text{ALMPS}^c_t) + 1.821 * \Delta\text{Divorce}^c_t - 3.554 * \Delta(\text{Divorce}^c_t * \text{ALMPS}^c_t) - 1.400 * \Delta\text{ALMPS}^c_t + 1.926 * \Delta\text{Expenditure on survivors}_t + \text{Year-specific fixed effect}_t - \text{Year-specific fixed effect}_{t\text{-}1}.$$

Using these equations, we estimated the predicted values of suicide rate in Japan and Korea, which are depicted in Figure 5.4 and Figure 5.5. Pearson's product-moment correlation coefficients between the predicted values and the observed values were 0.864 (in contrast with 0.845 between the previous-year observed values and the current observed values) in Japan and 0.947 (in contrast with 0.914) in Korea. Therefore, we can say that suicide rates were predicted with a certain effectiveness for both countries.

12 As for year-specific fixed effects, coefficients that were significant at the 10 percent level in the model were introduced into the predictive equations in order to assume as gradual effects as possible. In both Model 14 and Model 7, neither the country-specific linear time trend of Japan nor that of Korea were significant, and thus were not introduced into the predictive equations. In both these models, the constant was not significant, and thus was not introduced into the predictive equations.

TABLE 5.4 *Dynamic FD-GMM estimation of suicide rates with robust standard errors for 27 OECD countries, 1980–2007*

Model	Model 1	Model 2	Model 3	Model 4	Model 5	Model 6	Model 7	Model 8
Estimation	FD-GMM	FD-GMM	FD-GMM	FD-GMM	FD-GMM	FD-GMM	FD-GMM	FE-WG
Suicide rate [year-1]	0.525***	0.492***	0.448***	0.331***	0.303***	0.225*	0.214*	0.379***
GDP per capita[c]						0.000226	0.000204	6.45E-06
(GDP per capita[c])2						-4.94E-09	-3.74E-09	-1.68E-08
Unemployment						-0.0325	-0.0498	-0.00913
Annual change rate of unemployment[c]	0.00709	0.0105**	0.0110***	0.0139***	0.0136***	0.0128***	0.0128**	0.00118
Annual change rate of unemployment[c] * Public expenditure on ALMPs[c]					0.00746		-0.000197	
Annual change rate of unemployment[c] * Japan's dummy								
Annual change rate of unemployment[c] * Korea's dummy								
Working hours						-0.00239	-0.00156	-0.00134
Union density						0.0363	0.0549	0.00898
Female labor participation rate						0.0935	0.1	0.057
Male population rate						-1.313	-1.116	4.121
Child population rate						0.601*	0.561*	0.253
Elderly population rate						1.231	1.134	0.887
Marriage rate[c]		-0.387	-0.415	-0.590**	-0.567**	-1.023**	-0.933**	-0.647**
Marriage rate[c] * Public expenditure on ALMPs[c]					-1.173**		-1.550**	
Marriage rate[c] * Japan's dummy								
Marriage rate[c] * Korea's dummy								
Fertility rate						0.658	0.608	-1.862*
Divorce rate[c]			1.268**	1.173***	1.394***	1.675***	1.821***	0.851
Divorce rate[c] * Public expenditure on ALMPs[c]					-4.037***		-3.554***	
Divorce rate[c] * Japan's dummy								
Divorce rate[c] * Korea's dummy								
Alcohol consumption						0.187	0.187	0.294
Total tax revenue						0.0775	0.0576	0.00439
Rate of value added tax						0.0266	0.0299	-0.00761

Model 9	Model 10	Model 11	Model 12	Model 13	Model 14	Model 15	Model 16	Model 17	Model 18	Model 19
FE-WG	FD-GMM	FD-GMM	FD-GMM	FD-GMM	FD-GMM	FD-GMM	FD-GMM	FD-GMM	FD-GMM	FD-GMM
0.355***	0.233*	0.226*	0.200*	0.225*	0.186	0.243*	0.258*	0.254*	0.255*	0.209*
2.77E-05	0.000254	0.000237	0.00031	0.000223	0.000292	0.000187	0.00017	0.000178	0.000199	0.000141
-1.49E-08	-5.71E-09	-5.42E-09	-3.65E-09	-4.85E-09	-9.81E-10	-4.50E-09	-5.82E-09	-4.83E-09	-5.30E-09	-4.05E-09
-0.0374	-0.0288	-0.0334	-0.0192	-0.0326	-0.0324	-0.0296	-0.0258	-0.0316	-0.0286	-0.0441
7.65E-05	0.0112**	0.0123***	0.0131**	0.0127***	0.0123**	0.0110**	0.0115**	0.0115**	0.0115**	0.0123**
0.0142					0.000926					-0.00181
	0.0812***				0.0564**					
						0.101***				0.148***
-0.00149	-0.0016	-0.0022	-0.00199	-0.0024	-0.00108	-0.00216	-0.00154	-0.00206	-0.00219	-0.000174
0.0271	0.0362	0.0361	0.0481	0.0364	0.0701	0.0423	0.039	0.0426	0.0392	0.0571
0.0411	0.097	0.0937	0.1	0.0934	0.106	0.113*	0.110*	0.115*	0.105	0.116
3.651	-1.973	-1.592	-3.048	-1.256	-2.917	-0.875	-0.596	-0.801	-0.829	-0.733
0.204	0.688*	0.650*	0.733*	0.592*	0.638*	0.565*	0.563*	0.575*	0.588*	0.476*
0.733	1.195	1.229	0.863	1.24	0.715	1.135	1.116	1.133	1.175	0.953
-0.624*	-1.059**	-1.055**	-1.134**	-1.022**	-1.038**	-0.997**	-0.939**	-0.975**	-0.983**	-0.853*
-1.430***					-1.549**					-1.574**
		1.256			-1.973**					
							-5.949***			-13.90***
-2.334**	0.706	0.731	0.586	0.647	0.281	0.479	0.694	0.499	0.682	0.447
0.905	1.595***	1.640***	1.456**	1.679***	1.575***	1.427**	1.338**	1.365**	1.434**	1.590***
-0.461					-3.155**					-3.221**
			6.623***		7.990***					
								3.067***		-2.663**
0.316	0.162	0.178	0.162	0.189	0.173	0.205	0.183	0.184	0.202	0.166
0.00559	0.0983	0.0843	0.0921	0.0765	0.0744	0.0633	0.0613	0.0589	0.0643	0.0525
-0.00529	0.0254	0.0278	0.0281	0.0263	0.0262	0.0245	0.0249	0.0254	0.0258	0.0258

TABLE 5.4 *Dynamic FD-GMM estimation of suicide rates with robust standard errors for 27 OECD countries, 1980–2007* (cont.)

Model	Model 1	Model 2	Model 3	Model 4	Model 5	Model 6	Model 7	Model 8
Rate of basic (non-targeted) corporate income tax						0.0213	0.0157	0.0508**
Public non-social expenditure						0.0715	0.0618	-0.0598
Public expenditure on old age						-0.204	-0.149	-0.0632
Public expenditure on health						-0.0935	-0.113	0.144
Public expenditure on incapacity						-0.104	-0.064	0.368*
Public expenditure on family						0.348	0.398	0.379
Public expenditure on ALMPs[c]				-0.691*	-0.519	-0.878*	-1.400**	-0.392
Public expenditure on ALMPs[c] * Japan's dummy								
Public expenditure on ALMPs[c] * Korea's dummy								
Public expenditure on unemployment						0.129	0.115	0.196
Public expenditure on survivors						1.888*	1.926*	-0.0781
Public expenditure on housing						-0.362	-0.55	-0.99
Public expenditure on public assistance and other areas						-0.466	-0.0993	0.276
Year-specific fixed effects	included	included	included	included	included	included	included	included
Country-specific linear time trends	included	included	included	included	included	included	included	included
Country-specific linear time trends of Japan	0.0384***	-0.296*	-0.468**	-1.163***	-1.098*	-0.13	-0.0915	0.00458
Country-specific linear time trends of Korea	0.521***	0.152	-0.105	-0.949*	-0.868	0.724*	0.704	0.52
Constant	7.082***	14.59***	19.31***	40.24***	39.27***	40.89	30.97	-211.2
Number of observations	616	561	548	479	479	366	366	390
Number of countries	27	27	27	27	27	25	25	25
Number of instruments (GMM-type and standard)	617	562	549	480	480	367	367	
Sargan test of overidentifying restrictions (p)	0.2264	0.2582	0.1425	0.1277	0.1368	0.0946	0.114	
Arellano-Bond test for zero autocorrelation in first-differenced errors (p of second order)	0.6089	0.248	0.1371	0.1972	0.3338	0.5995	0.6243	

Model 9	Model 10	Model 11	Model 12	Model 13	Model 14	Model 15	Model 16	Model 17	Model 18	Model 19
0.0434*	0.021	0.0209	0.0272	0.0214	0.0239	0.0228	0.023	0.023	0.0217	0.0195
−0.0487	0.0602	0.0696	0.0538	0.0712	0.0345	0.0525	0.0547	0.052	0.0619	0.0398
−0.0295	−0.13	−0.174	−0.266	−0.204	−0.225	−0.204	−0.193	−0.206	−0.189	−0.161
0.0256	−0.142	−0.12	−0.128	−0.0903	−0.133	−0.07	−0.0353	−0.0642	−0.0727	−0.0321
0.400*	−0.157	−0.129	−0.144	−0.103	−0.101	−0.0548	−0.0571	−0.0448	−0.0696	−0.0333
0.365	0.382	0.347	0.525	0.35	0.641	0.389	0.346	0.365	0.323	0.507
−1.278***	−0.784*	−0.850*	−0.732	−0.878*	−1.254**	−0.771	−0.744	−0.759	−0.793*	−1.305**
				−2.525	−19.73***					
									−18.34***	50.57***
0.176	0.0983	0.117	0.0645	0.13	0.0445	0.124	0.1	0.112	0.119	0.0855
0.0576	1.967*	1.929*	1.867*	1.886*	1.874*	1.835*	1.833*	1.826*	1.859*	1.875*
−0.906	−0.276	−0.34	−0.285	−0.365	−0.401	−0.456	−0.5	−0.48	−0.437	−0.658
0.386*	−0.471	−0.467	−0.478	−0.468	−0.148	−0.456	−0.412	−0.398	−0.451	−0.0878
included	included	included	included	included	included	included	included	included	included	included
included	included	included	included	included	included	included	included	included	included	included
0.0587	−0.0703	−0.0981	−0.283	−0.148	−0.419	−0.061	−0.0385	−0.0515	−0.0862	0.0391
0.543	0.695	0.712	0.742	0.725*	0.733	0.335	0.606	0.795*	0.0602	1.634***
−183.9	70.18	53.11	127.5	38.2	123.2	19.85	4.106	15.21	16.73	11.28
390	366	366	366	366	366	366	366	366	366	366
25	25	25	25	25	25	25	25	25	25	25
	367	367	367	367	367	367	367	367	367	367
	0.135	0.1076	0.1271	0.0927	0.1869	0.1851	0.1542	0.1694	0.18	0.1078
	0.5298	0.6461	0.5588	0.5886	0.4896	0.5126	0.5938	0.6368	0.5899	0.6178

TABLE 5.4 *Dynamic FD-GMM estimation of suicide rates with robust standard errors for 27 OECD countries, 1980–2007* (cont.)

Model	Model 1	Model 2	Model 3	Model 4	Model 5	Model 6	Model 7	Model 8
Panel-level standard deviation								14.17
Standard deviation of $\varepsilon i,t$								0.808
Intraclass correlation (ρ)								0.997
R-squared between model								0.000838
R-squared within model								0.878
R-squared overall model								0.0063

† $p < 0.1$
* $p < 0.05$
** $p < 0.01$
*** $p < 0.001$
c Group-mean centered variables.
'E-n' represents '×10-n.'
'(X)2' represents the square of X.
Note: In dynamic fixed-effects within-group (FE-WG) estimation, not only suicide rate but also all the other independent variables are 1-year lagged.
SOURCE: SEE TABLE 5.1

Additionally, we estimated the predicted values under the assumption that ALMPs expenditure gradually increased at a constant rate from 1989 to 2007, to a higher level than observed in reality. For Japan, we assumed that ALMPs expenditure gradually increased from 0.327 (observed value) in 1989 to 0.675 (Austria's level) or 1.222 (Belgium's level) in 2007 (Figure 5.6). For Korea, we assumed that ALMPs expenditure gradually increased from 0.026 (observed value) in 1989 to 0.500 (Poland's level) or 1.222 (Belgium's level) in 2007 (Figure 5.7). Figures 5.6 and 5.7 suggest that the influence of ALMPs on suicide rate would not have been very large in either Japan or Korea, even if ALMPs had increased to the same high level as in Belgium. As we can see in Figures 5.4 and 5.5, the influence of change in unemployment and of divorce rate on suicide rate was much larger than the influence of ALMPs.

Discussion

On the basis of the above results, we can interpret our findings as follows:

1. Among OECD countries in recent years, ALMPs can prevent suicides, enhance the suicide-preventive effect of marriages, and decrease the

Model 9	Model 10	Model 11	Model 12	Model 13	Model 14	Model 15	Model 16	Model 17	Model 18	Model 19
13.41										
0.803										
0.996										
0.00306										
0.88										
0.0118										

suicide-stimulatory effect of divorces; but ALMPs do not seem to decrease the suicide-stimulatory effect of the increases in unemployment.

2. Both Japan and Korea follow the overall tendency for the suicide-preventive effect of ALMPs and marriage and the suicide-stimulatory effect of unemployment and divorce.
3. The influence of ALMPs on suicide rate was much smaller than the influence of change in unemployment and of divorce rate, at least in Japan and Korea.

Based upon these interpretations, we can tentatively answer the research questions raised at the beginning of this paper. Why did suicide rates increase in Japan and Korea sharply in the late 1990s, and why have they remained high? What are the main factors of change in suicide rate? In particular, what kinds of social policies can prevent suicide and reduce national suicide rates? How do social policies prevent suicide?

Leaving the first question aside for the moment and going straight to the second, the main factors that increase suicide rate are increases in unemployment (i.e., exclusion from public spheres) and divorce (i.e., loss of marital intimacy). On the other hand, the main factors that decrease suicide rate are increases in marriage (i.e., reintegration into marital intimacy) and public expenditure on ALMPs (i.e., reintegration into the public sphere).

Regarding the kinds of social policy that prevent suicide and the ways in which they do, ALMPs provide unemployed people with free-of-charge job training and other services, which reintegrate them into the public sphere by forming new social relationships through job training and other services. In

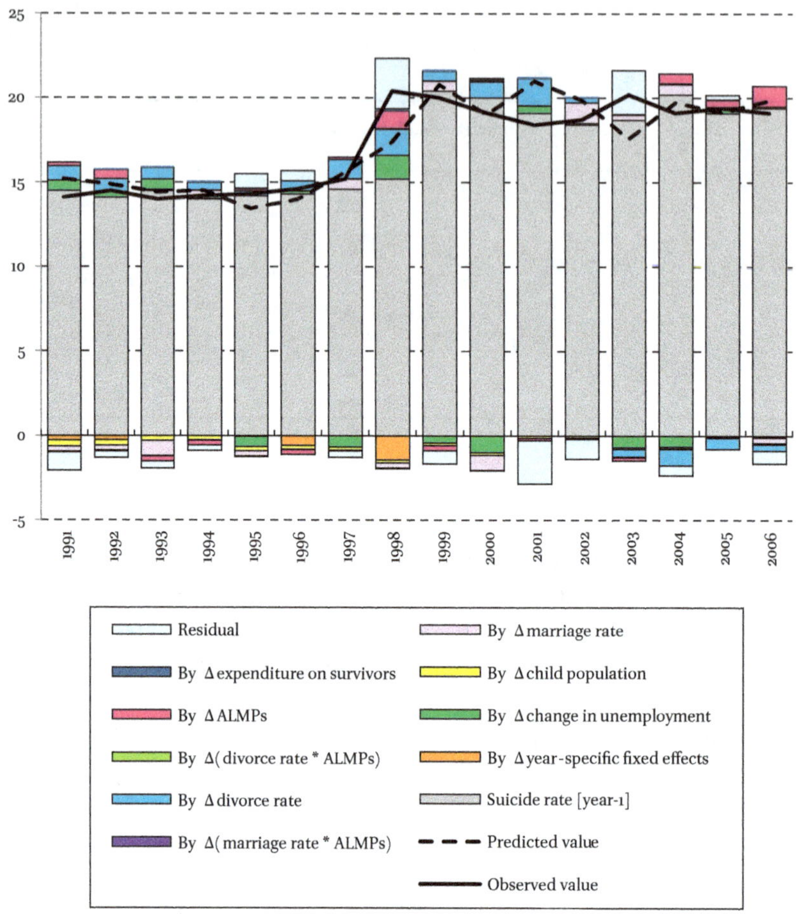

FIGURE 5.4 *Predicted values and observed values of suicide rate in Japan* ($r = 0.864$)
SOURCE: SEE TABLE 5.1

this way, ALMPs can prevent the isolation that may lead to suicide. Additionally, ALMPs provide working people with the chance to change workplaces, which can reduce dependence on their present workplaces, enhance work-life balance, increase happiness in marital relationships and promote other social relationships during leisure time, and enhance the suicide-preventive functions of various social relations.

Returning to the first question, concerning why suicide rates increased sharply in Japan and Korea in the 1990s, we can see the following features concerning the 11 countries with the highest suicide rates from the 1990s. (Figure 5.1)

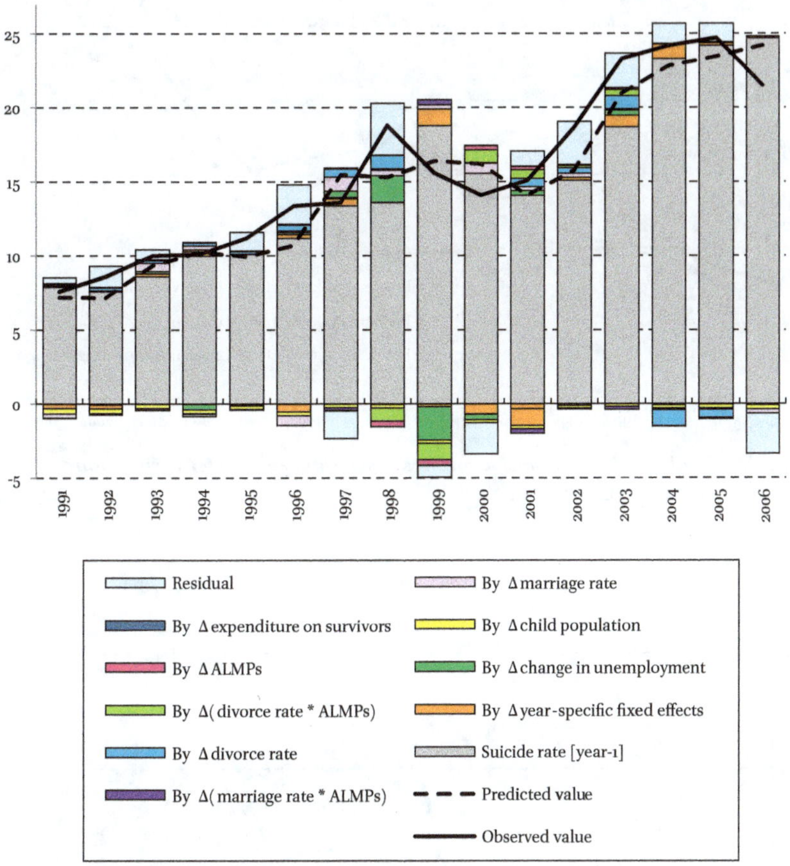

FIGURE 5.5 *Predicted values and observed values of suicide rate in Korea* ($r = 0.947$)
SOURCE: SEE TABLE 5.1

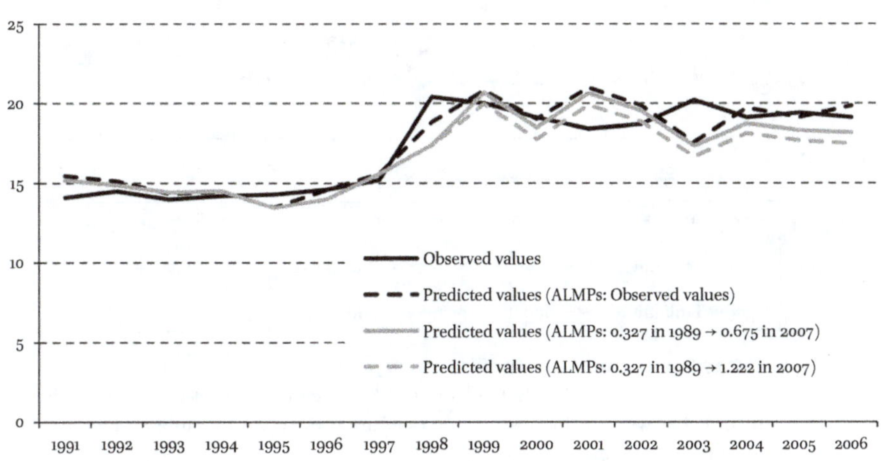

FIGURE 5.6 *Predicted values of suicide rate in Japan by growth in* ALMPs *expenditure*
SOURCE: SEE TABLE 5.1

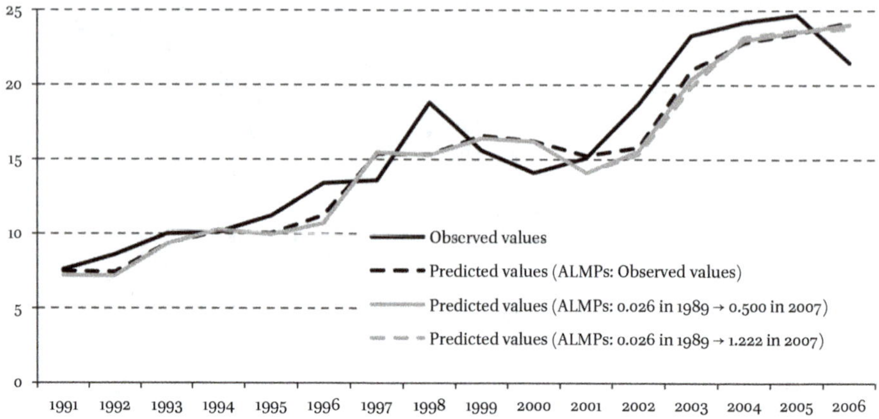

FIGURE 5.7 *Predicted values of suicide rate in Korea by growth in ALMPs expenditure*
SOURCE: SEE TABLE 5.1

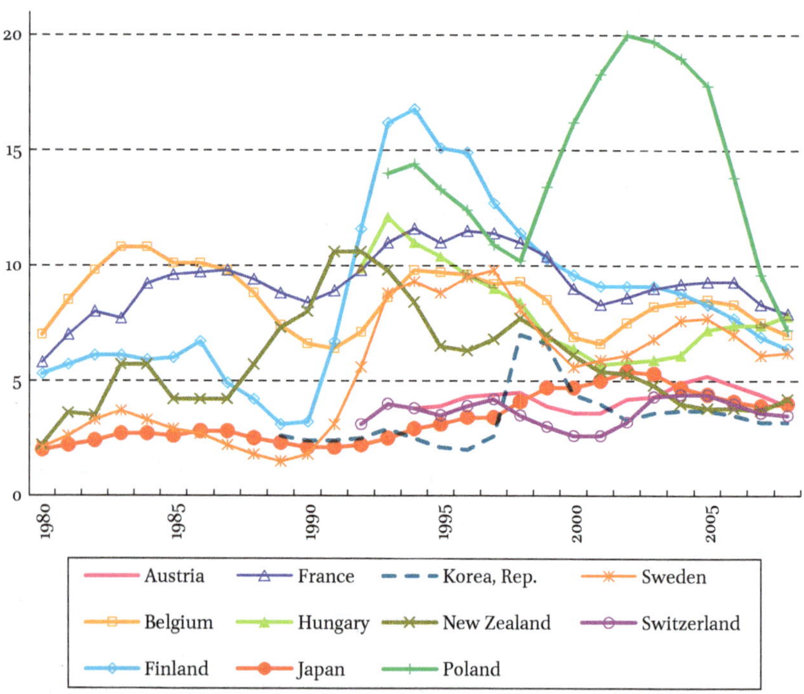

FIGURE 5.8 *Unemployment rate (percent of total labor force)*
Notes: Data are from World Bank (2010) *World Development Indicators 2010*. The 11 countries with the highest suicide rates are shown (see the notes of Figure. 5.1 for further information).

1. Unemployment increased in Japan and Korea (Figure 5.8),[13] divorce rates increased in Austria, Belgium, Switzerland, Japan, Korea, and Poland (Figure 5.3), and marriage rates decreased in all the countries except for Finland and Sweden (Figure 5.2). Therefore, Austria, Belgium, Switzerland, Poland, and especially Japan and Korea, may have higher risk of increases in the suicide rate.
2. Public expenditure on ALMPs decreased gradually in most countries including Japan and Korea, but also showed small increases in Austria, Switzerland, and Poland (Figure 5.9). Because of the suicide-preventive effects of ALMPs, these three countries may have suppressed the risk of increases in the suicide rate. On the other hand, the risk of the suicide

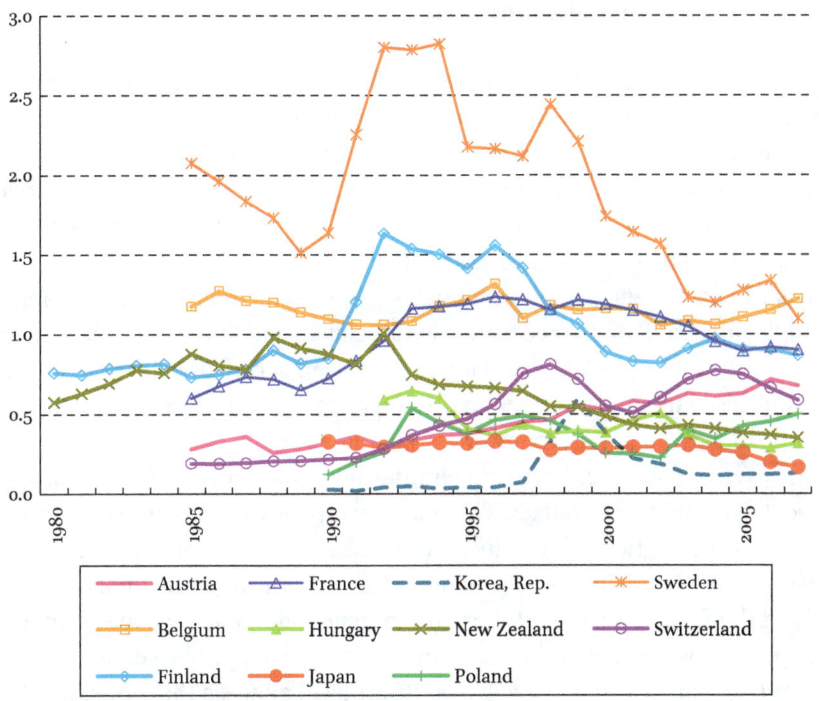

FIGURE 5.9 *Public expenditure on ALMPs (percent of GDP)*
Notes: Data are from OECD (2012) *Social Expenditure Database*. The 11 countries with the highest suicide rates are shown (see the notes of Figure. 5.1 for further information).

13 In Korea, unemployment has decreased since 1999. But, as Phang argues in Chapter 3 of this book, the segmented nature of the labor market in Korea has strengthened during the 10-year period following the economic crisis of 1998. Labor-market conditions for workers and job-seekers do not seem to have shown substantive improvement from 1999 to 2007.

rate rising in the other countries may increase (i.e., in Belgium, Japan, and Korea).

3. Taking the above points 1 and 2 together, Japan and Korea may be particularly at risk of increases in the suicide rate.

Thus, the reason that the suicide rate has increased since the late 1990s in both Japan and Korea and remains high there can be explained as follows. In Japan and Korea, increases in unemployment and divorce rates and a decrease in the marriage rate served to increase the risk of a higher suicide rate, and weak ALMPs were able to offer scarcely any mitigation of these risks.

Conclusions and Limitations

We interpret the results of our analyses as follows: (1) ALMPs can prevent suicides, enhance the suicide-preventive effect of marriages, and decrease the suicide-stimulatory effect of divorces, but they do not seem to decrease the suicide-stimulatory effect of increases in unemployment; (2) Both Japan and Korea follow the overall trends for the suicide-preventive effects of ALMPs and marriage and the suicide-stimulatory effect of unemployment and divorce; but (3) The influence of ALMPs on suicide rate was much smaller than the influence of change in unemployment and of divorce rate, at least in Japan and Korea. We thus conclude that since the late 1990s Japan and Korea have been at risk for higher suicide rates from increased unemployment and divorce rates and a decreased marriage rate, but this risk has scarcely been lowered by actual ALMPs.

However, our analyses have some limitations. First, we must be careful about the ecological inference fallacy. The relationship between divorce rate and suicide rate at the national level does not necessarily mean or support the relationship between divorce and suicide at the level of the individual. In further study in the future, we should therefore pursue individual-level panel analysis that specifically considers the usage of ALMPs-related public services by individuals (e.g., job training) as well as a multi-level analysis that considers both nation-level data on ALMPs and individual-level data on divorce and suicide.

Secondly, the significant effects of independent variables can include some confounding biases (i.e., spurious correlations/de-correlations) caused by some unobserved variables that were not included in the regression equations of our analyses. Thus, examination of various additional independent variables in the future will be beneficial. In addition, our data are limited to the period from 1980 to 2007, and additional unreleased data from 2008 should be included in future analyses, when available.

Lastly, the dynamic FD-GMM estimation used in our analyses is based upon the Sargan test of over-identifying restrictions for the exogeneity of all the instrumental variables and the Arellano-Bond test for zero autocorrelation in first-differenced errors. FD-GMM estimation requires that the results of both tests cannot reject the null hypothesis. However, when sample size is too small and statistical power too weak, it is always difficult to reject the null hypothesis. Thus, even if we cannot reject the null hypotheses in any of the two tests, it is possible that some instrumental variables are endogenous or that there is some auto-correlation in first-differenced errors because the statistical power of the model is too weak (Wooldridge 2010: 135). It will therefore be necessary to conduct power analyses on the two tests in the future.[14]

References

Alvarez, Javier and Manuel Arellano. 2003. "The Time Series and Cross-section Asymptotics of Dynamic Panel Data Estimators." *Econometrica* 71(4): 1121–1159.

Andrés, Antonio Rodríguez. 2005. "Income Inequality, Unemployment, and Suicide: A Panel Data Analysis of 15 European Countries." *Applied Economics* 37: 439–451.

Chen, Joe, Yun Jeong Choi and Yasuyuki Sawada. 2009. "How is Suicide Different in Japan?" *Japan and the World Economy* 21(2): 140–150.

Durkheim, Émile. 1897. *Le suicide: Etude de sociologie*. Paris: Presses Universitaires de France.

Fishback, Price V., Michael R. Haines and Shawn Kantor. 2007. "Births, Deaths, and New Deal Relief During the Great Depression." *Review of Economics and Statistics* 89(1): 1–14.

Flavin, Patrick and Benjamin Radcliff. 2009. "Public Policies and Suicide Rates in the American States." *Social Indicators Research* 90(2): 195–209.

Gerdtham, Ulf-G. and Christopher J. Ruhm, 2006. "Deaths Rise in Good Economic Times: Evidence from the OECD. *Economics & Human Biology* 4(3): 298–316.

Hedström, Peter, Liu Ka-Yue, and Monica K. Nordvik. 2008. "Interaction Domains and Suicide: A Population-based Panel Study of Suicides in Stockholm, 1991–1999." *Social Forces* 87: 713–740.

Helliwell, John F. 2007. "Well-Being and Social Capital: Does Suicide Pose a Puzzle?" *Social Indicators Research* 81(3): 455–496.

14 We conducted a power analysis on the Sargan test, which showed the existence of enough statistical power in our estimation. However, technical limitations meant that we could not conduct any power analysis on the Arellano-Bond test.

Hooijdonk, Carolien van, Mariël Droomers, Ingeborg M. Deerenberg, Johan P. Mackenbach and Anton E. Kunst. 2008. "The Diversity in Associations between Community Social Capital and Health per Health Outcome, Population Group and Location Studied." *International Journal of Epidemiology* 37(6): 1384–1392.

Japan Ministry of Health, Labour and Welfare. 2010. *An Analysis on the Features of Suicides Based on Population Survey Report.* (in Japanese) http://ikiru.ncnp.go.jp/ikiru-hp/pdf/1003301.pdf (accessed February 1, 2011).

Kelly, Brendan D., Mary Davoren, Áine Ní Mhaoláin, Eugene G. Breen and Patricia Casey. 2009. "Social Capital and Suicide in 11 European Countries: An Ecological Analysis." *Social Psychiatry and Psychiatric Epidemiology* 44(11): 971–977.

Maimon, David and Danielle C. Kuhl. 2008. "Social Control and Youth Suicidality: Situating Durkheim's Ideas in a Multilevel Framework." *American Sociological Review* 73: 921–943.

Masocco, Maria, Maurizio Pompili, Monica Vichi, Nicola Vanacore, David Lester and Roberto Tatarelli. 2008. "Suicide and Marital Status in Italy." *Psychiatric Quarterly* 79 (4): 275–285.

Neumayer, Eric. 2003. "Are Socioeconomic Factors Valid Determinants of Suicide? Controlling for National Cultures of Suicide with Fixed-effects Estimation." *Cross-Cultural Research* 37(3): 307–329.

———. 2004. "Recessions Lower (Some) Mortality Rates: Evidence from Germany." *Social Science & Medicine* 58(6): 1037–1047.

OECD. 2010. *Employment Database 2010* (http://www.oecd.org/els/emp/onlineoecdemploymentdatabase.htm), *Factbook 2010* (http://www.oecd-ilibrary.org/economics/oecd-factbook-2010_factbook-2010-en), *Society at a Glance 2009* (http://www.oecd-ilibrary.org/social-issues-migration-health/society-at-a-glance-2009_soc_glance-2008-en), *Tax Database* (http://www.oecd.org/tax/tax-policy/tax-database.htm) (all accessed March 25, 2015).

———. 2012. *Health Data 2011* (http://stats.oecd.org/index.aspx?DataSetCode=HEALTH_STAT), *Social Expenditure Database* (http://www.oecd-ilibrary.org/content/datacollection/socx-data-en) (both accessed January 15, 2012).

Ruhm, Christopher J. 2000. "Are Recessions Good for Your Health?" *Quarterly Journal of Economics* 115: 617–650.

Stack, Steven. 1990. "New Micro-Level Data on the Impact of Divorce on Suicide, 1959–1980: A Test of Two Theories." *Journal of Marriage and Family* 52(1): 119–127.

———. 1996. "The Effect of the Media on Suicide: Evidence from Japan, 1955–1985." *Suicide and Life-Threatening Behavior* 26(2): 132–142

Stuckler, David, Sanjay Basu, Marc Suhrcke, Adam Coutts and Martin McKee. 2009. "The Public Health Effect of Economic Crises and Alternative Policy Responses in Europe: An Empirical Analysis." *Lancet* 374: 315–323.

West, Mark D. 2003. "Dying to Get out of Debt: Consumer Insolvency Law and Suicide in Japan." *Michigan Law and Economics Research Paper* 03–015; *U of Michigan Law, Public Law Working Paper* 37, http://papers.ssrn.com/sol3/papers.cfm?abstract_id=479844 (accessed December 20, 2010).

Wooldridge, Jeffrey M. 2010. *Econometric Analysis of Cross Section and Panel Data. Second Edition*. Cambridge, MA: MIT Press.

World Bank. 2010. *World Development Indicators*. http://databank.worldbank.org/ddp/home.do?Step=12&id=4&CNO=2 (accessed September 1, 2010).

Wyder, Marianne, Patrick Ward and Diego De Leo. 2009. "Separation as a Suicide Risk Factor." *Journal of Affective Disorders* 116: 208–213.

Yoon, Jangho and Tim A. Bruckner, 2009. "Does Deinstitutionalization Increase Suicide?" *Health Services Research* 44(4): 1385–1405.

Zimmerman, Shirley L. 1992. *Family Policies and Family Well-being: The Role of Political Culture.* CA: Sage.

———. 1993. "Political Culture, Policy Choices, and Unmet Needs." In A. Leenaars, ed., *Suicidology: Essays in Honor of Edwin Shneidman Northvale*, 42–60. NJ: Jason Aronson.

———. 1995. "Psychache in Context: States' Spending for Public Welfare and Their Suicide Rates." *Journal of Nervous and Mental Disease* 183: 425–434.

———. 2002. "States' Spending for Public Welfare and Their Suicide Rates, 1960 to 1995: What is the Problem?" *Journal of Nervous and Mental Disease* 190: 349–360.

CHAPTER 6

An Inter Regional Comparison of Occupational Gender Segregation in Japan

Oda Akiko, Tarohmaru Hiroshi, and Yamato Reiko

1 Introduction

In many Western capitalist countries, the gender gap in labor force participation rate and average years in employment significantly narrowed following World War II. This was due mainly to increased participation in the labor force by women, particularly married women. Nevertheless, the wage gap remained, and it remains, relatively large, as does the gap in workplace power and authority.

Table 6.1 presents gender disparity in terms of labor force participation rate, average years in employment, and wages in three Western countries that represent the three kinds of welfare regimes identified by Esping-Andersen (1990)—Swedish social democracy, German conservatism, and American liberalism—and Japan. The number means the ratio of female workers to male workers in Table 6.1 (male as 100). The smaller number indicates the larger gender disparity. Although gender disparity in labor force participation rate and years in employment is small in the three Western countries, in wages the gender disparity is relatively large. To understand the persistence of gaps in

TABLE 6.1 *Gender disparity in labor force participation rate, years in employment, and wages (male as 100)*

	Sweden	Germany	U.S.	Japan
Labor force participation rate[a]	92.3	80.5	87.6	70.4
Years in employment[b]	97.2	80.2	86.1	67.2
Wage[c]	88.4	73.6	76.5	65.7

a 2003.
b The average length of years per same employer. In 1996 for the United States, in 2004 for Japan, and in 1995 for others.
c Monthly average. In 1999 for the United States, in 2004 for Japan, and in 2001 for others.
SOURCE: JAPAN INSTITUTE FOR LABOUR POLICY AND TRAINING, *DATA BOOK OF INTERNATIONAL LABOUR STATISTICS 2006*.

 | DOI 10.1163/9789004262737_007

wages and perhaps in workplace power, much research on gender and employment in Europe and the United States has focused on occupational gender segregation, where men and women are concentrated in different occupations (doctors tend to be men while nurses tend to be women, for example) as well as the social processes behind such segregation.

Table 6.1 shows that the gender gaps in labor force participation rate and years of continuous employment in Japan are larger than in Europe and the United States. Many researchers consider that these gaps lead to gender gaps in wage, power, and authority since women with shorter tenure are likely allocated to lower level positions. Research has therefore focused either on women's exit at marriage or childbirth as a factor that reduces labor force participation rate and length in employment, or on their re-entry into the labor market after childrearing as a factor that counters the reduction of labor participation or years in employment (Nakai 2009; Osawa Machiko 1993; Otobe 2010; Takeishi 2006a; Wakisaka and Tomita 2001; Yamato 2009). However, little research has been conducted on workplace gender segregation. It may be that workplace gender segregation has a negative impact on female labor participation rate and years in employment, for the reason that if women cannot find employment with sufficient appeal they more easily quit their jobs at marriage or childbirth.

This chapter focuses on occupational gender segregation in Japan to understand Japanese women's employment from a different perspective from previous studies. We use the framework presented by Charles and Grusky (2004) to analyze how global social changes such as the spread of gender egalitarianism and the advancement of post industrialization have affected occupational gender segregation in Japan. We then compare the results of the analysis with those in Europe and the United States as analyzed by Charles and Grusky (2004), and examine how the impacts of such global social changes differ accordance with country-specific socioeconomic structure.

2 Frameworks for Research on Workplace Gender Segregation

This section examines various research frameworks on workplace gender segregation and clarifies the framework of this study.

2.1 *Classifications of Jobs or Workplaces*

(1) Segregation by Industry

Workplace gender segregation can be analyzed by industry, sector (public or private), occupation, firm size, employment status, and career track. Here we will give an overview of the characteristics of workplace gender segregation in Japan according to this classification.

With regard to gender segregation by industry, Table 6.2 shows the ratio of male to all workers by industry in the same four countries as shown in Table 6.1. In the two European countries and the United States, men are distributed between various types of industries, while women are concentrated in a small number of industries such as hotel and restaurant management, health and social services, and education. The same tendency is seen in an analysis on 15 countries in the European Union (Glover and Kirton 2006). The female-dominated industries tend to employ a large number of part-time workers. As a result of women being concentrated in a small number of industries, women are highly susceptible to the effects of economic fluctuations, and thus their employment is unstable (Glover and Kirton 2006).

In comparison with the Western countries, Japan has a lower extent of gender segregation by industry. Although the proportion of women in the hotel and restaurant industry, health and social work, and education is high in Japan, the ratio of women to men in agriculture, hunting and forestry, fishing, mining, and construction is higher in Japan than in all the other three. (The higher proportion of women is indicated in the lower percentage figures for men in Table 6.2.)

(2) Segregation by Sector

Gender segregation can also be analyzed by public versus private sectors. If we classify "public administration, defense, and compulsory social security" in Table 6.2 into the public sector and the remainder into the private sector, the ratio of male to female workers is high in the private sector and almost equal in the public sector in the two European countries and in the United States. Thus, women are mostly concentrated in the public sector in these countries. Although not shown here, the same is true for most Western European countries (Glover and Kirton 2006; ILO, LABORSTA Internet). Regarding the effect of women's concentration in the public sector on women's economic status, findings of studies in Europe and the United States are inconsistent. Some studies argue that women's concentration in the public sector lowers women's economic status because wages in the public sector are lower than those in the private sector. Other studies argue that it improves women's economic status, because employment in the public sector provides higher social status and greater job security than employment in the private sector (Glover and Kirton 2006).

In Japan, the proportion of men is high not only in the private sector but also in the public sector (Table 6.2). One explanation for this is that the job

TABLE 6.2 *Proportion of males to all workers by industry (2008)*

Industry (ISIC Rev.4)	Sweden (15–74) (%)	Industry (ISIC Rev.3)	Germany (aged 15 and over) (%)	U.S. (aged 16 and over) (%)	Japan (aged 15 and over) (%)
Agriculture, forestry and fishing	*81.4*	Agriculture, hunting and forestry	*67.6*	*76.1*	57.1
		Fishing	*83.3*	↑	*73.9*
Mining and quarrying	*88.9*	Mining and quarrying	*87.2*	*87.2*	66.7
Manufacturing	*76.7*	Manufacturing	*72.1*	*70.7*	*69.2*
Electricity, gas, steam and air conditioning supply	*77.3*	Electricity, gas and water supply	*77.2*	*80.6*	*90.6*
Water supply; sewerage, waste management and remediation activities	*83.3*				
Construction	*92.2*	Construction	*87.9*	*90.3*	*85.5*
Wholesale and retail trade; repair of motor vehicles and motorcycles	56.4	Wholesale and retail trade; repair of motor vehicles, motorcycles and personal and household goods	47.5	55.0	51.2
Accommodation and food service activities	43.9	Hotels and restaurants	42.2	46.9	41.0
Transportation and storage	*75.5*	Transport, storage and communications	*72.3*	*76.2*	*79.3*
Information and communication	*69.8*				
Financial and insurance activities	47.9	Financial intermediation	49.3	42.0	48.8
Real estate activities	*65.2*	Real estate, renting and business activities	53.3	56.9	61.5
Public administration and defense; compulsory social security	44.8	Public administration and defense; compulsory social security	54.2	54.8	*77.1*

TABLE 6.2 *Proportion of males to all workers by industry (2008)* (cont.)

Industry (ISIC Rev.4)	Sweden (15–74) (%)	Industry (ISIC Rev.3)	Germany (aged 15 and over) (%)	U.S. (aged 16 and over) (%)	Japan (aged 15 and over) (%)
Education	50.0	Education	32.7	30.3	45.1
Human health and social work activities	38.7	Health and social work	24.5	20.9	24.1
Professional, scientific and technical activities	59.4	Other community, social and personal service activities	43.1	52.2	50.1
Administrative and support service activities	53.8				
Arts, entertainment and recreation	0.0				
Other service activities	***100.0***				
Activities of households as employers; undifferentiated goods- and services-producing activities of households for own use	25.4	Private households with employed persons	6.9	(Contained above)	–
Activities of extraterritorial organizations and bodies	16.7	Extra-territorial organizations and bodies	57.6	(Contained above)	–
Unclassifiable industry	50.0	Unclassifiable industry	–	(Contained above)	58.1
(Total)	52.7	(Total)	54.7	53.3	58.4

Note: ***Bold italic*** script indicates industries with males over-represented, as compared to the average of all industries. Underlined script indicates industries with males under-represented as compared with the average of all industries.
SOURCE: ILO, LABORSTA INTERNET

security and the social security of the public sector are attractive for men. This high proportion of men in the public sector further strengthens gender inequality in Japan.

(3) Segregation by Occupation

Much of the research on workplace gender segregation in Europe and the United States has focused on occupation. This is probably because in these countries, gender inequality in terms of wages, power, and workplace authority is more closely linked to occupation than other aspects of work such as industry or firm size. Occupational segregation is often classified into two dimensions: horizontal and vertical segregations (Hakim 1979). Horizontal segregation is the phenomenon in which men and women are concentrated in different occupations. In vertical segregation men and women have different wages, power, and authority within the same occupations. In this study, however, vertical and horizontal segregations are used in a more specific meaning, as delineated by Charles and Grusky (2004).

Table 6.3 shows the ratio of male to all workers by occupation in the same four countries as in previous tables. In Europe and the United States, the horizontal segregation is evident: women are concentrated in clerical, service, and sales industries, whereas men are concentrated in agriculture, forestry, fishery, and manual occupations. Vertical segregation in the non-manual occupations is relatively weak: the male-to-female ratio in managerial occupations is more equal. In Japan, on the other hand, the opposite is true: horizontal segregation is weaker than in Europe and the United States but vertical segregation is much stronger in that the male-to-female ratio in managerial occupations is strongly biased toward men.

(4) Segregation by Firm Size

Gender segregation can also be analyzed in terms of firm size. The gender disparity in wage and benefits according to firm size is large in Japan. Further, the gap in benefits tends to be larger than the wage gap. The amount of extra-legal corporate welfare provided by companies with more than 5,000 employees is over four times that of companies with 30–99 employees (Takeuchi 2004). In Japan, men are concentrated in larger firms and women in smaller firms. According to the 2010 labor force survey (Statistics Bureau, Ministry of Internal Affairs and Communications 2010), among those who are employed in large companies, 61.7 percent are male and 38.3 percent are female; while among those in small- to medium-sized enterprises, 55.5 percent are male and 44.5 percent are female. The concentration of male workers in large firms further strengthens inequality of wages and benefits. In Europe and the United States,

TABLE 6.3 *Proportions of male to all workers by occupation* (2008)

(ISCO-88)	Sweden (15–74) (%)	Germany (aged 15 and over) (%)	U.S. (aged 16 and over) (%)	(ISCO-1968)	Japan (aged 15 and over) (%)
(Total)	52.7	54.7	53.3	(Total)	58.4
Legislators, senior officials and managers	68.1	62.2	57.3	Administrative and managerial workers	90.7
Professionals	49.4	60.0	43.3	Professional, technical and related workers	53.4
Technicians and associate professionals	49.4	42.4	(Contained above)		
Clerks	31.2	32.7	25.2	Clerical and related workers	38.9
Service workers and shop and market sales workers	25.2	25.7	45.9	Sales workers	62.3
				Service workers	43.5
Skilled agricultural and fishery workers	77.2	69.3	78.9	Agriculture, animal husbandry and forestry workers, fishermen and hunters	59.8
Craft and related trade workers	94.5	90.4	86.1	Production and related workers, transport equipment operators and laborers	74.7
Plant and machine operators and Assemblers	85.1	84.7	(Contained above)		
Elementary occupations	39.5	47.8	–		

TABLE 6.3 *Proportions of male to all workers by occupation (2008)* (cont.)

(ISCO-88)	Sweden (15–74) (%)	Germany (aged 15 and over) (%)	U.S. (aged 16 and over) (%)	(ISCO-1968)	Japan (aged 15 and over) (%)
Armed forces	100.0	95.0	–		
Workers not classifiable by occupation	71.4	55.9	–	Workers not classifiable by occupation	59.4
(Total)	52.7	54.7	53.3	(Total)	58.4

SOURCE: ILO, LABORSTA INTERNET

wage structures are different from those in Japan and wages are more likely to be paid according to occupational skills. Therefore, gender disparity in wages by firm size is smaller than that in Japan.

(5) Employment Status and Career Track

On the whole, studies of labor market segmentation tend to pay more attention to segregation by employment status or career track than studies of workplace gender segregation (Marshall 1998). However, there is a strong tendency in Japan for men and women to be concentrated in different employment statuses or on different career tracks. This is one of major causes of gender inequality in wage, authority, and workplace power (Osawa Mari 1993). We will therefore briefly touch on research on segregation by employment status or career track here.

Employment status refers to distinctions of employment involving fixed-term versus permanent employment, or full-time versus part-time. In Japan, regular employment is overwhelmingly full-time and permanent, while irregular employment is fixed-term. For women, the majority of fixed-term employment is part-time. Even in the same occupation, regular employees receive more advantageous treatment in terms of wages, benefits, job security, promotion, and training compared to irregular employees. In Japan, irregular employment is largely held by women (Osawa Mari 1993). In the Japanese employment system, a further distinction among regular employment is that between core and peripheral employment tracks (particularly amongst white-collar workers in large companies). Men are more often found in the former and women in the latter track (Takeishi 2006a). After the Equal Employment Opportunity Law was enacted in 1985, such gender distinctions were camouflaged with the use of more gender-neutral terms such as "main career track" (*sōgō shoku*) and "general staff track" (*ippan shoku*) (Takenobu 1994). Actually, almost all of men are assigned to the "main career track," and most women are assigned "general staff track." Limited women are assigned to the "main career track," they are treated as executive trainee as their male colleagues, while women in "general staff track" work in assistant jobs.

Much research has been conducted on gender segregation by employment status and career track in Japan (Kawaguchi 2008; Kimoto 1999, Otobe 2006, 2010; Osawa Machiko 1993; Takeishi 2006a; Wakisaka and Tomita 2001; Yamato 2009). Gender segregation by employment status and career track are a major source of workplace gender inequality in Japan. In comparison, studies on gender segregation by occupation in Japan are rather less than in Europe and the United States. However, segregation by occupation certainly exists. If women have far fewer opportunities of finding favorable occupations than men, this could explain why the majority of Japanese women, even women with high educational qualifications, quit employment at marriage or childbirth. Our research focuses on occupational gender segregation to examine workplace gender inequality, taking a different perspective from existing research in Japan, which tends to focus more on employment status.

2.2 *Occupational Gender Segregation at National, Regional, and Organizational Levels*

Occupational gender segregation can be analyzed at national, regional, and organizational levels. At the national level, occupational gender segregation is greatly influenced by factors such as laws and institutions (welfare and employment regimes, for example), economic situations (industrialization, post-industrialization), and cultural norms (gender role ideology). Considerable research has been conducted on how occupational gender segregation has historically changed within a country (Charles et al. 2004; Goldin 1990) and how it differs between countries (Chang 2000; Charles and Grusky 2004; Glover and Kirton 2006).

Even within the same country, regional differences in industrialization can be significant, and they become particularly so during times of rapid industrialization and post-industrialization. Such regional differences exert an influence on the degree and pattern of occupational gender segregation, and have become the subject of comparative regional studies (Scott 1994, and others).

Occupational gender segregation can also be studied at the organizational level—the level of, for example, a workplace or corporation. Organizational level analysis is useful because the extent and pattern of the segregation is affected by what kinds of business environment the organization is located in and the types of workers the employer hires to adapt the environment (Reskin 1993; Kimoto 1999).

In Japan, some scholars have used qualitative case study data to conduct such organizational level research (Kimoto 1999; Shutou 2003). Other scholars have conducted historical comparisons using quantitative data at the national level. Very few studies use the level of regions within Japan, despite the considerable variations in socioeconomic structures that exist even today in various regions. This study therefore focuses on differences by region (particularly by prefecture), and examines how occupational gender segregation is affected by regional differences in cultural and socioeconomic factors.

Our focus on the regional differences has substantial and analytical advantages. Firstly, by scrutinizing regional differences we get a better picture of the diversity of a given society. Society is often used in a very general way, to refer to a whole nation, and regional differences are often ignored. However, regional differences even without one country are sometimes considerable (Lobao et al. 2007). Labor markets can often be geographically segregated, making regional differences in industrial structure large. Ignoring these regional differences may hinder accurate understanding of gender segregation. Secondly, regional comparisons offer a higher comparability level than cross-national comparisons, which can be very fruitful, but very difficult to perform. Cross-national comparison of gender ideology, for example, can be challenging because of the diversity of social contexts surrounding gender issues, and concomitant difficulties in translation. In contrast, regions in Japan share the same language and despite their differences many similar social contexts as well. Even so, certain aspects such as industrial structure and local culture show significant dissimilarities. For these reasons, regional comparison has an analytical advantage over cross-national comparison.

2.3 *Frameworks to Measure Occupational Gender Segregation*

(1) One-Dimensional Framework

How has occupational gender segregation has been conceptualized and measured in previous studies?

Up until the 1990s, the conventional way of measuring the degree of gender segregation, particularly in quantitative research, was to use a one-dimensional scale. A typical example was the index of dissimilarity, which indicated the percentage of all workers that would have to be moved into different occupational categories to reach a hypothetical scenario in which no gender segregation exists in any occupational category (that is, the ratio of men to women in all occupational categories is exactly the same as the ratio of men to women, for all workers). No segregation is represented by 0 percent, and complete segregation is represented by 100 percent (Charles and Grusky 2004).

However, this index of dissimilarity as an indicator of gender inequality can be less than helpful. Scholars are interested in the question of gender segregation because it might explain workplace gender inequality. Nevertheless, the index of dissimilarity is not always consistent with gender differences in wage or the socioeconomic index (SEI), an index showing the extent of prestige inhering in various occupations. For instance, the index of dissimilarity is high in Sweden, although gender disparity in wages and SEI is low; in Japan the index of dissimilarity is low, despite the fact that there are considerable wage inequalities (Table 6.1). These inconsistencies occur because the extent to which Swedish women are concentrated in non-manual labor (where wages and SEI are relatively high) and the extent to which Swedish men are concentrated in manual labor (where wages and SEI are relatively low), are much higher than in Japan. In other words, the extent of gender segregation is higher in Sweden than in Japan, but women's economic status is higher in Sweden (Charles and Grusky 2004). This kind of complexity suggests that it is necessary to understand gender segregation not in a single dimension but in multiple dimensions where segregation between different occupations, such as manual versus non-manual, is distinguished from the segregation between higher and lower positions within the same occupation.

(2) Three-Dimensional Framework

This study, following Charles and Grusky (2004), measures occupational gender segregation in Japan in three dimensions. First, it distinguishes between horizontal and vertical segregation. Charles and Grusky define horizontal segregation as the tendency for women to be concentrated in non-manual labor and men in manual labor. Vertical segregation is the tendency for men to be concentrated in occupations with a high SEI, and for women in occupations with a low SEI. Second, vertical segregation is further divided into vertical segregation in non-manual labor and vertical segregation in manual labor. The former is the tendency to place men in positions with a high SEI and women in positions with a low SEI within the field of non-manual occupations. The latter is the same tendency in the field of manual labor. The three dimensions are thus (1) horizontal segregation, (2) vertical segregation in non-manual occupations, and (3) vertical segregation in manual occupations. This three-dimensional approach is adopted to allow for a better model since as discussed later vertical segregation in non-manual occupations is different from that in manual occupations both in terms of empirical evidence and theoretical implications.

2.4 *Determinants of Occupational Gender Segregation*

Occupational gender segregation has paid a great deal of attention not only to describing the extent and pattern of segregation but also to finding their determinants. Arguments as to whether segregation should be viewed on one or multiple dimensions, examined above, are closely related to theories of their determinants, the subject of this section.

Structural functionalists[1] argue on the basis of Parsons' role theory that men and women are functionally different and thus specialized to different social roles, which has resulted in occupational gender segregation (Parsons and Bales 1956; Yamane 1998). Feminists criticize this approach. Feminist theories of occupational gender segregation can be classified into two basic types. Liberalist feminists regard gender segregation as a remnant of pre-modern sexism in modern society (Friedan 1963; Ehara 1985). They believe that in a modern society, gender segregation is irrational and inefficient, and will be gradually eliminated as modernization, marketization, rational bureaucratic systems, and egalitarian cultural norms permeate society (Charles and Grusky 2004). Marxist feminists claim that gender segregation is based on patriarchal systems that have existed throughout history, and that continue to exist even in modern society (Beechey 1987; Kuba 1986; Ueno 1990). Both structural functionalists and feminists see the main cause of occupational gender segregation in one-dimensional terms, although they differ in the factor identified as a major cause. As stated in the previous section, however, gender segregation is multi-dimensional in reality, and is best understood with multi-dimensional theory.

Charles and Grusky (2004) propose a multi-dimensional framework for occupational gender segregation. They argue first that two cultural factors are the primary causes of gender segregation: gender essentialism and male primacy. Gender essentialism is a cultural system that considers women as inherently suited to nurturing and dealing with people, and men as naturally suited to physical labor and dealing with objects, such as commodities and materials. Male primacy is a cultural system that considers men inherently suited to occupy and exercise positions of authority. Under gender essentialism, the tendency for women to work in non-manual labor and men in manual labor is strengthened, and horizontal segregation prevails. Under male primacy, on the

1 Structural functionalism is a sociological theory emphasizing normative integration of a society and focusing on the contribution of action, norm, and organization to the maintenance of a society.

other hand, the tendency for men to work in jobs with a high SEI and women to work in those with a low SEI is strengthened, both in non-manual and manual occupations, which leads to vertical segregation. Although both gender essentialism and male primacy are cultural and institutional factors that exist at the macro level, they affect the preferences and actions of individuals, through which gender segregation is reproduced.

Charles and Grusky further argue that two types of social changes that affect occupational gender segregation have recently occurred in developed countries. The first is a change in ideology: an intensification of gender egalitarianism since the 1960s. The second is an economic change: the spread of post-industrialism since the 1970s. These social changes have had various effects. With regard to the effect of gender egalitarianism on the three dimensions of occupational gender segregation (horizontal segregation, vertical segregation in non-manual occupations, and vertical segregation in manual occupations), Charles and Grusky (2004) set up the following hypotheses.

(G1) Horizontal segregation will not be affected to any great degree by gender egalitarianism. Although gender essentialism (which recognizes and respects different natures of each sex) produces horizontal segregation, it does not necessarily oppose gender egalitarianism (in which the gendered nature of each sex can be regarded as "different but equal").

(G2) Vertical segregation in non-manual occupations will weaken as gender egalitarianism spreads in society. Although the cultural system of male primacy reproduces vertical segregation, it is weakened by gender egalitarianism. Gender egalitarianism is most likely to penetrate workplaces of non-manual occupations because, for one thing, non-manual occupations are more likely to be exposed to public scrutiny than manual ones; workplaces of non-manual occupations also often allocate workers to different positions according to qualifications or examinations through a meritocratic selection system.

(G3) Vertical segregation in manual occupations will not be affected to any great degree by gender egalitarianism. Workplaces for manual occupations are different from those for non-manual occupations and are less likely to have the conditions mentioned above in G2 conducive to the spread of gender egalitarianism.

The second social change seen in recent years, post-industrialism, has brought two other social changes. The first is an increase in non-manual occupations as post-industrialism and the service economy have grown. The second is the increasing rationalization and deskillization of organizations and tasks in the service industries as non-manual occupations are undertaken by unskilled workers (for example, the self-employed shopkeeper is replaced by a salesperson at a chain store).

Charles and Grusky (2004) hypothesize that post-industrialism and its accompanying changes will have the following effects on the three dimensions of gender segregation.

(P1) Horizontal segregation will further increase. Non-manual occupations, which will grow with the expansion of the service economy, tend to be seen as "women's work," and women will thus be concentrated in these occupations.

(P2) Vertical segregation in non-manual occupations will further increase. Women are concentrated in non-manual occupations. If unskilled occupations in non-manual work increase, women will be concentrated in such non-manual occupations with a low SEI.

(P3) Vertical segregation in manual occupations will not be significantly affected by post-industrialism. Charles and Grusky believe that, as hypothesized in P2, it is not in manual work but in non-manual work that post-industrialism will affect and deskill occupations.

These six hypotheses by Charles and Grusky are summarized in Table 6.4.

On the basis of the six aforementioned hypotheses, Charles and Grusky (2004) analyzed data from 10 countries: eight European countries (Italy, Portugal, Sweden, Belgium, France, West Germany, Switzerland, and the United Kingdom), the United States, and Japan. The overall results are shown in

TABLE 6.4 *Effects of gender egalitarianism and post-industrialism on three dimensions of occupational gender segregation; hypotheses and results by Charles and Grusky (2004) and hypotheses of this study for Japan*

	Gender essentialism		Male primacy			
	Horizontal segregation		Vertical segregation in non-manual		Vertical segregation in manual	
Effect of gender egalitarianism	+	(o)^{G1}	–	(–)^{G2}	+	(o)^{G3}
Effect of post-industrialism	+	(+)^{P1}	+	(+)^{P2} (–)$^{P2\_J}$	–	(o)^{P3} (+)$^{P3\_J}$

Notes: '+' indicates a positive effect, '–' indicates a negative effect, and 'o' indicates no effect on gender segregation. The signs '+,' '–,' or 'o' with no parentheses indicate the results by Charles and Grusky (2004), and those in parentheses indicate hypotheses by Charles and Grusky (2004) or by this study. Subscripts indicate the hypotheses in Section 2-4 and 3-2 to which the signs correspond.

SOURCE: CHARLES AND GRUSKY (2004)

Table 6.4, by '+,' '–,' or '0' signs with no parentheses. Among the six hypotheses, three that anticipate positive or negative effects (G2, P1, and P2 in Table 6.4) are supported by the analysis results (see the signs having no parentheses and corresponding to G2, P1, and P2, respectively in Table 6.4). This indicates that gender egalitarianism weakens vertical segregation in non-manual occupations whereas post-industrialism strengthens both horizontal segregation and vertical segregation in non-manual occupations. However, the coefficients for gender egalitarianism are rather small compared to those of post-industrialism, indicating that post-industrialism has larger effects on occupational gender segregation than gender egalitarianism does. With regard to the remaining three hypotheses, which anticipate no effect (G1, G3, and P3 in Table 6.4), the results reveal that there are weak positive or negative effects in the actual data. However, because the coefficients for these (particularly those for gender egalitarianism) are so small, it is possible to argue that these positive or negative effects are not drastically deviant from the hypotheses predicting no effect.

3 Analysis

3.1 *Framework of Analysis*

Employing Charles and Grusky's framework (2004), this study analyzes data for Japan and focuses on differences between regions, particularly between prefectures. The extents of gender egalitarianism and of post-industrialism differ between prefectures in Japan. This study analyzes what kind of impact the extent of gender egalitarianism and post-industrialism has on three dimensions of occupational gender segregations: horizontal segregation, vertical segregation in non-manual occupations, and vertical segregation in manual occupations. This study therefore does *not* analyze gender segregation either by employment status, firm size, industry, or sector.

This study follows Charles and Grusky's study in being a comparative study between geographical areas, but it should be noted that the units of comparison are different: Charles and Grusky's is an international comparison whereas this study is a comparison between prefectures within one country. As stated above, this study bases itself on the fact that there are often substantial differences in industrial structures between regions, which may give rise to differences in extent and pattern of occupational gender segregation. In Japan, industrial structures differ between prefectures (see Section 3.5). Women's employment rates also vary significantly: generally speaking, they are lower in prefectures with large cities and higher in prefectures with large rural areas. Even the gendered division of labor in the household differs between prefectures

(Sechiyama 1996; Hashimoto and Miyagawa 2008). Although some of these regional differences are attributed to the prevalence of three-generation households and low male income, some differences remain unexplained (Abe et al. 2008; Takeishi 2006b). These facts suggest that there may also be differences between prefectures in the type of occupation that women are more likely to be employed in. Insufficient work has been done on regional differences in women's occupations in Japan. This study will shed new light not only on regional differences but also how occupational gender segregations may vary between prefectures in Japan.

3.2 *Hypotheses*

This study proposes the following hypotheses. Regarding the effects of gender egalitarianism on the three dimensions of gender segregation (horizontal segregation, and vertical segregation in non-manual and manual occupations), we adopt the same hypotheses as those of Charles and Grusky (2004) (G1, G2, and G3 in the top panel of Table 6.4). We also adopt Charles and Grusky's hypothesis regarding the effect of post-industrialism on horizontal segregation (P1 in the bottom panel of Table 6.4).

However, with regard to the effects of post-industrialism on the two dimensions of vertical segregation (non-manual and manual occupations), we propose different hypotheses from those of Charles and Grusky (P2-J and P3-J in the bottom panel of Table 6.4). We do this because industrial structures in Japan are substantially different to those in Europe or the United States. Comparing statistics for 2008, the proportion of non-manual workers in all working populations is higher in Sweden (72.2 percent) and the United States (77.6 percent) than in Japan (64.5 percent), although the proportion in Germany (66.7 percent) is almost the same as that in Japan. The proportion of non-manual workers in female working populations is also higher in Sweden (88.2 percent), Germany (83.1 percent) and the United States (93.2 percent) than in Japan (76.9 percent), indicating that women are concentrated in non-manual occupations in Western Europe and the United States but to a lesser extent in Japan (ILO, LABORSTA Internet).

The hypotheses of Charles and Grusky laid out in Section 2-4 are based on industrial structures that prevail in Europe and the United States, as summarized in Table 6.5. In these societies, post-industrialism is more advanced and the ratio of non-manual workers in working populations is higher than in Japan. Post-industrialism replaces skilled jobs with unskilled jobs and creates societies with more non-manual occupations than manual ones. Charles and Grusky suppose that the social impacts of labor being rationalized and deskilled are larger and more prevalent in non-manual occupations than in manual ones. Moreover, in these countries, the proportion of women in non-manual occupations, particularly in lower non-manual occupations, is much higher than in Japan (Table 6.3). Consequently, deskillization of labor concentrates women in lower strata within non-manual occupations such as clerical, service, and sales occupations.

As shown in Table 6.5, the industrial structures in Japan are quite different to those in Europe and the United States. In Japan, post-industrialism is less advanced than in Europe and the United States, and the ratio of manual workers in the working population is higher than in Europe and the United States. In societies with more manual occupations, the social impacts of the rationalization and deskillization of labor are larger and more wide-ranging in manual occupations than in non-manual ones. In Japan, the proportion of women in manual occupations is higher than that in Europe and the United States, and it is possible to predict that in an area where post-industrialization is more advanced, the deskillization of labor will produce a larger number of lower manual occupations and women will be concentrated in such occupations involving unskilled or elementary work.

Thus our first hypothesis for Japan is that post-industrialism *strengthens* vertical segregation in manual occupation. This is different from both the hypothesis and results obtained by Charles and Grusky. On the basis of the industrial structures in Europe and the United States, they presuppose that it is mainly in non-manual occupations that post-industrialism deskillizes labor (Charles and Grusky 2004: 30). In the Japanese context, on the contrary, it is possible to argue

TABLE 6.5 *Comparisons of occupational structure between Europe or the United States and Japan*

	Europe and the U.S.	vs.	Japan
The manual-to-non-manual ratio			
For all workers	More non-manual		More manual
For female workers	More non-manual		More manual
The male-to-female ratio			
In manual occupations	More male		More female
In non-manual occupations with lower status	More female		More male
In non-manual occupations with higher status	Similar to Japan		Similar to Europe and the U.S.

that, as our hypothesis states, it is in manual occupations rather than in non-manual occupations that deskillization is more apparent and influential.

Second, looking at women in higher non-manual occupations (professional or technical) as per Table 6.3, the proportion of women in these occupations in Japan is as high as that in Europe and the United States (see also Table 6.5). This is probably because in general in a country like Japan where there is less post-industrialism, even in prefectures where post-industrialism is comparatively more advanced than in other areas, non-manual occupations such as "feminine" human services are less likely to be created and professional or technical occupations more likely to be created. In fact, feminization of lower service jobs did not occur in Japan between 1950 and 1995 despite the expansion of non-manual jobs (Charles et al. 2004). In the professional occupations, employment is more likely to be based on merit such as qualification or examination. It is therefore also possible to predict that if a woman lives in a prefecture where post-industrialism advances and a comparatively larger number of employment opportunities for non-manual occupations are provided than in less post-industrialized prefectures, and if she has a higher human capital, she will have more chance of being employed in a non-manual occupation with higher status, such as professional or technical occupation, than women in less post-industrialized prefectures.

On the basis of this discussion, our second hypothesis for Japan is that post-industrialism *weakens* vertical segregation in non-manual occupations. Charles and Grusky themselves acknowledge that this could be seen in countries where post-industrialism has not progressed far (Charles and Grusky 2004: 30).

The arguments so far in this section can be summarized as follows. As post-industrialism progresses, in Europe and the United States women are concentrated in lower non-manual occupations, whereas we predict that in Japan occupations in which women are concentrated will be polarized between lower manual and higher non-manual occupations.

Here, then, are the hypotheses of this study for Japan. Our hypotheses on the effects of gender egalitarianism on the three dimensions of segregation (G1, G2, and G3) and the hypothesis on the effects of post-industrialism on horizontal segregation (P1) are the same as Charles and Grusky's. However, we have set up our own hypotheses on the effects of post-industrialism on two dimensions of vertical segregation.

(P2-J) Post-industrialism weakens vertical segregation in *non-manual* occupations. In Japanese prefectures where post-industrialism has progressed, women (particularly those with higher human capital) will be more likely than women in other prefectures to be employed in higher-status, non-manual occupations such as managerial or professional occupations.

(P3-J) Post-industrialism strengthens vertical segregation in *manual* occupations. In Japanese prefectures where post-industrialism has progressed, the amount of unskilled occupations in manual work increases. Women in these prefectures, particularly those with low human capital, will be more likely than women in other prefectures to be employed in these low-status manual occupations.

3.3 *Models for Analysis*

The results of Charles and Grusky's analysis were in fact partially inconsistent with their hypotheses, but there are some possible reasons. Firstly, their study compares only 10 countries, and it is possible that this sample size is insufficient for multivariate analysis with two independent variables, gender egalitarianism and post-industrialism. Secondly, the statistical model that they used may have been inappropriate. Charles and Grusky used a log multiplicative model, but the results were extremely complicated. The model used was thus not appropriate for the structure of the data analyzed. Although the data had two levels of variables (national and individual), their analytical model did not take this structure into consideration. The estimations of standard errors were therefore too small, and so the magnitudes of the coefficients at the national level were not properly evaluated.

This study therefore uses a multilevel logistic regression model[2] with a male dummy as the dependent variable. It is true that when analyzing the tripartite relationship between gender, occupation, and region, gender cannot be necessarily regarded as a dependent variable and the rest as independent variables (particularly when the unit of analysis is the individual). This may be why Charles and Grusky used a log multiplicative model. However, because their study predicts the proportions of women in working populations based on differences in country and occupational type, a logistic regression model would be more appropriate. In addition, like their data set, the data set used in this study has two levels (national/prefectural and individual), so it is more appropriate to explicitly incorporate these two levels into the model.

The model used in this study is as follows. Horizontal segregation is represented by whether a worker is in a manual or non-manual occupation. Each vertical segregation in manual occupations and in non-manual ones is represented by the SEI of the occupation. Assuming that the proportion of men employed in an occupation j ($j = 1, \ldots, 273$) in a prefecture i ($i = 1, \ldots, 47$) is r_{ij}, the

2 Multilevel logistic regression model is a multi-level model for a binary dependent variable. The multilevel model is a regression model to deal with several levels of variables such as individuals and organizations they belong to.

SEI of occupation j is SEI_j,[3] and the dummy variable indicating whether occupation j is a manual occupation or not is man_j. Then the individual-level model gives the following equation:

$$\log \frac{r_{ij}}{1-r_{ij}} = \beta_{i0} + \beta_{i1}\,\text{man}_j + \beta_{i2}\,\text{SEI}_j \times \text{man}_j + \beta_{i3}\,\text{SEI}_j \times (1 - \text{man}_j) \tag{1}$$

where β_{i1} represents the extent of horizontal segregation, β_{i2} is vertical segregation in manual occupations, and β_{i3} is vertical segregation in non-manual occupations. This model does not estimate the main effect of SEI, but it estimates the slope of SEI in each of manual and non-manual occupations, which is mathematically equivalent to the model with normal interaction effects. Actually, the normal interaction model can be derived from Equation (1).

Next, the prefecture-level model gives the following equations, taking gender egalitarianism in prefecture i as G_i, and post-industrialism there as P_i.

$$\beta_{i0} = \gamma_{00} + \gamma_{10} G_i + \gamma_{20} P_i + e_{i0}. \tag{2}$$

$$\beta_{i1} = \gamma_{01} + \gamma_{11} G_i + \gamma_{21} P_i + e_{i1}. \tag{3}$$

$$\beta_{i2} = \gamma_{02} + \gamma_{12} G_i + \gamma_{22} P_i + e_{i2}. \tag{4}$$

$$\beta_{i3} = \gamma_{03} + \gamma_{13} G_i + \gamma_{23} P_i + e_{i3}. \tag{5}$$

As the central question of this study is on the influences of gender egalitarianism and of post-industrialism on the three dimensions of occupational gender segregation, the values of γ_{11}, γ_{12}, and γ_{13} and the values of γ_{21}, γ_{22}, and γ_{23} are to be estimated. These represent the effects of gender egalitarianism and of post-industrialism on the extents of the three dimensions of occupational gender segregation represented by β_{i1}, β_{i2}, and β_{i3}.

3.4 *Data*

The data used in this study is a triple cross-tabulation by prefecture (47), gender (2), and minor occupational group (273) for the Japanese working population

3 SEIs are included in the model after adjusting the average for all samples to be zero. The same procedures are applied to all other continuous variables.

(aged 15 and over). This cross-tabulation is made from publicly available aggregated data extracted from Japan's 2005 population census. Workers with unclassifiable occupations were excluded from the analysis. Although the census covers all Japanese residents, the aggregated data extract takes approximately 11.1 percent of the collected surveys (Statistics Bureau, Ministry of Internal Affairs and Communications 2008). As the publicly available cell frequencies are frequencies estimated from the extracted sample, the reversal calculation of multiplying the publicly available frequencies by 0.111 enables us to estimate the original frequencies of the extracted samples. This study uses a triple cross-tabulation with cell frequencies of these estimated samples. The statistical program R version 2.12.0 (R Development Core Team 2011) was used for the analysis.

3.5 *Variables*

The dependent variable is the proportion of men in each occupation. The independent variables are classified as variables at the individual level or those at the prefectural level. At the individual level, we create two variables representing each occupation's SEI and whether the occupation is manual or non-manual. At the prefecture level, we also create two variables representing the extent of gender egalitarianism and of post-industrialism.

At the individual level, the SEI allocated to each occupation is determined as follows. First, following the procedures employed by Kanomata et al. (2007) and Ganzeboom and Treiman (1996) as closely as possible, we match the minor occupational groups for Japan's population census corresponding with those in the 1988 version of the minor (three-digit) international standard classification of occupations (ISCO88).[4] Next, to each of these occupational groups matched, the SEI for ISCO88's minor occupational groups made by Ganzeboom and Treiman are allocated.[5] Next, the dummy variable of whether an occupation is manual or not is made by classifying ISCO88's major occupational

4 When there is no minor occupational group equivalent to that used in Japan's census in the ISCO 88, we use SEI of the most equivalent occupational group in the mid-level (2-digit) or major (3-digit) occupational classifications.

5 Charles (2003) and Charles and Grusky (2004) use SEI for the major occupational groups, not those for the minor occupational groups. In other words, in their analysis every occupation in the same major occupational group is assumed to have the same SEI. They claim that the results of the analysis are almost the same regardless of whether they use SEI for the minor occupational groups or for the major ones. Our study seems to show that this claim might be true. However, it is also true that the fitness of the model is better when we use t SEI for the minor occupational groups instead of for the major ones. We have therefore chosen to use the SEI for the minor occupational groups.

groups of 6 (agriculture, forestry and fishery), 7 (craft), 8 (operative), and 9 (laborer) as manual, and those of 1 (professional), 2 (management), 3 (semi-professional), 4 (clerical), and 5 (sales and service) as non-manual.[6]

At the prefecture level,the gender egalitarianism variable is created by modifying Yoshida's (2010) gender equality index.[7] This index ranks prefectures into four levels in terms of the male-to-female ratio of population 15–64 years old, the male-to-female ratio of students in higher education, the male-to-female ratio of the labor force participation rate, the male-to-female wage ratio, the proportion of female parliamentarians, the proportion of females who completed compulsory education, the female higher education graduate rate, the female labor force participation rate, and the female average wage. The average value of these rankings for each prefecture is then calculated. Although this index is suitable for this study as it is an index by prefecture, three elements (the male-to-female wage ratio, the female average wage, and the proportion of female parliamentarians) can be regarded as identical to the indicators of occupational gender segregation. We therefore exclude these three elements and average those remaining to determine the index of gender egalitarianism for this study. According to the index, the prefecture where the gender egalitarianism is the highest is Gifu, followed by Kyoto, Kagawa, Ishikawa, and Tokushima, while the lowest is Kanagawa, followed by Ibaraki, Chiba, Saitama, and Akita.

As the index of post-industrialism, the second prefecture-level variable, we use the Z score of the proportion of the tertiary industry populations in each prefecture calculated from Japan's 2005 census. For this indicator Charles and Grusky use proportions of employees in addition to the proportion of the tertiary industry populations, calculating the Z score for each and averaging the two scores. However, our preliminary analysis reveals that it is the tertiary

6 See the Appendix for the variables at the prefecture level.

7 In Charles and Grusky's international comparison (2004), they use the average value for each nation of attitudes toward the statement, "When unemployment rates are high, men have the priority to be hired before women" in the 1990 World Values Survey. Although our study requires the average value for each prefecture in Japan, the sample size of the World Value Survey is too small for our purposes and is therefore ignored. Moreover, the cross-national/regional comparability of this one-item scale is questionable, since the response to this item would be dependent on male unemployment rate in a region or a country and its comparability is not examined. Although our ideology index is constructed from objective instead of subjective attributes of each prefecture, it is reasonable to assume that objective attributes reflect subjective and ideological states of a region. Despite this difference, we reached a conclusion consistent with Charles and Grusky (2004), as we discuss in Sections 4 and 5. We believe this reflexively shows the validity of our ideology index.

industry ratio—not the ratio of employees—that correlates with occupational gender segregation. Moreover, the reason as to why they regard the ratio of employees as representing the extent of post-industrialism is vague. Our study thus uses the ratio of the tertiary industry populations as an index of post-industrialization. The prefecture with the highest ratio of tertiary industry population is Tokyo, followed by Okinawa, Kanagawa, Fukuoka, and Chiba. Prefectures with the lowest ratio were Nagano, Yamagata, Fukushima, Tochigi, and Shizuoka.

4 Results

4.1 *Distributions of Occupations*

We first summarize the male-to-female ratio in the minor occupational groups. Table 6.6 presents the 15 highest and lowest occupations in terms of the proportion of male to all workers. We can see that the proportion of women tends to be low in skilled or semi-skilled manual occupations and in professional occupations, and high in semi-professional, service, and physical elementary occupations. In Figure 6.1, taking the minor occupational group as a single case, a scatter plot was made with the SEI of the occupation on the horizontal axis and the proportion of men in that occupation on the vertical axis. It can be observed that the proportion of men is higher in manual occupations (triangles in Figure 6.1), while those of women are high in non-manual occupations (circles in Figure 6.1). Moreover, there is a tendency that men are more likely to be found in both manual and non-manual occupations with higher SEIs, and the tendency is stronger in manual than non-manual occupations because the slope for manual occupations is steeper than that for non-manual occupations, although the correlation between the SEI and the proportion of men for each occupation is larger for non-manual than manual occupations.

4.2 *Multilevel Model*

Models 1 and 2 in Table 6.7 present the results of logistic regression analysis with the proportion of male to all workers as the dependent variable. Model 1 includes the effects of SEI and of the manual dummy as the main effects, and Model 2 includes the interaction effects between SEI and the manual dummy. The fitness of the model is remarkably improved in Model 2. This indicates that it is more appropriate to distinguish between manual and non-manual occupations to measure occupational gender segregation. Model 2 shows that gender differences are about three times larger in manual than in non-manual occupations. Next, random effects were added to the intercept in Model 3, to

TABLE 6.6 *The 15 highest and lowest occupational groups in terms of proportion of male to all workers in Japan*

The highest 15			The lowest 15		
121	Ship controllers and technicians and navigator (fishery)	100.0%	*22*	***Dental hygienist***	0.0%
129	***Aircraft controllers and technicians***	100.0%	*18*	***Midwife***	0.0%
265	Rail line construction worker	100.0%	*17*	***Public health nurses***	0.9%
246	Boiler operator	99.9%	83	House-keeper and domestic help	1.4%
250	Power-production and related plant operators	99.8%	*135*	***Telephone operator***	1.4%
251	Electric wire mechanics and fitters	99.7%	*27*	***Nursery teacher***	2.2%
247	Crane winch operator	99.5%	*94*	***Geisha and dancer***	2.8%
248	Construction machinery operator	99.5%	*24*	***Nutritionist***	4.2%
174	Railroad vehicle assembly and servicing operator	99.5%	*19*	***Nurse***	4.8%
125	Train drivers and related workers	99.4%	*35*	***Kindergarten teacher***	6.2%
128	***Ship controllers and technicians (except for fishery)***	99.2%	84	Home care worker	6.4%
249	Other stationary engine and construction machinery operator	99.0%	*93*	***Attendant and hostess***	6.9%
257	Carpenter	99.0%	207	Japanese clothes tailor	9.3%
138	Metal-processing-plant operator	98.9%	*49*	***Musician (teaching individually)***	10.0%
258	Construction assistant	98.9%	*103*	***Advertising***	10.1%

Note: ***Bold italic*** indicates non-manual occupations.
SOURCE: CENSUS 2005

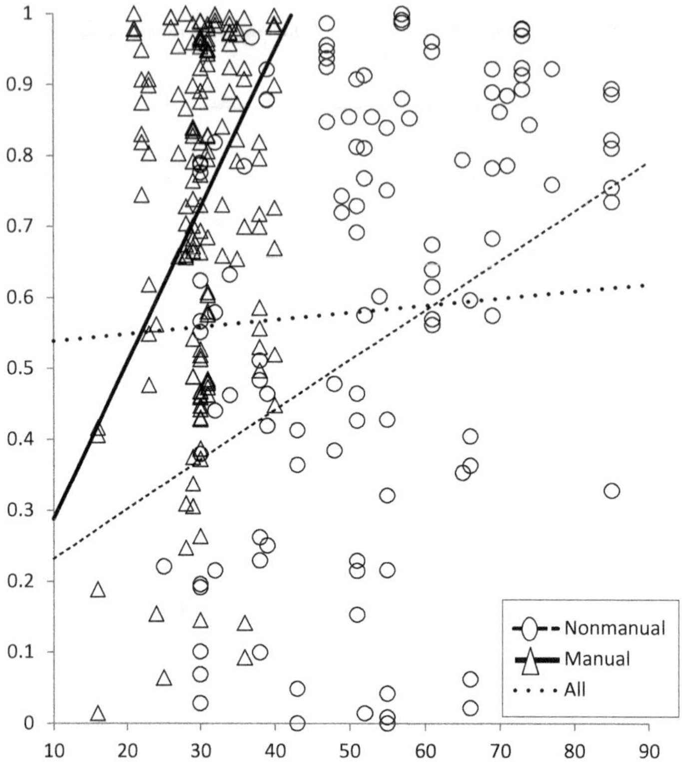

FIGURE 6.1 *A scatter plot of the* SEI *of the minor occupational groups on the horizontal axis and the proportion of males to all workers in the occupation on the vertical axis*
Note: Three regression lines are presented, for non-manual occupations only, for manual occupations only, and for all occupations. Each of the lines is estimated by the least-square method weighted by the number of workers.
SOURCE: CENSUS 2005

the manual dummy in Model 4, and to the interaction effects between SEI and the manual dummy in Models 5. It is observed that the Bayesian information criterion (BIC) improves when the random effect is added in each of these models, which indicates that the intercepts and slopes for these variables differ between prefectures.

Next, by including two prefectural-level variables of gender egalitarianism and of post-industrialism in models, the effects of these two variables on the manual dummy, on the slope of SEI for non-manual occupations (or the interaction effect between the two), and on the slope of SEI for manual occupations (or the interaction effect between the two), are estimated. The results are presented in Table 6.8. As the effects on the intercept are beyond the scope of this study, we focus on interpretations of the effects on other variables. Looking at the effects of gender egalitarianism and of post-industrialism on the slope of

TABLE 6.7 *Logistic regressions predicting the proportion of male to all workers*

	Model 1	Model 2	Model 3	Model 4	Model 5
Intercept	−0.199***	−0.161***	−0.231***	−0.243***	−0.243***
	(0.001)	(0.001)	(0.013)	(0.016)	(0.016)
Manual	1.516***	2.346***	2.366***	2.409***	2.345***
	(0.002)	(0.004)	(0.004)	(0.019)	(0.045)
SEI/10	0.381***				
	(0.001)				
SEI/10 * non-manual		0.313***	0.312***	0.312***	0.312***
		(0.001)	(0.001)	(0.001)	(0.004)
SEI/10 * manual		1.099***	1.091***	1.097***	1.045***
		(0.003)	(0.003)	(0.003)	(0.027)
The variance of random effects					
Intercept			0.008	0.011	0.012
Manual				0.016	0.095
SEI * non-manual					0.001
SEI * manual					0.034
Nagelkerke R^2	0.235	0.271			
Log likelihood/10,000	−104.6	−100.5	−97.2	−97.0	−96.8
BIC/10,000	209.1	200.9	194.3	194.1	193.6

$N = 6{,}715{,}562$, $^{***}p < 0.001$.
Notes: Models 1 and 2 are the normal logistic regression models, and Models 3, 4 and 5 are the random intercept and random slope models. The values of log likelihood and BIC are so large that 1/10,000 of their original values are presented to save space.
SOURCE: CENSUS 2005

the manual dummy (second panel from the top in Table 6.8), as the hypothesis predicts, only the effect of post-industrialism is significant. This indicates that in prefectures where post-industrialism is more advanced, the difference in the male-to-female ratio between manual and non-manual occupations is larger than in other prefectures. In other words, post-industrialism strengthens horizontal segregation.

Looking at the effects of gender egalitarianism and of post-industrialism on the slope of SEI in *non-manual* occupations (third panel of Table 6.8), both gender egalitarianism and post-industrialism have significant negative effects on gender segregation in non-manual occupations, as the hypotheses suggested. For non-manual occupations, gender disparity in SEI is lower in prefectures either with a higher degree of gender egalitarianism or with a higher

TABLE 6.8 *Multi-level model predicting the proportion of male (only parameters at the prefecture level presented)*

	Model 6	Model 7	Model 8
Effect on intercept			
Gender egalitarianism		−0.034* (0.015)	−0.031* (0.013)
Post-industrialism	0.054*** (0.014)		0.053*** (0.013)
Pseudo R^2	0.248	0.096	0.329
Effect on manual dummy			
Gender egalitarianism		0.007 (0.046)	0.018 (0.034)
Post-industrialism	0.204*** (0.034)		0.205*** (0.034)
Pseudo R^2	0.434	0.001	0.437
Effect on SEI * non-manual			
Gender egalitarianism		−0.008* (0.003)	−0.009** (0.003)
Post-industrialism	−0.010** (0.003)		−0.011** (0.003)
Pseudo R^2	0.198	0.123	0.340
Effect on SEI * manual			
Gender egalitarianism		−0.014 (0.027)	−0.007 (0.019)
Post-industrialism	0.134*** (0.019)		0.134*** (0.019)
Pseudo R^2	0.522	0.007	0.523
Log likelihood + 967,000	−769.0	−793.0	−762.0
BIC − 1,935,000	708.0	756.0	732.0

***$p < 0.001$, **$p < 0.01$, *$p < 0.05$.
Notes: Coefficients at the occupational level are not presented in Table 6.8. Pseudo coefficients of determination are a PRE scale that represents how the variance of random effects becomes smaller in a model compared with that in the baseline model, Model 5 in Table 6.7. The absolute values of log likelihood and BIC in each model are so large and thus inconvenient to present in a table that the original values are uniformly adjusted to be smaller in term of the absolute value.
SOURCE: CENSUS 2005

degree of post-industrialism. In other words, vertical segregation in non-manual occupations is lower in prefectures where gender egalitarianism or post-industrialism advances.

Next, looking at the effects of gender egalitarianism and of post-industrialism on the slope of SEI in *manual* occupations (bottom panel of Table 6.8), the figure for effects of gender egalitarianism is not significant, whereas the figure for effects of post-industrialism is positively significant, again as the hypotheses suggested. In manual occupations, gender egalitarianism has no effect on vertical segregation, but post-industrialism strengthens it.

We will now summarize the results of prefecture-level analyses. With regard to the effect on horizontal segregation, gender egalitarianism has no effect on it; however, post-industrialism strengthens it. As to the effects on vertical segregations, the first factor of gender egalitarianism weakens vertical segregation in non-manual occupations, but has no effect in manual occupations. The second factor of post-industrialism weakens vertical segregation in non-manual occupations but strengthens it in manual occupations. All of these results are consistent with our hypotheses. However, comparing our results for Japan with Charles and Grusky's results, which concern mainly European countries, there are some similarities and some differences. The most interesting differences are the effects of post-industrialism on the two dimensions of vertical segregation. In Charles and Grusky's study, post-industrialism strengthens vertical segregation in non-manual occupations but weakens it in manual occupations, whereas in Japan the opposite is true: post-industrialism weakens vertical segregation in non-manual occupations but strengthens it in manual occupations.

Finally, Table 6.9 presents the correlation coefficients between the effects of the manual dummy, the interaction effect between SEI and the non-manual dummy, and the interaction effect between SEI and the manual dummy, all of which are estimated for each of all 47 prefectures in Model 5 in Table 6.7. Figure 6.2 presents a scatter plot of the effect of the manual dummy on the horizontal axis and the interaction effect between SEI and the non-manual dummy on the vertical axis. It can be observed that if a prefecture has a larger effect of the manual dummy, it also has a larger interaction effect between SEI and the manual dummy. In other words, if prefectures have a higher level of horizontal segregation, they also have a higher level of vertical segregation within manual occupations. This is probably because when the ratio of men in manual occupations is large, men are likely to be concentrated in occupations with higher SEIs, and conversely when the ratio of women in manual occupations is large, women are likely to be concentrated in occupations with lower SEIs.

Some other significant correlations are observed in Table 6.9. First, there is a weak correlation between the intercept (representing the ratio of male to all workers) and the interaction effect between SEI and the manual dummy. This indicates that if prefectures have a higher ratio of male to all workers, they have slightly higher vertical segregation in manual occupations. In other words, in prefectures where gender relations are more egalitarian in terms of higher rates of female labor participation, vertical segregation in manual occupation may weaken. Second, Table 6.9 indicates that the correlations between the effects of the manual dummy and the interaction effect between SEI and the non-manual dummy are negative, albeit only slightly, which indicates that

TABLE 6.9 *Correlations between coefficients of four variables for 47 prefectures*

	Intercept	Manual	SEI * non-manual	SEI * manual
Intercept		−0.01	−0.09	0.29*
Manual	−0.01		−0.32*	0.93***
SEI * non-manual	−0.09	−0.32		−0.27
SEI * manual	0.29*	0.93***	−0.27	

N = 47, ***p < 0.001, **p < 0.01, *p < 0.05.
Note: Correlations between the random effects in Model 5 in Table 6.7 are presented.
SOURCE: CENSUS 2005

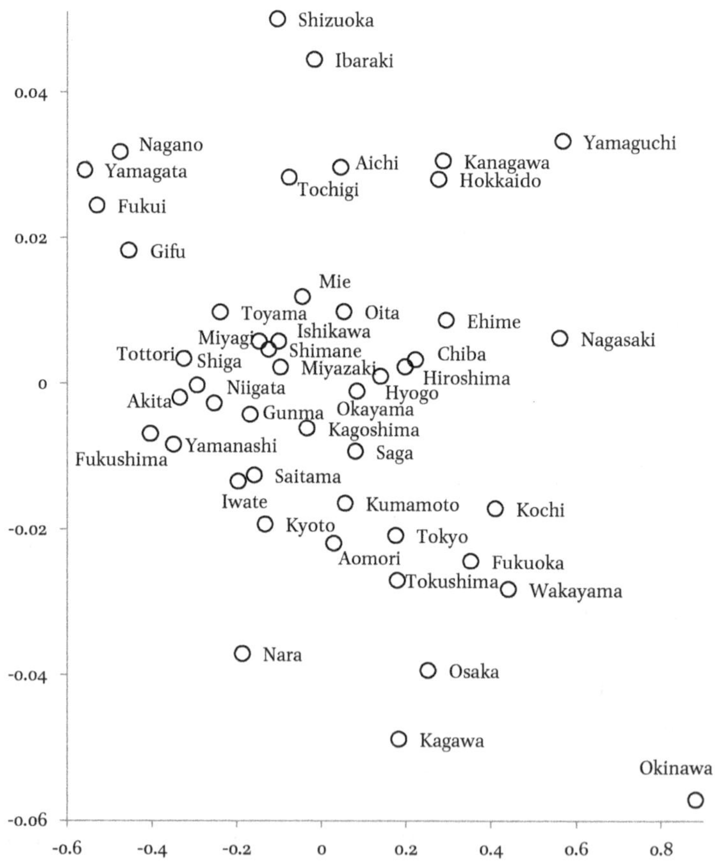

FIGURE 6.2 *A scatter plot of the effects of the manual dummy on the horizontal axis and the interaction effects between SEI and the non-manual dummy on the vertical axis for 47 prefectures estimated from Model 5 in Table 6.7 (deviations from the average)*
SOURCE: CENSUS 2005

in prefectures with strong horizontal segregation, vertical segregation in non-manual occupations is relatively weak. This, however, seems to be due to the influence of the outlier Okinawa (see bottom-right corner in Figure 6.2).

5 Discussion and Suggestions for Future Research

5.1 *Discussion*

Our study on gender segregation in Japan allows us to present the following findings. First, gender egalitarianism has no effect on horizontal segregation or on vertical segregation in manual occupations, but weakens vertical segregation in non-manual occupations. Second, post-industrialism strengthens horizontal segregation and vertical segregation in manual occupations, but weakens vertical segregation in non-manual occupations. All of these results are consistent to the hypotheses for Japan (see Table 6.4).

Comparing these results with those of Charles and Grusky (2004), we see both similarities and differences (see Table 6.10). In both studies, gender egalitarianism is shown to weaken vertical segregation in non-manual occupations, and post-industrialism to strengthen horizontal segregation in non-manual occupations. The differences between the two studies concern the effects of gender egalitarianism on horizontal segregation and on vertical segregation in manual occupations. These differences, however, are not so important because, for one thing, the effects of gender egalitarianism are extremely limited compared to the effect of post-industrialism. Also, the direction of these effects,

TABLE 6.10 *Effects of gender egalitarianism and of post-industrialism on three dimensions of occupational gender segregation: A comparison of the results between this study and the study by Charles and Grusky (2004)*

	On horizontal segregation		On vertical segregation			
			In non-manual		In manual	
Effect of gender egalitarianism	o	[+]	–	[–]	o	[+]
Effect of post-industrialism	+	[+]	–	[+]	+	[–]

Note: Signs '+,' '–,' or 'o' with no parentheses indicates the results of this study, and those in parentheses indicate the results by Charles and Grusky (2004).
SOURCE: CHARLES AND GRUSKY (2004)

positive, is the same in both studies, although they differ slightly in statistical significance; the effects in Charles and Grusky's study are not statistically significant, whereas those in our study are statistically significant.

The most striking and important differences in the results between the two studies are in the effects of post-industrialism on the two dimensions of vertical segregation. In Europe and the United States, the major targets of Charles and Grusky's study, post-industrialism strengthens vertical segregation in non-manual occupations but weakens it in manual occupations; while in Japan, the opposite is true: post-industrialism weakens vertical segregation in non-manual occupations but strengthens it in manual occupations.

What is the reason for these opposite effects? The answer may lie in the differences in the industrial structures of western Europe and the United States on the one hand, and Japan on the other. In comparison with Japan, post-industrialism is much more advanced in western Europe and the United States, and there are more non-manual occupations than manual ones. Charles and Grusky claim that the deskillization of labor brought by post-industrialism is more prominent in non-manual occupations than in manual occupations. Women tend to exit from lower-status manual occupations where men remain, and get concentrated in lower-status non-manual occupations characterized as "feminine." As a result, post-industrialism strengthens vertical segregation in non-manual occupations while it weakens that in manual ones. In other words, it is lower-status non-manual occupations such as sales or service that post-industrialism "feminizes" in these societies.

In contrast, in Japan there are many more manual occupations remaining, for women as well as for men. In such an industrial structure, deskillization of labor by post-industrialism will be more prominent in manual occupations than in non-manual occupations. Women will remain in manual occupations and be concentrated in lower-status de-skilled manual occupations, particularly in prefectures where rationalization of work by post-industrialism is intensified.

In contrast, deskillization in non-manual occupations is less well advanced and widespread in Japan than in Europe or the United States. In Japanese prefectures where post-industrialism is more advanced, there will be more skilled non-manual occupations, such as professional or technical jobs, and women in such prefectures will be more easily employed in such higher-status non-manual occupations than those in less post-industrialized prefectures. Thus, unlike Europe and the United States, in Japan post-industrialism weakens vertical segregation in non-manual occupations while it strengthens it in manual ones. In other words, in Japan, it will be lower-status manual occupations such as unskilled and elementary jobs that post-industrialism "feminizes."

On the basis of the results of this study, it can be argued that the effect of gender egalitarianism as a normative factor is almost the same between societies with different industrial structures, as for the effects of post-industrialism on horizontal segregation. However, the effects of post-industrialism on vertical segregation, whether in the manual or non-manual spheres, differ according to industrial structures.

5.2 *Suggestions for Future Research*

The results of this study show that the effects of post-industrialism in Japan on two dimensions of vertical segregation are different from those reported in Charles and Grusky's (2004) study focusing mainly on Europe and the United States. Nevertheless, it does not pretend to give a full, empirically based explanation of why exactly these effects in Japan are different from those in Europe or the United States, nor by what mechanisms post-industrialism in Japan helps women be employed in higher-status non-manual occupations on the one hand, and squeezes them into lower-status manual occupations on the other. We have given only hypothetical explanations, which should be empirically tested in the future.

This study is a comparative analysis of regions within a country in East Asia while Charles and Grusky's study compares countries mainly in the West. It would be interesting to compare regions within another country in Europe or in the United States and compare those results with the results of this study of Japan. The focus of this study has been on gender segregation in terms of occupation only. However, in Japan, there are large gender gaps in wages, and in authority and power between employment types and firm sizes. The various career tracks that exist within the same employment status cause further disparities in promotion and pay raises between men and women (Shutou 2003). Analyses on gender segregation in terms of these factors will also be useful and necessary to understand workplace gender segregation as a whole.

Appendix

APPENDIX 6.1 *Variables at the prefecture level*

Prefecture	Gender equality index (GEI)	Ranking	Proportion of tertiary industries	Ranking
Hokkaido	1.250	42	0.727	6
Aomori	1.417	37	0.643	25
Iwate	1.667	25	0.603	42
Miyagi	1.333	39	0.699	12
Akita	1.167	43	0.619	32
Yamagata	1.417	38	0.585	46
Fukushima	1.500	33	0.598	45
Ibaraki	1.083	46	0.617	34
Tochigi	1.500	34	0.601	44
Gunma	1.750	22	0.604	41
Saitama	1.167	44	0.702	10
Chiba	1.167	45	0.739	5
Tokyo	1.750	23	0.801	1
Kanagawa	1.000	47	0.745	3
Niigata	1.333	40	0.611	38
Toyama	2.000	6	0.607	39
Ishikawa	2.083	4	0.661	18
Fukui	1.917	11	0.619	33
Yamanashi	1.500	35	0.606	40
Nagano	1.833	17	0.574	47
Gifu	2.167	1	0.613	36
Shizuoka	1.667	26	0.602	43
Aichi	1.833	18	0.623	31
Mie	1.833	19	0.614	35
Shiga	1.667	27	0.613	37
Kyoto	2.167	2	0.715	8
Osaka	2.000	7	0.726	7
Hyogo	1.833	20	0.698	13
Nara	2.000	8	0.709	9
Wakayama	1.583	30	0.659	21
Tottori	1.917	12	0.638	30
Shimane	1.750	24	0.645	23

Prefecture	Gender equality index (GEI)	Ranking	Proportion of tertiary industries	Ranking
Okayama	2.000	9	0.638	29
Hiroshima	2.000	10	0.680	14
Yamaguchi	1.583	31	0.659	22
Tokushima	2.083	5	0.641	27
Kagawa	2.167	3	0.660	20
Ehime	1.917	13	0.645	24
Kochi	1.917	14	0.677	15
Fukuoka	1.667	28	0.744	4
Saga	1.917	15	0.641	28
Nagasaki	1.500	36	0.701	11
Kumamoto	1.667	29	0.661	19
Oita	1.833	21	0.668	17
Miyazaki	1.583	32	0.642	26
Kagoshima	1.333	41	0.670	16
Okinawa	1.917	16	0.775	2

SOURCE: YOSHIDA (2010) AND CENSUS 2005

References

Abe, Yukiko, Shiori Kondo and Kunie Mori. 2008. "On the Regional Differences of Women's Labor Supply: An Analysis of the Regular Employment Ratios Using Aggregate Data." *Japanese Journal of Research on Household Economics* 80: 64–74 (in Japanese).

Beechey, Veronica. 1987. *Unequal Work*. London: Verso.

Chang, Mariko L. 2000. "The Evolution of Sex Segregation Regimes." *American Journal of Sociology* 105(6): 1658–1701.

Charles, Maria. 2003. "Deciphering Sex Segregation: Vertical and Horizontal Inequalities in Ten National Labor mMarkets." *Acta Sociologica* 46(4): 267–287.

Charles, Maria, Mariko Chang and Joon Han. 2004. "Gender and Age in the Japanese Labor Market, 1950–1995." In Charles and Grusky, eds., 179–212.

Charles, Maria and David B. Grusky, 2004. *Occupational Ghettos: The Worldwide Segregation of Women*. Stanford, CA: Stanford University Press.

Ehara, Yumiko. 1985. *The Concept of Liberation of Women*. Tokyo: Keiso Shobo (in Japanese).

Esping-Andersen, Gosta. 1990. *The Three Worlds of Welfare Capitalism*. Cambridge: Polity Press.

Friedan, Betty. 1963. *The Feminine Mystique*. New York: Curtis Brown Ltd.

Ganzeboom, Harry B.G. and Donald J. Treiman. 1996. "Internationally Comparable Measures of Occupational Status for the 1988 International Standard Classification of Occupations." *Social Science Research* 25: 201–239.

Glover, Judith and Gill Kirton. 2006. *Women, Employment and Organizations*. Milton Park: Routledge.

Goldin, Claudia. 1990. *Understanding the Gender Gap: An Economic History of American Women*. New York: Oxford University Press.

Hakim, Catherin. 1979. *Occupational Segregation*. London: Department of Employment.

Hashimoto, Yuki and Shuko Miyagawa. 2008. "Why is Women's Labor Force Participation in Metropolitan Areas Low? A Re-examination of the Current Situation and of the Issues." *Research Institute of Economy, Trade & Industry Discussion Paper Series* (URL: http://www.rieti.go.jp/jp/publications/dp/08j043.pdf). Accessed June 17, 2015.

ILO, LABORSTA Internet (URL: http://laborsta.ilo.org/). Accessed December 17, 2009.

Kanomata, Nobuo, Shunsuke Tanabe and Hirohisa Takenoshita. 2007. "SSM Occupational Classification and International Class Index: Conversion to EGP Classification, SIOPS and ISEI." In T. Maeda, ed., *2005 SSM Series 12 Problems Involving Measurement and Method in a Social Survey*, 69–94. 2005 SSM Chosa Kenkyukai (in Japanese).

Kawaguchi, Akira. 2008. *The Gender Gap in Labor Market Status: Why is a Gap Produced and What is the Key to Overcoming It?* Tokyo: Keiso Shobo (in Japanese).

Kimoto, Kimiko. 1999. "Female Jobs and Male Jobs." In Toshiko Kamata, Sumiko Yazawa and Kimiko Kimoto, eds., *Lecture Sociology 14: Gender*, 151–178. University of Tokyo Press (in Japanese).

Kuba, Yoshiko. 1986. "Marxist Feminism and Its Theoretical Scope." In Socialist Theoretical Forum, ed., *Challenging Feminism*, 86–100. Shakai Hyoronsha (in Japanese).

Lobao, Linda M., Gregory Hooks and Ann R. Tickamyer. 2007. "Introduction: Advancing the Sociology of Spatial Inequality." In Lobao, Hooks, and Tickamyer eds., *The Sociology of Spatial Inequality*, 1–25. New York: State University of New York Press.

Marshall, Gordon. 1998. *Oxford Dictionary of Sociology*. Oxford: Oxford University Press.

Nakai, Miki. 2009. "Job Opportunities, Access to Workplace Authority and Gender." *Shakaigaku Hyoron* 59(4): 699–715 (in Japanese).

Osawa, Machiko. 1993. *Economic Change and Women in the Labor Force: A Japan–U.S. Comparative Study*. Nihon Keizai Hyoronsha (in Japanese).

Osawa, Mari. 1993. *Exceeding Company-Oriented Society: Reading Contemporary Japan by Gender*. Tokyo: Jiji Tsushinsha (in Japanese).

Otobe, Yuko. 2006. *Middle-Aged Women's Life Cycles and Part Time Jobs: The Women Who Work in a Supermarket.* Tokyo: Minerva Shobo (in Japanese).

———. 2010. *Female Career Continuation: Between Regular and Non-regular Work.* Tokyo: Keiso Shobo (in Japanese).

Parsons, Talcott and Robert F. Bales. 1956. *Family: Socialization and Interaction Process.* Routledge and Kagan Paul.

R Development Core Team. 2011. *R: A Language and Environment for Statistical Computing.*

Reskin, Barbara. 1993. "Sex Segregation in the Workplace." *Annual Review of Sociology* 19: 241–270.

Scott, Alison M., ed. 1994. *Gender Segregation and Social Change: Men and Women in Changing Labor Markets.* Oxford: Oxford University Press.

Sechiyama, Kaku. 1996. *Patriarchy in East Asia: Comparative Sociology of Gender.* Keiso Shobo (in Japanese).

Shutou, Wakana. 2003. *Integrated Men's and Women's Workplaces.* Tokyo: Keiso Shobo (in Japanese).

Statistics Bureau, Ministry of Internal Affairs and Communications, eds. 2008. *National Census Report: The Industry (Small Classification), The Occupation (Small Classification). Extraction Detailed Total: Part 1 Whole Country.* Statistics Bureau, Ministry of Internal Affairs and Communications (in Japanese).

———. 2010. *Labor Force Survey* (URL: http://www.e-stat.go.jp/SG1/estat/Xlsdl.do?sinfid=000008597965). Accessed June 30, 2015.

Takeishi, Emiko. 2006a. *The Employment System and Women's Careers.* Tokyo: Keiso Shobo (in Japanese).

———. 2006b. "Aspects of Regional Differences in the Female Participation Rate (the 'M-shaped Curve')." In Gender Equality Council Expert Committee on Low Fertility and Gender Equality, eds., *Report on Analysis of Domestic Social Environment for Low Fertility and Gender Equality*, Vol. 3, 1–41 (in Japanese).

Takenobu, Mieko. 1994. *The Women of Japan Inc.* Tokyo: Asahi Shinbun Shuppansha (in Japanese).

Takeuchi, Tomohiko. 2004. "The Gap between Size of Company in Welfare Expenses." *Keizai Ronso* 173(5–6): 38–50 (in Japanese).

The Japan Institute for Labour Policy and Training. 2006. *Data Book of International Labour Statistics 2006* (in Japanese).

Ueno, Chizuko. 1990. *Paternalism and Capital System: The Ground Level of Marxist Feminism.* Tokyo: Iwanami Shoten (in Japanese).

Wakisaka, Akira and Yasunobu Tomita, eds. 2001. *Labor Patterns of College-Educated Women.* The Japan Institute of Labor (in Japanese).

Yamane, Mari. 1998. "Gender Studies in Japanese Family Sociology: A Review since the 1970s." *Kazoku Shakaigaku Kenkyu* 10(1): 5–29 (in Japanese).

Yamato, Reiko. 2009. "A Comparison of Women's M-Curve Life Course between Japan and Korea: Focusing on Re-entry into the Labor Market after Childbirth." In Yoshimichi Sato and Fumiaki Ojima, eds., *Social Stratification in Contemporary Japan: 1: Disparity and Diversity*, 161–175. University of Tokyo Press (in Japanese).

Yoshida, Hiroshi. 2010. "Development of A Gender Equality Index in Japan: With Reference to the Norwegian Gender Equality Index." *GEMC Journal* 3: 82–92 (in Japanese).

CHAPTER 7

Who Succeeds in Self-Employment? The Role of Family, Gender, and Labor Market Structures

Takenoshita Hirohisa

1 Introduction

Self-employment has received considerable attention from researchers of social stratification. Traditional Marxist theories predicted that the petty bourgeoisie, small employers and self-employed workers, would gradually disappear over time (Steinmetz and Wright 1989), but recent studies on stratification claim that the petty bourgeoisie has in fact persisted through intergenerational inheritance of class position (Erikson and Goldthorpe 1992). Family plays a greater role in entry to self-employment than in attainment of higher occupational positions in wage sectors because of resources mobilized from other family members that help people initiate and stabilize their own businesses (Mueller and Arum 2004). Self-employment, in other words, can be embedded within family institutions (Aldrich et al. 1998).

Gender inequality, in the form of male dominance and the exploitation of women in the family, has been shown to persist in family-run small businesses. As previous research has argued, in agricultural production the family has served as a central unit due to the organic unity of workplace and home. Consequently, patriarchy within the household, men's dominance over women, has played a critical role in maintaining women's subordinate position in the family (Hakim 2004; Ochiai 1996). Although the rate of female participation in the labor force declined during the early stage of industrialization as production moved out of the home and into the factory, late industrialization expanded the scale of the service economy, drawing more women into the labor force (see the Section 2.2 of Chapter 1, regarding the effect of industrialization on female employment). Thus, in recent years, increasing numbers of women in industrialized countries have worked outside the home and become economically independent and autonomous (Brinton 2001; Goldin 1990). Nevertheless, it cannot be assumed that women who work in small family businesses, as family workers, avoid becoming subordinate to male control and obtain economic independence. The question of the ways in which gender inequality and

 | DOI 10.1163/9789004262737_008

female working conditions differ between self-employment and wage employment deserves investigation.

In this chapter, I will consider how the gendered division of labor within households influences gender disparity in self-employment. Married women with young children face certain difficult challenges in self-employment activities because family responsibilities are still allocated to women and men unequally, and women are still expected to be care providers for their children and other family members (Hakim 2004; Ochiai 1996). This gender inequality in family responsibilities has led married women to choose part-time employment to accommodate the competing demands of work and family (Blossfeld and Hakim 1997; see Chapters 4 and 6 of this book for details on women and part-time employment in Japan). The number of female self-employed workers increased in a number of countries in the 1980s and 1990s because self-employment offers female entrepreneurs greater autonomy and flexibility in determining time and place of work, as well as allowing women to balance work and family demands (Carr 1996; Taniguchi 2002). However, because women tend to have the primary responsibility for childcare, they tend to be more involved in marginal, part-time or unskilled self-employment occupations, which are more associated with flexible work arrangements (Mueller and Arum 2004).

Several existing studies on female self-employment have relied on cross-sectional data, derived from a survey implemented at a certain point in time (Carr 1996; Kim et al. 2002). However, this type of data makes it difficult to clearly identify the mechanisms by which people move into and out of the self-employment sector. To capture the dynamic process of people's self-employment activities over their life course, longitudinal data that repeatedly observe several indicators over a long period of time are required. Arum and Mueller's seminal cross-national comparison of self-employment activities explained how the macro-structural arrangements of the labor market and family institutions influence people's patterns of entry into and exit from self-employment. However, their study lacks a theoretical perspective on gender inequality in self-employment (Mueller and Arum 2004). Previous longitudinal studies on gender and self-employment have largely focused on the process by which people enter self-employment rather than the way that the self-employed remain in this sector once they enter it (Budig 2006; Takenoshita 2012; Taniguchi 2002). It is thought that female entrepreneurs may suffer from instability of self-employment due to their involvement in marginal, part-time, and unskilled self-employment, which allows women to reconcile work and family responsibilities. Thus, a gender-based allocation of work and family responsibilities appears to lead to gender disparity in the stability of self-employment. The purpose of this study is to contribute to the further understanding of such gender inequality in self-employment stability.

With a focus on how stability of self-employment differs between women and men, this study compares gender disparity across three East Asian countries: Japan, Korea, and Taiwan. These three countries are chosen for the three following reasons. First, self-employment has played a more critical role in postwar industrialization in East Asian countries than it has in North American and European countries (Ishida 2004; Sato and Arita 2004). The large number of self-employed workers in the total labor force in the East Asian region enables a clear observation of self-employment situations.

Second, the Confucian patriarchal ideology that has shaped the institutional settings of family forms and values in these countries, in contrast to their Western counterparts, has strengthened male dominance in small family businesses and has often resulted in exploitation of unpaid family workers, especially wives (Basu 1991; Lu 2001). The advantages that sons have over daughters in inheriting family assets and businesses also have its basis in Confucian ideology (Lebra 1998; Ochiai 1996). Women are less likely than men to gain significant support from their parents and husbands, and female entrepreneurs may thus suffer from instability of self-employment activities despite having successfully started their own businesses.

Finally, despite cultural similarities in family and gender ideology, considerable variation exists in female employment across East Asian countries (see also Chapter 1 in this volume). Japanese and Korean women are more likely than Taiwanese women to leave the labor force while their children are young (Brinton 2001). Conversely, Taiwanese married women often continue to work as entrepreneurs or as family workers. Such cross-national differences raise questions as to how female employment structures are linked to self-employment stability.

In this study, I investigate in particular how the effects of family situations in non-agricultural self-employment differ by gender, comparing the differences across Japan, Korea, and Taiwan. I first consider how the institutional arrangements of family structures and the labor market in this region affect the stability of female self-employment. I then suggest hypotheses that predict relationships between family situations and the stability of self-employment. Finally, I draw conclusions on the basis of my empirical findings.

2 Differences in Female and Male Self-Employment Across Countries

The institutional contexts of family in Japan, Korea, and Taiwan are characterized by Confucian ideology. The tradition of Confucian doctrine stresses hierarchy, cooperation, industriousness, deference to elders, and most important, the subordination of the individual to family, group and state (Deyo 1988). This ideology has been embedded in welfare policies, in which the family is assumed to provide care for the elderly and children (Aspalter 2006). These family values and structures influence female self-employment activities by legitimizing the subordinate female position in the family (Lu 2001; Yu 2001b). Such family conditions make it less likely that female entrepreneurs will obtain significant support from other family members. In Japan, Korea, and Taiwan, family-based social capital, which implies strong ties with extended kin and interdependence with parents throughout one's life course, has played a crucial role in shaping the social structure and conditions facilitating self-employment (Mueller and Arum 2004), although these three countries differ with respect to employment conditions among married women. In the following section, I will illustrate these institutional contexts in the three countries.[1]

2.1 *Labor Market Structures and Self-Employment Activities*

The rate of self-employment varies widely in Japan, Korea, and Taiwan. The difference has been explained with reference to the certain institutional characteristics of their labor market structures. These include labor market flexibility and employment protection for dependent employees, which may or may not encourage wage earners to become self-employed, and the overall barriers to self-employment that stem from the occupational composition of self-employed workers in a country (Mueller and Arum 2004; Takenoshita 2011).

In this section, I describe the labor market structures and patterns of self-employment in Japan, Korea, and Taiwan. The Japanese labor market has long been characterized by lifetime employment and seniority-based earnings, resulting in a higher level of employment protection for regular workers.[2] Nevertheless, substantial disparities exist between large and small firms with respect to employment stability, economic rewards, and opportunities for promotion. Employees in small firms are more likely to transfer to other employers or to become self-employed because of smaller economic rewards and fewer opportunities for promotion (Hara and Seiyama 2005). Conversely, unskilled workers face greater difficulties in entering self-employment in Japan than in Korea and Taiwan because more entrepreneurs are engaged in skilled occupations as opposed to unskilled self-employment. This occupational composition in the self-employment sector has the effect of making small businesses relatively stable in the labor market.

---

1 Discussions in this section draw from my previous work (Takenoshita 2011; Takenoshita 2012).

2 "Regular" workers in Japan refer to "core" workers in a firm, who are guaranteed employment security and promotion opportunities through personnel management practices (Koike 1988).

In Korea, large conglomerates called *Chaebol* have played a critical role in postwar economic development (Deyo 1989). Prior research has suggested that significant gaps exist between large and small firms with respect to economic rewards and opportunities for promotion (Brinton 2001). Nevertheless, employment in large conglomerates has been quite unstable in Korea, a phenomenon that is largely attributable to the early retirement programs adopted by many large companies (Amsden 1989; OECD 2004). The economic crisis of the late 1990s increased labor market flexibility in Korea (Kye 2008), impelling people to become self-employed. However, self-employment in Korea has tended to be marginalized because of the higher concentration of unskilled jobs in self-employment, such as street food vendors and shop owners (Cheng and Gereffi 1994; Park 2010). One study highlighted the finding that Korean workers are more likely to move into self-employment involuntarily to avoid unemployment (Kim and Cho 2009). As access to self-employment in Korea is easy because of its low entry barrier, the Korean self-employment sector is unstable and marginalized.

In Taiwan, small firms contributed substantially to postwar economic development (Hamilton and Biggart 1988). The subcontracting system in Taiwan has played a crucial role in shaping inter-firm relationships and dividing production processes into numerous segments (Shieh 1992), resulting in higher labor market flexibility and a reduced opportunity cost for employees in becoming self-employed (Luo 1997). In comparison with Korea, self-employment in Taiwan is less marginalized in the labor market. The subcontracting relationships that have evolved in the manufacturing industry have also contributed to the development of a skilled workforce in the Taiwanese self-employment sector (Hsu and Cheng 2002). In contrast with their Korean counterparts, the Taiwanese tend to enter self-employment voluntarily for further occupational advancement rather than to avoid unemployment (Chang 2003). However, a considerable share of unskilled self-employment in the service sector also exists in Taiwan (Takenoshita 2011). There may be larger occupational variations in the stability of self-employment in Taiwan than in Japan and Korea.

2.2 *Female Employment in the Labor Market*

One difference across the three studied Asian countries lies in women's employment patterns throughout their life cycle, including their decisions to leave the labor force at the time of marriage or childbirth (Brinton 2001). In North American and many European countries, the level of female participation in the labor force has increased over recent decades, and many married women continue to work uninterrupted throughout their lives (Brinton 1993). In contrast, women in Japan and Korea tend to withdraw from the labor force at the time of marriage or childbirth (Tsuya and Bumpass 2004). Taiwan is much more similar to western nations in that married women with young children continue to work.

These differences among the three countries can be largely explained by the organizational structures of companies (Brinton 2001; Hamilton and Biggart 1988). In Japan, lifetime employment and a firm internal labor market within large companies have applied exclusively to male employees. Regular workers are expected to work long hours away from home, preventing married women with young children from continuing to work. Many married women in Japan thus choose part-time employment as a way to have sufficient time for performing household chores and providing care to children (Brinton 1993; Yu 2009).

This is also the case with Korean female workers. As in Japan, non-agricultural jobs are likely to be located in large firms in large cities, requiring a long commute to the workplace and long, inflexible work hours (Brinton 2001). Additionally, capital-intensive production has led to lower labor demands in Korea, providing less incentive for employers to abolish traditional marriage bars to female employment (Hamilton and Biggart 1988). In contrast, in Taiwan, small firms play an important role in the labor market. Here, overtime work at night is less common than in Japan, and the arrangements between management and employees are relatively informal and personal in small firms, making it easier for women to negotiate with employers to reduce work-family conflicts (Yu 2001a).

2.3 *Gender, Family Structure, and Self-Employment*

In general, family support is crucial to starting one's own business. Family support brings advantages such as the intergenerational inheritance of a family business, socialization of entrepreneurship in a self-employed family, and support from and co-ownership with one's spouse (Laferrere 2001; Yu and Su 2004). Prior research in many countries has found that having a self-employed father significantly facilitates individuals' entry into self-employment and helps to stabilize small businesses (Sikora and Evans 2009). Nevertheless, men and women may not be provided with equal support from their parents and spouses for starting and running small businesses.

Confucian patriarchal ideology has had a considerable influence on the nature of familial relationships between men and women and between generations in East Asia (Brinton 2001). This ideology has defined the division of labor in families, leading to a strong expectation for wives to perform household chores and to provide care for their children (Slote 1998). Male dominance in the family has been facilitated by the transfer of household assets from fathers to sons, excluding women in many cases (Lebra 1998).[3] A preference for sons has traditionally been strong in Japan, Korea, and Taiwan, and women have been expected to have at least one son as the inheritor of the family business. Although the preference for sons seems to have weakened over the past decades in Japan (Brinton, 2001), the situation for those who engage in family businesses differs from that of wage earners because small businesses are meant to be bequeathed to children—specifically, sons—according to Confucian ideology.

The increase in the number of female wage earners in recent years has brought changes in the division of labor between husbands and wives. Conversely, female family workers in small firms have persisted in Japan, Korea, and Taiwan, although their numbers have declined over the past decades. Wives in family businesses are expected to support their husbands in accordance with the traditional gendered division of labor (Lu 2001; Yu 2001b), whereas female entrepreneurs find it difficult or impossible to obtain significant support from their spouses and other family members. Prior research in Chinese family enterprises has indicated that the traditional gendered division of labor is reproduced through wives' participation in family firms (Basu 1991; Greenhalgh 1994), through which wives are likely to be exploited by their husbands.

3 Hypotheses

This study examines and compares the effects of family characteristics on transitions out of self-employment by women and men in three countries. The primary focus is on gender differences in the effects of marital status and children, parental self-employment, and spouse's employment status on the likelihood of exiting self-employment in Japan, Korea, and Taiwan. Educational attainment and work experience prior to leaving self-employment are controlled in this study.[4]

We pose the following hypotheses regarding what shapes the stability of self-employment among women. Previous studies on female self-employment in the United States have suggested that married women with young children

3 In Japan, a family with only daughters generally expects one daughter to stay in the family and to marry a husband who will become an heir (Ochiai 1996).

4 See Takenoshita (2012) with respect to gender differences in the effect of family and labor market positions on entry into self-employment in Japan, Korea, and Taiwan.

tend to choose self-employment because this sector provides women with more flexibility and autonomy to reconcile work and family responsibilities (Budig 2006; Taniguchi 2002). Therefore, it is assumed that married women with young children would prefer to remain in the self-employment sector to accommodate the demands of work and family.

H1a: *Married women with young children are less likely to leave self-employment than are unmarried women or those without children.*

Given that women have primary responsibilities for childcare, they also tend to have greater involvement in marginal, part-time, and unskilled self-employment that is associated with flexible work arrangements. Therefore, married women with young children may suffer from more instability of self-employment than their male counterparts.

H1b: *Married women with young children are more likely to leave self-employment than are unmarried women or those without children.*

The extent to which the stability of female entrepreneurship depends on family situations is linked to the institutional arrangements of the labor market. In Japan, married women tend to choose part-time employment to reduce work and family conflicts. Given the higher barrier to entry into self-employment, Japanese married women cannot easily start small businesses unless they have significant skills and work experience. Therefore, I expect that the stability of self-employment among Japanese women does not depend significantly on marital status and the number of children. Conversely, Korean and Taiwanese women are more likely to choose self-employment to balance work and family because a large number of unskilled jobs in the service sector, which is associated with flexible work arrangements, are available in the self-employment sector in both countries (Yu and Su 2004). Accordingly, I expect Korean and Taiwanese married women with young children to remain in the self-employment sector. Given the large proportion of unskilled self-employment among women in these two countries, it is also assumed that married women may suffer from instability in self-employment. Although it is difficult to presuppose which hypothesis of H1a and H1b is correct, the likelihood that Korean and Taiwanese women leave self-employment would depend on their marital status and the number of their children.

I also focus on the effects of self-employed fathers on the stability of self-employment and differences in this relationship by gender. In East Asia, the patriarchal Confucian ideology argues that sons (especially the eldest son, in

Japan and Korea) inherit the family business, assets, and authority from their parents to carry on the family line into the future, thus preventing women from becoming family successors (Takenoshita 2012). Because women cannot obtain significant support from their parents, female entrepreneurs suffer from more instability in self-employment, regardless of whether they have a self-employed father.

H2: *Compared with their male counterparts, women do not benefit from having a self-employed father with respect to the stability in self-employment.*

This hypothesis may not hold true for Korean entrepreneurs because the self-employment sector has been highly marginalized due to a concentration there of unskilled jobs in the service industry. The Korean individuals who enter self-employment may thus be highly motivated to exit it. Because even Korean entrepreneurs who have self-employed fathers would likely hope to leave self-employment, having a self-employed father may have no significant effect on the stability of self-employment in Korea.

Finally, I examine the impact of a spouse's employment status on the likelihood of exiting self-employment. The Confucian patriarchal ideology that prevails in East Asian countries holds that a son should inherit the family assets and authority, and a wife is expected to help her husband and to take a subordinate role in the family. Such ideology serves to maintain gender inequality in family businesses. A male entrepreneur is more likely to obtain considerable support from his wife, who works as a family worker, whereas it will be rare for a husband to help his wife run her own business. Because there are few male family workers in the self-employment sector in this region, it is assumed that whether a husband works as a family worker or a self-employed owner has no significant impact on women's likelihood of remaining in self-employment.

H3: *Compared with their male counterparts, spousal support does not help female entrepreneurs to remain in self-employment.*

4 Data, Method, and Variables

This study uses data derived from the Social Stratification and Mobility (hereafter SSM) survey conducted in Japan, Korea, and Taiwan in 2005.[5] Although these surveys were cross-sectional, they had the advantage of asking respondents to

5 I use the SSM survey data sets with the kind permission of the SSM Research Committee.

think retrospectively about their entire work histories. These surveys are also advantageous because they adopted a comparative research design, allowing social stratification researchers to compare work history patterns across the three Asian countries. All of the surveys conducted in these countries used a systemic sampling method with nationally representative samples consisting of respondents aged 20 to 69. These data included complete work histories and information on many job characteristics; they are thus useful for assessing the hypotheses associated with the stability of self-employment. The usable sample sizes were 5,742, 2,080, and 5,379 in Japan, Korea, and Taiwan, respectively, and the response rates were 44.1, 40.0, and 51.8 percent, respectively. Minor discrepancies were reported between the population and the samples in terms of gender and age distributions for the Japanese and Korean data sets. Therefore, weights were used to match the survey and census data. For the Taiwanese data sets, based on previous research, the number of samples consisting of people living in urban areas was intentionally inflated because people in urban areas are more likely to refuse to be survey respondents than are people in rural areas. Because this sampling procedure produced few discrepancies between the population and the samples, weights were not used in this particular data set.

The units of observation in the analyses of exit from self-employment were job spells rather than individuals.[6] I constructed person-year files using complete work histories. If the same individuals became self-employed more than twice, these cases were also included in the data set. All cases with missing information on independent variables used in this study were eliminated. By constructing the person-year data sets, the numbers of observations for the event history analyses were 13,938, 5,512, and 16,231 in Japan, Korea, and Taiwan, respectively.

In this study, self-employment was defined as non-agricultural self-employment (Mueller and Arum 2004), and respondents who engaged in agricultural occupations were excluded. By definition, a self-employed person is someone who earns an income, at least in part, through his or her own labor, but not by selling his or her labor to an employer for a wage (Steinmetz and Wright 1989). Employers who hire a large number of workers tend to be extensively involved in managerial activities rather than in producing goods or providing services through their own labor. Therefore, it is reasonable to eliminate employers who hired more than 30 employees from the self-employment category. In other words, in this study, employers

6 If an individual spent nine years before leaving self-employment, nine observations would be necessary to examine how time-variant covariates, such as family and employment conditions, affect the hazard rate of exit from self-employment.

with fewer than 29 employees and self-employed workers without employees were regarded as self-employed (Erikson and Goldthorpe 1992; Ishida 2004).

To examine the impacts of family and employment conditions on exit from self-employment, this study used the discrete-time logit model, one of several different types of event history model. The event history model is frequently used to capture an occurrence of a specific event at a given time point. Sociologists apply the event history model to consider the timing of marriage, childbirth, quitting a job, and so forth.

The discrete-time logit model can be expressed in a logistic regression form as follows:

$$\log\left(\frac{h(t_j|X)}{1-h(t_j|X)}\right) = a_j + \sum_k b_k X_k$$

where $h(t_j|X)$ is the conditional probability of having an event at time t_j for a given covariate vector $X = (X_1,\ldots, X_k)$, b_k, $k = 1,\ldots, k$ are parameters, and a_j is equal to $\log(h_0(t_j)/1-h_0(t_j))$, that is, the logged odds for the baseline group.

Using the event history model, I was able to identify the underlying mechanisms through which people left self-employment. This model allowed me to incorporate time-varying covariates into the analyses of exit from self-employment. For the analyses, respondents who were self-employed were considered at risk of leaving self-employment. To explore gender differences in transitions out of self-employment, the discrete-time logit model was applied to men and women separately.

The models included two types of independent variables: time-constant and time-varying. The set of independent variables included the characteristics of family situations, educational background, and self-employment situations. My primary focus was on gender, marital status, conditions related to entrepreneur's children, paternal self-employment, and spouse's employment status. Marital status was categorized as married or unmarried (the reference category). I used two indicators to measure the conditions related to the respondents' children, such as the number of children aged 6 or younger and the number of children aged 7 to 18. Regarding the self-employment of the respondents' fathers, respondents who had a self-employed father were coded as 1, and those who did not were coded as 0. Spouse's employment status was classified into three categories: self-employment, family employment, and other (the reference category). Given the causal mechanisms through which people left self-employment, I did not use the spouse's employment status at the time of the survey.[7] The SSM survey conducted in Japan and Taiwan measured the spouse's employment status at the time of marriage, whereas the Korean SSM survey did not. Therefore, I did not estimate the effects of the spouse's employment status on exit from self-employment in Korea.

Other characteristics of family background, educational attainment, and conditions for self-employment were used as control variables. As another indicator of family background, I used the father's class position according to six categories based on the Erikson, Goldthorpe, and Portocarero (EGP) class schema[8] (Erikson and Goldthorpe 1992): non-manual job (Classes I, II, and IIIa); sales and service occupation (Classes IIIb, V, VI, and VIIa in the sales and service sector); skilled job (Classes V and VI in the industrial sector); unskilled job (Class VIIa in the industrial sector); agriculture (Classes IVc and VIIb); and respondents providing no information on their father's class. The reference category was the unskilled class. Age was used as a time-varying covariate. The respondent's education was classified according to three categories: compulsory education (the reference category), secondary education, and tertiary education.

Other sets of time-varying covariates were created to represent the conditions for respondents' self-employment activities. I used nearly the same occupational categories for self-employed jobs as those used for the father's class position: non-manual jobs, sales and service jobs, skilled jobs, and unskilled jobs (the reference category). Firm size was dichotomized into employers who hired other workers and self-employed workers without employees (the reference category). The duration of self-employment was a time-varying covariate to identify the timing of transition out of self-employment. Previous experience of self-employment was treated as a dummy variable.

5 Descriptive Results

Figure 7.1 shows the shares of self-employed and family workers in Japan, Korea, and Taiwan over time using macro-level statistics.[9] Because this

7 The SSM survey conducted in Taiwan also followed the career trajectories of the spouses of the respondents, whereas the Japanese SSM survey measured spouses' employment conditions at the time of marriage and at the time of the survey. To ensure the comparability of these two data sets, information on the spouse's employment status at the time of marriage was used in the multivariate analyses.

8 The EGP class schema was created to grasp the extent to which class positions are inherited across generations, and it has been used for cross-national comparison of intergenerational reproduction of social class.

9 Macro-level statistics in Japan and Korea were derived from the statistical database of the OECD. Taiwanese statistics were derived from the Directorate-General of Budget, Accounting and Statistics, Executive Yuan, Republic of China.

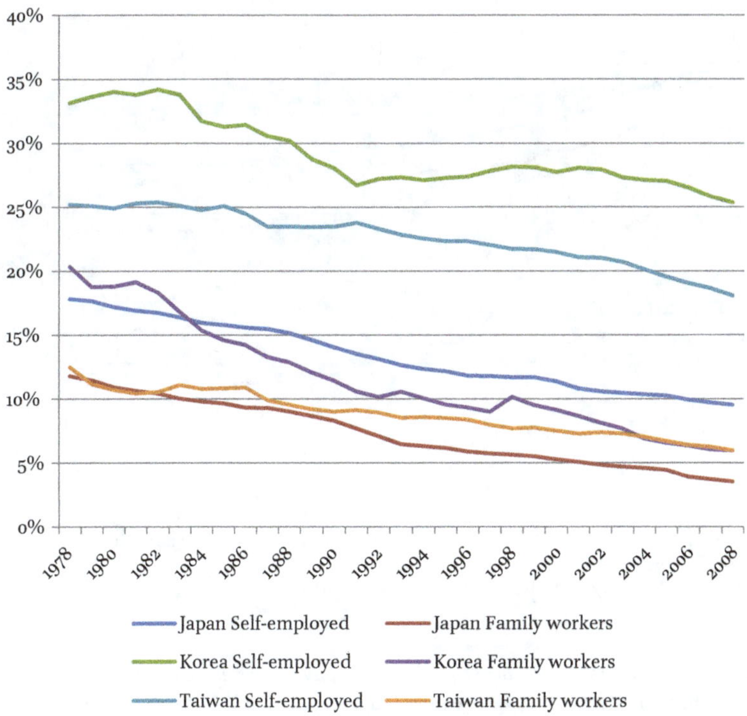

FIGURE 7.1 *The proportions of self-employed and family workers over time in Japan, Korea, and Taiwan.*
Note: Japanese and Korean data are derived from OECD (Organisation for Economic Corporation and Development) statistics, whereas Taiwanese data are drawn from the Manpower Survey Statistics, conducted by Directorate General of Budget, Accounting and Statistics (DGBAS), Executive Yuan, Republic of China.

figure includes a number of self-employed farmers, temporal changes in the share of the agricultural sector should also be taken into account. The proportions of farmers tended to converge over time across the three countries (data not shown). In 2000, the share of agriculture declined to less than 10 percent in all three countries, whereas the share of self-employment differed considerably across these countries over time. In 2005, more than 30 percent of workers in Korea were self-employed, and nearly a quarter of workers in Taiwan were self-employed. In Japan, this figure was only 15 percent, although the share of self-employment in Japan was slightly higher than in other developed countries. The proportions of family workers have recently converged across the three countries, declining to ten percent from 1978 to 2000.

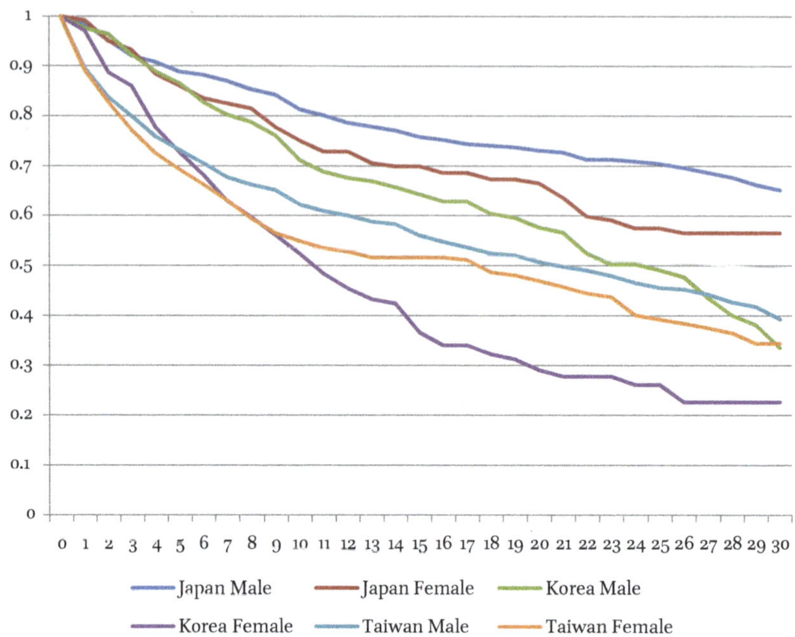

FIGURE 7.2 *Survival curves for the exit from self-employment by gender and country.*
Note: These survival curves were estimated using the Kaplan-Meyer method.
SOURCE: SSM 2005.

Figure 7.2 uses the SSM data sets to show the survival curves for self-employment by gender in the three countries, indicating the shares of those who remain in self-employment over time. Overall, this graph suggests that men were more likely to remain in self-employment than were women over their life cycle. In addition, significant differences across countries existed in the hazard rates of the transition out of self-employment. Japanese men and women tended to remain in self-employment. Gender differences in stability of self-employment were larger in Korea than in Taiwan. Korean women had greater disadvantages in the stability of self-employment than Korean men, whereas this gender gap appeared to be smaller in Taiwan. Ten years after they initiated their own businesses, three-quarters of Japanese women remained in self-employment, whereas almost half of Korean and Taiwanese women left self-employment.

Table 7.1 shows the average scores of the variables used in multivariate analyses. Regarding family background, the shares of respondents with self-employed fathers among all entrepreneurs were higher among men than

TABLE 7.1 *Average scores of variables used in multivariate analyses*

	Japan		Korea		Taiwan	
	Male	Female	Male	Female	Male	Female
Age	41.919	42.678	39.016	38.683	37.799	36.499
Father's self-employment	0.402	0.229	0.186	0.171	0.281	0.234
Father's occupation						
Non-manual	0.150	0.168	0.091	0.118	0.110	0.159
Service	0.205	0.148	0.115	0.144	0.206	0.160
Skilled	0.216	0.093	0.067	0.061	0.112	0.079
Agriculture	0.206	0.257	0.499	0.504	0.367	0.372
Missing	0.148	0.248	0.179	0.147	0.104	0.164
Respondent's education						
Compulsory	0.289	0.296	0.337	0.561	0.544	0.622
Secondary	0.499	0.550	0.420	0.295	0.318	0.244
Tertiary	0.211	0.154	0.243	0.144	0.137	0.134
Self-employed occupation						
Non-manual	0.218	0.311	0.157	0.121	0.191	0.145
Service	0.320	0.575	0.545	0.813	0.456	0.723
Skilled in manufacturing	0.375	0.076	0.191	0.041	0.259	0.104
Unskilled in manufacturing	0.086	0.037	0.107	0.024	0.094	0.028
Self-employment with employees	0.735	0.583	0.629	0.468	0.667	0.518
Self-employment duration (years)	14.293	13.957	10.526	9.181	11.888	11.119
Self-employment experience	0.032	0.021	0.049	0.068	0.171	0.111
Marriage	0.791	0.816	0.814	0.766	0.805	0.809
Number of children aged 6 or younger	0.384	0.308	0.572	0.414	0.611	0.450
Number of children aged 7 to 18	0.682	0.698	0.885	0.880	0.921	0.858
Spouse's self-employment	0.023	0.132			0.073	0.307

TABLE 7.1 *Average scores of variables used in multivariate analyses* (cont.)

	Japan		Korea		Taiwan	
	Male	**Female**	**Male**	**Female**	**Male**	**Female**
Spouse's family employment	0.075	0.019			0.220	0.048
N	9989	3949	3261	2251	11585	4646

Notes: The units of observations are job spells rather than individuals. The numbers of observations in this table differ from those of the original samples in these surveys. The average scores of the variables included were estimated using the weights provided by these data sets.
SOURCE: SSM 2005

among women, although these gaps between men and women differed substantially across nations. Among male entrepreneurs, 40 percent in Japan, 19 percent in Korea, and 28 percent in Taiwan had self-employed fathers. The self-employed occupations differed considerably by gender and by country. Overall, the share of skilled occupations in the industrial sector was larger in Japan than in the other two countries. In Korea and Taiwan, more entrepreneurs engaged in jobs in the service sector. Conversely, female entrepreneurs were more concentrated in jobs in the service sector than were their male counterparts. 80 percent of women in Korea, 70 percent in Taiwan, and almost 60 percent in Japan were involved in sales and service jobs. More Japanese women (30 percent) than Korean and Taiwanese women engaged in non-manual occupations. Regarding the share of employers hiring workers, more Japanese entrepreneurs tended to hire other employees, whereas more Korean and Taiwanese entrepreneurs tended to be self-employed workers without employees. This result reflects the fact that firm size in the self-employment sector is larger in Japan than in Korea and Taiwan.

Table 7.2 presents the occupational distributions by country, using a detailed classification. Among the non-manual jobs, more Japanese and Korean women than Taiwanese women worked as teachers and instructors. Some were piano instructors, and others were private tutors or ran small cram schools. More Japanese female entrepreneurs were involved in clerical jobs in the self-employment sector than were their Korean and Taiwanese counterparts. Overall, women tended to concentrate in jobs in the service sector. Comparing the three countries, more Korean and Taiwanese women than Japanese women were retailers and shop owners. Furthermore, Japanese and Korean women often ran small restaurants. Interestingly, more than 1 in 10 female entrepreneurs

TABLE 7.2 *The distributions of occupations among self-employed workers by gender in the three countries*

	Japan		Korea		Taiwan	
	Men	Women	Men	Women	Men	Women
Medical professionals	3.2	1.3	1.2	0.4	2.3	1.0
Teachers and instructors	0.9	8.5	1.2	8.2	0.8	3.7
Estate agents and trade brokers	7.8	1.3	2.0	0.0	11.1	2.2
Clerical workers (e.g., accounting)	4.7	16.2	4.3	3.3	1.3	4.7
Retailers and shop owners	14.8	14.1	30.9	39.3	23.0	30.7
Restaurant owners	10.5	23.5	10.5	24.6	10.3	18.2
Hairdressers, barbers, and beauticians	3.2	10.3	1.6	8.6	1.3	15.7
Childcare and domestic workers	0.2	3.0	0.0	0.8	0.0	6.5
Automobile drivers	2.2	0.9	9.4	0.0	7.9	0.2
Construction-related workers	21.3	1.7	9.4	0.0	8.8	0.0
Production-related workers	19.3	11.1	19.1	8.6	23.1	11.5
N	554	234	256	244	857	401

Note: The figures in this table represent the percentage points by column. These occupational distributions are derived from jobs only when people started their own businesses. The percentages in these categories do not total 100 percent in each country because this table does not represent all of the occupational categories for the self-employed.

SOURCE: SSM 2005

in Japan and Taiwan worked as hairdressers, barbers, and beauticians. The higher number of female entrepreneurs working as childcare providers or domestic helpers in Taiwan may reflect the fact that more married women with young children worked in the labor market. Few women worked as automobile drivers across the three countries, although this is a typical job in the service sector. A small number of women across the three countries worked in the industrial sector; almost no women in these countries were involved in construction-related jobs.

6 Multivariate Analyses

Table 7.3 presents the results of event history models of the transitions out of self-employment in Japan, Korea, and Taiwan. The coefficients of the variables used in the models were estimated separately for men and women. In pooled samples, I investigated the gender differences in the hazard rates of exit from self-employment. After family situations, educational attainment, and occupational conditions were controlled for, Korean female entrepreneurs were twice as likely to leave self-employment as their male counterparts. In contrast, there was no significant evidence to support this gender difference in Japan and Taiwan. This result indicates that female entrepreneurs in Japan and Taiwan do not always suffer from instability in self-employment. In other words, female self-employment remains as stable as male self-employment, even if women are less committed to self-employment activities than male entrepreneurs are because of the greater family responsibilities allocated to married women.

In this section, I address the question of whether the hypotheses specified above are supported by the empirical results. I describe the results for the effect of marriage and the number of children on leaving self-employment.

In pooled samples in Japan, married people or those with school-aged children were less likely to leave self-employment, but this tendency was found solely among male entrepreneurs. Among Japanese women, the stability of self-employment did not depend significantly on their marital status and did not depend at all on their number of children. This finding seems to result from the fact that Japanese female entrepreneurs are highly selected according to their work experience and their ability to run small businesses because the barrier to moving into self-employment is relatively higher in Japan than in the other two countries (Takenoshita 2011; Takenoshita 2012). In contrast, married women in Korea and Taiwan were less likely to leave self-employment, as were Korean women with school-aged children. This finding highlights the fact that married women in these two countries tend to choose self-employment to accommodate the demands of work and family. Although this tendency may lead to the instability of female self-employment, the empirical results do not support this hypothesis. Korean and Taiwanese married women continue to engage in the self-employment sector. As I argued previously, the flexibility of the work schedule and job autonomy enable female entrepreneurs to successfully remain in self-employment.

Regarding the effect of family background (paternal self-employment) on the exit from self-employment, Japanese and Taiwanese entrepreneurs with self-employed fathers were less likely to leave self-employment in pooled samples, whereas the stability of self-employment in Korea did not depend significantly on paternal self-employment. These findings are consistent with those of previous studies in Korea, which suggested that the high concentration of unskilled jobs in the self-employment sector causes people with self-employed fathers to avoid the same class position (Park 2010; Takenoshita 2007; Takenoshita 2011). When the results were separated by gender, male entrepreneurs in Japan benefited from paternal self-employment in terms of the stability of self-employment, whereas females did not. Surprisingly, in Taiwan, this benefit was limited to female entrepreneurs rather than to male entrepreneurs.

The findings in Japan are completely consistent with the second hypothesis. The significant gender gap in the likelihood of becoming the family successor as a result of the patriarchal Confucian system made paternal self-employment of female entrepreneurs less beneficial in terms of the stability of self-employment. In contrast, the results in Taiwan show a tendency that opposes the hypothesis. This association is quite reasonable in Taiwan because married men with children were highly motivated to become self-employed, as indicated by Table 7.3. In the Taiwanese economy, where small firms have predominated, earnings in wage employment are insufficient to feed a family, employment in small firms is unstable, and there are fewer prospects for promotion because of the small number of managerial positions in organizations (Yu and Su 2004). However, Taiwanese women are not required to become their own bosses to the same extent as men because of the greater family responsibilities allocated to women; instead, women have been expected to become family workers to help their husbands run their small businesses (Takenoshita 2012). Under these circumstances, paternal self-employment would provide female workers with the skills to run small organizations effectively.

Regarding the effects of a spouse's employment status at the time of marriage,[10] I expected to find a significant gender difference in this effect on the stability of self-employment because of the patriarchal family structures in the region of the study. The results in Japan and Taiwan support the third hypothesis. In these two countries, male entrepreneurs whose wives were family workers were less likely to leave self-employment, whereas females did not receive this type of benefit from their husbands. Hence, the patriarchal Confucian ideology produces a gender inequality in receiving significant support from other family labor, leading to disadvantages for women in the stability of self-employment. Conversely, in Taiwan, female entrepreneurs with

10 Due to a lack of this indicator in the Korean SSM survey, I did not estimate the effect of spouse's employment status on the stability of self-employment.

TABLE 7.3 *Discrete time logit models predicting transitions out of self-employment in the three countries*

Japan	All		Male		Female	
	Coef.	s.e.	Coef.	s.e.	Coef.	s.e.
Gender (Reference: Male)	0.179	0.157				
Age	0.029**	0.008	0.034**	0.010	0.026+	0.014
Father's self-employment	−0.489**	0.185	−0.672**	0.227	0.112	0.355
Education (Reference: Compulsory or less)						
Secondary	−0.415**	0.156	−0.386+	0.201	−0.551*	0.261
Tertiary	−0.278	0.223	−0.268	0.273	−0.437	0.403
Occupation (Reference: Non-manual)						
Sales and Service	0.193	0.187	0.404+	0.241	0.100	0.313
Skilled in manufacturing	−0.101	0.221	−0.232	0.269	0.742+	0.407
Unskilled in manufacturing	0.483+	0.258	0.579+	0.299	0.464	0.594
Firms with other employees	−0.167	0.140	−0.301+	0.181	0.002	0.231
Duration of self-employment	−0.032**	0.008	−0.027**	0.010	−0.032*	0.015
Marriage	−0.506**	0.160	−0.672**	0.208	−0.316	0.278
Number of children aged 6 or younger	−0.083	0.118	−0.014	0.141	−0.103	0.223
Number of children aged 7 to 18	−0.217*	0.084	−0.227*	0.108	−0.127	0.140
Spouse's self-employment	−0.251	0.340	−0.368	0.730	−0.380	0.415
Spouse's family employment	−1.266*	0.589	−1.152+	0.595		
Constant	−3.686**	0.415	−3.516**	0.508	−4.217	0.781
N	13938		9989		3949	
Pseudo R^2	0.039		0.054		0.034	
Log likelihood	−1184		−768		−404	

TABLE 7.3 *Discrete time logit models predicting transitions out of self-employment in the three countries* (cont.)

Korea	All		Male		Female	
	Coef.	s.e.	Coef.	s.e.	Coef.	s.e.
Gender (Reference: Male)	0.671**	0.179				
Age	0.004	0.012	−0.004	0.022	0.006	0.015
Father's self-employment	0.268	0.294	0.048	0.498	0.092	0.428
Education (Reference: Compulsory or less)						
Secondary	0.315	0.200	0.700*	0.307	−0.118	0.302
Tertiary	0.136	0.288	0.332	0.391	−0.471	0.525
Occupation (Reference: Non-manual)						
Sales and Service	0.159	0.278	0.636	0.412	−0.262	0.454
Skilled in the industrial sector	−0.150	0.384	0.110	0.502	−0.554	0.768
Unskilled in the industrial sector	0.371	0.387	0.344	0.523	0.469	0.682
Firms with other employees	−0.031	0.164	−0.160	0.256	0.120	0.224
Duration of self-employment	0.004	0.014	0.019	0.023	−0.011	0.017
Marriage	−0.596**	0.205	0.066	0.403	−1.018**	0.260
Number of children aged 6 or younger	0.021	0.122	−0.029	0.182	0.050	0.171
Number of children aged 7 to 18	−0.159+	0.090	−0.126	0.122	−0.225+	0.133
Constant	−3.718**	0.683	−4.782**	1.122	−2.03	0.931
N	5512		3261		2251	
Pseudo R^2	0.033		0.026		0.049	
Log likelihood	-721		-333		-375	

TABLE 7.3 *Discrete time logit models predicting transitions out of self-employment in the three countries* (cont.)

Taiwan	All		Male		Female	
	Coef.	s.e.	Coef.	s.e.	Coef.	s.e.
Gender (Reference: Male)	0.145	0.098				
Age	−0.007	0.006	−0.016+	0.008	−0.005	0.009
Education (Reference: Compulsory or less)						
Secondary	0.113	0.100	0.102	0.123	0.158	0.180
Tertiary	0.120	0.144	0.200	0.174	0.016	0.271
Occupation (Reference: Non-manual)						
Sales and Service	0.302*	0.130	0.315*	0.154	0.298	0.254
Skilled in manufacturing	−0.053	0.158	−0.074	0.179	0.099	0.362
Unskilled in manufacturing	0.462*	0.188	0.385+	0.214	1.025*	0.421
Firms with other employees	0.118	0.092	0.008	0.113	0.361*	0.162
Duration of self-employment	−0.027**	0.007	−0.020*	0.010	−0.035**	0.013
Marriage	−0.637**	0.103	−0.341*	0.155	−0.668**	0.184
Number of children aged 6 or younger	0.008	0.031	−0.190*	0.077	0.041	0.054
Number of children aged 7 to 18	−0.027	0.031	−0.126*	0.057	−0.060	0.054
Spouse's self-employment	−0.266+	0.149	−0.138	0.225	−0.365+	0.210
Spouse's family employment	−0.658**	0.168	−0.743**	0.189	0.023	0.375
Constant	−2.329**	0.257	−2.155**	0.321	−2.189**	0.437
N	16231		11585		4646	
Pseudo R^2	0.043		0.048		0.052	
Log likelihood	−2468		−1672		−779	

+ $p < 0.10$; * $p < 0.05$; ** $p < 0.01$.

SOURCE: SSM 2005

self-employed spouses tended to remain in self-employment, an association unseen among Japanese women. This tendency indicates that a husband's self-employment contributes significantly to the stability of his wife's self-employment in Taiwan. Although patriarchal family structures continue to be reproduced through practices of small family businesses in Taiwan (Lu 2001; Takenoshita 2012), the findings suggest that married women are also supported by their self-employed spouses in stabilizing their small businesses.

7 Conclusions

This study addressed the question of how gender differences in the stability of self-employment across three Asian countries are associated with the broader structures of the family and the labor market. Based on gender inequality in the labor market, I expected women to suffer from more instability in self-employment than men. However, empirical findings suggest that this prediction is correct solely for Korean female self-employment; this particular gender gap does not arise in Japan or Taiwan. Despite this finding, we are unable to conclude that Japanese and Taiwanese women have been in a similar condition of self-employment. Japan and Taiwan differ considerably in their employment and industrial structures, as argued previously. The Japanese labor market has a higher level of employment protection for regular workers, such as employment practices associated with long-term employment and firm-based labor unions. In contrast, in Taiwan, labor market flexibility is relatively higher because small firms run by family members have played a crucial role in economic development. In addition, more unskilled self-employment exists in Taiwan. Consequently, self-employment among Japanese men and women is relatively stable over the course of their lives, whereas more Taiwanese men and women (30 percent) leave self-employment, even five years after starting small businesses. Taken together, the presence and extent of marginalization among female entrepreneurs in the self-employment sector depends on the institutional arrangements of the labor market that have persisted in these countries.

The empirical findings correspond in several ways to the four hypotheses specified above. These associations are summarized in Table 7.4. Hypothesis 1 assumes two different working hypotheses. In H1a, it is assumed that self-employment among married women with children is relatively stable because self-employment provides female entrepreneurs with more flexibility and autonomy. In H1b, it is assumed that married women with children suffer from the instability of self-employment because they tend to have greater involvement in the marginal, part-time or unskilled self-employment occupations

TABLE 7.4 *Summary of empirical tests concerning hypotheses of family and self-employment*

	Japan	Korea	Taiwan
H1: marital status and number of children			
H1a: work-family balance	R	S	S
H1b: marginalization	R	R	R
H2: gender disparity in inheritance of self-employment	S	R	R
H3: female disadvantage in spouse's support	S	–	S

Note: S denotes the fact that the hypothesis was supported by empirical findings in this study, and R denotes that the hypothesis was rejected by the findings.

associated with flexible work arrangements. The results indicate that, although Hypothesis 1b was rejected across all three countries, Hypothesis 1a proved to be correct for Korean and Taiwanese self-employment, showing that married women were less likely to leave self-employment. This hypothesis was not applicable to self-employment in Japan because the higher barrier to moving into self-employment required people to have more skills and experience when starting their small businesses (Takenoshita 2012). It seems likely that Japanese self-employment does not allow married women to accommodate work and family responsibilities. In contrast, a large share of unskilled jobs in the self-employment sector in Korea and Taiwan enables married women to engage in self-employment to reduce the conflict between work and family. In sum, whether married women consistently work in the self-employment sector depends on the industrial structures of this sector.

Hypotheses 2 and 3 originate from a consideration of patriarchal Confucian family structures, which focus on the intergenerational inheritance of assets and authority and an unequal relationship between husbands and wives. The results of Japanese self-employment were consistent with these two hypotheses. In Japan, male entrepreneurs experienced greater stability in self-employment as a result of paternal self-employment and support from their wives, whereas these factors did not contribute to the stability of self-employment among female entrepreneurs. In Taiwan, the results supported Hypothesis 3, but not Hypothesis 2. In Japan and Taiwan, the Confucian patriarchal ideology has continued to shape gender inequality in the stability of self-employment.

In contrast, Korean self-employment does not correspond to these two hypotheses. No gender disparity in the effect of paternal self-employment and spousal support exists in Korea because of the marginalized situations for this country's self-employment sector. The intergenerational reproduction of self-employment, therefore, does not arise in Korea. In other words, both men and women, even those who have self-employed fathers, tend to avoid inheriting their parents' small businesses.

On the basis of the empirical findings presented above, I will now discuss the theoretical implications of this study. One contribution of this study lies in its exploration of the association between family conditions and gender inequality in the stability of self-employment. There is a lack of studies that focus on this topic, although there are several studies on gender differences in the patterns through which women enter self-employment. In particular, it was previously unclear how the stability of self-employment among married women is affected by the need to balance work and family life. The results in this study indicate that Korean and Taiwanese married women have tended to remain in self-employment. Interestingly, this tendency was not found among Japanese women. This finding suggests that the ability of married women to stay in self-employment depends on the institutional arrangements of the industrial structures in the self-employment sector, such as whether unskilled self-employment that allows married women to have flexible working arrangements exists.

Another contribution of this study is its investigation of how women's disadvantaged position in family relationships as a result of patriarchal Confucian ideology affects the stability of their self-employment. By examining three East Asian societies in which Confucian ideology continues to prevail, I clearly identify how one variant of patriarchy has created gender inequality in self-employment. Through this careful investigation, we have learned that the effect of the patriarchy on the stability of self-employment depends on the location of self-employment in the hierarchy of social stratification. In a country where mobility into self-employment is a desirable option, men who hold privileged familial assets are highly motivated to move to and remain in self-employment because entrepreneurial jobs ranked higher in occupational hierarchy. In contrast, in a country where self-employment is marginalized in the labor market and regarded as an undesirable position, gender inequality in familial relationships does not play a significant role in shaping the stability of self-employment because even those who hold privileged resources or status in a family tend to avoid moving into self-employment or to move to the employment sector.

Female entrepreneurs are generally depicted using two contradictory and inconsistent images. The first image suggests that these women successfully acquired upward socioeconomic mobility, became their own boss, and are not subject to anyone in conducting their businesses. In contrast, the second image assumes that many married women choose self-employment to reconcile work and family responsibilities (Taniguchi 2002). The findings in this study indicate that people's motivation to become self-employed differs significantly by gender and by country. In several Western countries, female labor force participation rates have grown consistently since the 1970s because of the significant expansion of the service economy and the increasing number of highly educated women. Recent female employment scenarios in Western countries, such as the expansion of employment opportunities in the wage sector, have allowed more women to become economically independent and autonomous. However, this is not the case with female workers in self-employment in East Asia because women's choice of self-employment is substantially associated with the reconciliation of work and family responsibilities. Under this situation, women tend to choose unskilled jobs in self-employment because of lower mobility barrier into this type of self-employment. Since family small business are deeply embedded in the patriarchal structure, self-employment among women in East Asian countries may hinder them from becoming economically independent and autonomous, unlike the cases of female workers in Western countries.

This study has left certain issues unresolved. First, this study did not examine the effect of a spouse's employment status on the stability of self-employment in Korea because of a lack of this indicator in the Korean SSM survey. Future studies should examine whether this effect arises in Korea. Second, this study focused on the transition out of self-employment among three East Asian countries with similar but different institutional contexts. Nevertheless, it did not explore whether these findings were unique when compared with those in other industrialized countries, especially North American and European countries. Although it underlined the importance of the Confucian patriarchal structures specific to the East Asian region for gender inequality in self-employment, similar family structures may play a role in other countries. Future studies should investigate whether, and to what extent, this study's findings are unique to East Asian countries.

References

Aldrich, Howard E., Linda A. Renzulli and Nancy Langton. 1998. "Passing on Privilege: Resources Provided by Self-employed Parents to their Self-employed Children." *Research in Social Stratification and Mobility* 16: 291–317.

Amsden, Alice H. 1989. *Asia's Next Giant: South Korea and Late Industrialization.* New York: Oxford University Press.

Aspalter, Christian. 2006. "The East Asian Welfare Model." *International Journal of Social Welfare* 15: 290–301.

Basu, Ellen, O. 1991. "The Sexual Division of Labor and the Organization of Family and Firm in an Overseas Chinese Community." *American Ethnologist* 18: 700–718.

Blossfeld, Hans-Peter. and Catherine Hakim. 1997. *Between Equalization and Marginalization: Women Working Part-time in Europe and the United States of America*. New York: Oxford University Press.

Brinton, Mary C. 1993. *Women and the Economic Miracle: Gender and Work in Postwar Japan*. Berkeley: University of California Press.

———. 2001. "Married Women's Labor in East Asian Economies." In M.C. Brinton, ed., *Women's Working Lives in East Asia*, 1–37. Stanford: Stanford University Press.

Budig, Michelle. J. 2006. "Intersections on the Road to Self-employment: Gender, Family and Occupational Class." *Social Forces* 84: 2223–2239.

Carr, Deborah. 1996. "Two Paths to Self-employment? Women's and Men's Self-Employment in the United States, 1980." *Work and Occupations* 23: 26–53.

Chang, Feng-bin. 2003. "Career Dynamic of Self-Employment for Men and Women in Taiwan and Korea." Paper presented at the Annual Meeting of the American Sociological Association, Atlanta.

Cheng, Lu L. and Gary Gereffi. 1994. "The Informal Economy in East Asian Development." *International Journal of Urban and Regional Research* 18: 194–219.

Deyo, Frederic C. 1989. *Beneath the Miracle: Labor Subordination in the New Asian Industrialism*. Berkeley: University of California Press.

Erikson, Robert and John H. Goldthorpe. 1992. *The Constant Flux: A Study of Class Mobility in Industrial Societies*. Oxford: Clarendon Press.

Goldin, Claudia. 1990. *Understanding the Gender Gap: An Economic History of American Women*. Oxford: Oxford University Press.

Greenhalgh, Susan. 1994. "De-orientalizing the Chinese Family Firm." *American Ethnologist* 21: 746–775.

Hakim, Catherine. 2004. *Key Issues in Women's Work: Female Diversity and the Polarisation of Women's Employment*. London: Routledge.

Hamilton, Gary and Nicole W. Biggart. 1988, "Market, Culture, and Authority: A Comparative Analysis of Management and Organization in the Far East." *American Journal of Sociology* 94: S52–S94.

Hara, Junsuke and Kazuo Seiyama. 2005. *Inequality Amid Affluence: Social Stratification in Japan*. Melbourne: Trans Pacific Press.

Hsu, Jinn Yuh and Lu-Lin Cheng. 2002. "Revisiting Economic Development in Post-war Taiwan: The Dynamic Process of Geographical Industrialization." *Regional Studies* 36: 897–908.

Ishida, Hiroshi. 2004. "Entry into and Exit from Self-employment in Japan." In Richard Arum and Walter Mueller, eds., *The Reemergence of Self-employment: A Comparative Study of Self-employment Dynamics and Social Inequality*, 348–387. Princeton: Princeton University Press.

Kim, GiSeung and Joonmo. Cho. 2009. "Entry Dynamics of Self-Employment in South Korea," *Entrepreneurship and Regional Development* 21:303–323.

Kim, Sung-Hee, Deanna L. Sharpe and Hye-Yeon Kim. 2002. "Factors Influencing the Likelihood of Leaving Self-Employment in Korea." *Family and Consumer Sciences Research Journal* 30: 554–569.

Koike, Kazuo. 1988. *Understanding Industrial Relations in Modern Japan*. New York: St. Martin's Press.

Kye, Bongoh. 2008. "Internal Labor Markets and the Effects of Structural Change: Job Mobility in Korean Labor Markets between 1998 and 2000." *Research in Social Stratification and Mobility* 26: 15–27.

Laferrere, Anne, 2001. "Self-Employment and Intergenerational Transfers." *International Journal of Sociology* 31: 3–26.

Lebra, Takie S. 1998. "Confucian Gender Roles and Personal Fulfillment for Japanese Women." In Walter H. Slote and George A. De Vos, eds., *Confucianism and the Family*, 209–230. Albany: State University of New York Press.

Lu, Yu-Hsia. 2001. "The 'Boss's Wife' and Taiwanese Small Family Business." In Mary C. Brinton, ed., *Women's Working Lives in East Asia*, 263–297. Stanford: Stanford University Press.

Luo, Jar. D. 1997. "The Significance of Networks in the Initiation of Small Businesses in Taiwan." *Sociological Forum* 12: 297–317.

Mueller, Walter and Richard Arum. 2004. "Self-Employment Dynamics in Advanced Economies." In Richard Arum and Walter Mueller, eds., *The Re-emergence of Self-employment: A Comparative Study of Self-employment Dynamics and Social Inequality*, 1–35. Princeton: Princeton University Press.

Ochiai, Emiko. 1996. *The Japanese Family System in Transition: A Sociological Analysis of Family Change in Postwar Japan*. Tokyo: LTCB International Library Foundation.

OECD. 2004. *Ageing and Employment Policies in Korea*. Paris: OECD.

Park, Hyunjoon. 2010. "The Stability of Self-Employment: A Comparison between Japan and Korea." *International Sociology* 25: 98–122.

Sato, Yoshimichi and Shin Arita. 2004. "Impact of Globalization on Social Mobility in Japan and Korea: Focusing on Middle Classes in Fluid Societies." *International Journal of Japanese Sociology* 13: 36–52.

Shieh, Gwo Shyong. 1992. *Boss Island: The Subcontracting Network and Micro-entrepreneurship in Taiwan's Development*. New York: Peter Lang Publishing.

Sikora, Joanna, and Mariah D.R. Evans. 2009. "Self-employment: Determinants and Rewards in 33 Countries." Paper presented at the Australian Sociological Association, Australian National University, Canberra.

Slote, Walter H. 1998. "Psychocultural Dynamics Within the Confucian Family." In W.H. Slote and G.A. De Vos, eds., *Confucianism and the Family*, 37–52. Albany: State University of New York Press.

Steinmetz, George and Erik O. Wright. 1989. "The Fall and Rise of the Petty Bourgeoisie: Changing Patterns of Self-Employment in the Postwar United States." *American Journal of Sociology* 94: 973–1018.

Takenoshita, Hirohisa. 2007. "Intergenerational Mobility in East Asian Countries: A Comparative Study of Japan, Korea and China." *International Journal of Japanese Sociology* 16: 64–79.

———. 2011. "Labor Market Structure and Self-Employment in Three Asian Countries: A Comparative Study of Japan, Korea, and Taiwan." In K. Misumi, ed., *Study of an East Asian Stratification Model*, 21–47. Fukuoka: Working Papers of Grant-in-Aid for Scientific Research Project.

———. 2012. "Family, Labour Market Structures and the Dynamics of Self-employment in Three Asian Countries: Gender Differences in Self-employment Entry in Japan, Korea and Taiwan." *Comparative Social Research* 29: 85–112.

Taniguchi, Hiromi. 2002. "Determinants of Women's Entry into Self-Employment." *Social Science Quarterly* 83: 875–893.

Tsuya, Noriko O., and Larry L. Bumpass. 2004. *Marriage, Work, and Family Life in A Comparative Perspective: Japan, South Korea, and the United States*. Honolulu: University of Hawai'i Press.

Yu, Wei-Hsin. 2001a. "Family Demands, Gender Attitudes, and Married Women's Labor Force Participation." In Mary C. Brinton, ed., *Women's working lives in East Asia*, 70–95. Stanford: Stanford University Press.

———. 2001b. "Taking Informality into Account: Women's Work in the Formal and Informal Sectors in Taiwan." In Mary C. Brinton, ed., *Women's Working Lives in East Asia*, 233–262. Stanford: Stanford University Press.

———. 2009. *Gendered Trajectories: Women, Work, and Social Change in Japan and Taiwan*. Stanford: Stanford University Press.

Yu, Wei-Hsin and Kuo-Hsien Su. 2004. "On One's Own: Self-employment Activity in Taiwan." In Richard Arum and Walter Mueller, eds., *The Re-emergence of Self-employment: A Comparative Study of Self-employment Dynamics and Social Inequality*, 388–425. Princeton: Princeton University Press.

CHAPTER 8

Where Materialism Still Matters: Status Identity in East Asia

Chang Chin-Fen, Xie Guihua, Takamatsu Rie and Kim Young-Mi

> "With some over-simplification, one might thus say 'classes' are stratified according to their relations to the production and acquisition of goods; whereas 'status groups' are stratified according to the principles of their consumption of goods as represented by special 'styles of life'."
>
> — MAX WEBER

1 Preface

The statement by Max Weber (Gerth and Mills 1958: 193) in the quotation above provides a neat encapsulation of the difference between class and status. Social hierarchy is shaped simultaneously by several sources of power, and the economic dimension is only one (Swartz 1997: 146). Following arguments made by Pierre Bourdieu (1984), Chan and Goldthorpe (2010) show on the one hand how class structure defines discrepancies in material capital, and on the other how objective ranking of social status is decided by cultural capital. "Status," they say, "has to be seen as the symbolic aspect of the class structure" (Chan and Goldthorpe 2010: 13). While it makes sense to define the class structure by objective indicators, another approach to social hierarchy is to examine the subjective identification of individual positions within it. A multivariate analysis reveals how objective factors such as socio-economic background, employment status, and/or cultural capital affect subjective social status.

Previous studies of the subjective identification of position have mainly adopted categorical class differences in the analysis (e.g., Simpson et al. 1988). Following a traditional stratification scheme based on Marx's arguments regarding class, these studies analyzed questions that typically asked respondents to identify their positions using a scheme of upper, middle, lower, and working class (Davis and Robinson 1988). Some research focused on identification with the working class or not (Simpson et al. 1988). Recognizing the complexities within occupational structure, later studies turned to a multidimensional scale of identification based on authority, skill or knowledge. For instance, Baxter

 | DOI 10.1163/9789004262737_009

(1994) used six concepts to represent class structure: employers, petty bourgeoisie, expert managers, managers, experts, and workers.

The limitations with using categorical schemes to study class identity are threefold. First, by focusing on the contrast between the working class and other classes, the studies tended to use samples with paid jobs only (e.g., Simpson et al. 1988). People who are not in formal labor markets are thus excluded from the analysis. Such people include homemakers, the unemployed, adult students, and retired persons. Taken together, these groups constitute a considerable proportion of the population. The results of such an analysis thus cannot represent the class identity profile of a given society in an accurate way.

The second limitation concerns the compatibilities of schemes of categories used in different surveys. It is likely that many respondents would change the choice of categories for self-identification depending on the typologies used. The same individual identifying herself as working class in one survey might identify instead with lower class or middle class when the latter two items are also available in the questionnaire. The findings would be even more incomparable among studies that use different class schemes.

The third limitation concerns cross-national comparability. Even using the same combinations of class categories may affect the reliability of comparisons because of a lack of consensus as to the meanings of class in different societies. For instance, the choice of class categories may reflect the correct political ideology in some socialist regimes but not the real identity of respondents (Evans et al. 1992). In some societies the concept of working class is usually associated with blue-collar workers, labor unions and/or strikes in the public image. Accordingly non-manual workers may not view themselves as labor and show little interest in being organized as such—as, for instance, in Taiwan (Chang and Chang 2010).

We thus agree with Kelley and Evans (1995) and Evans and Kelley (2004) that self-identification measured on a continuous scale is more comparable than using distinct categories in a cross-national comparison. The study in this chapter therefore investigates social identity[1] by using a job-unrelated, continuous measure obtained from a collaborative survey conducted in East Asia. The survey asked respondents to identify their social status on a 1 to 10 scale. All respondents, whether they had paid jobs or not, could complete this question. Since the ranking is a continuous measure, the results of analysis will be

1 Social identity is a general term that includes both class identity and status identity. Class identity is a feeling of identification with a particular class category, while status identity is identification with a status on a continuous social ranking scale.

more comparable among societies in the region—China, Japan, South Korea (hereafter "Korea"), and Taiwan.

In the following sections, we explain the various factors that may affect variations of status identity among individuals as well as the possible differences among the four societies. We then introduce the data set used in the analyses and present our findings. In the last section we summarize our main findings and their theoretical implications for the study of status identity.

2 Literature Review

Following the arguments made by Weber cited above (Gerth and Mills 1958), we define social status in both economic and social terms. When people identify their positions in the social hierarchy, they may consider native family backgrounds, personal achievements in education or the labor market, and/or respect obtained in the community, in evaluations. Economic circumstances such as personal or household income, accumulated wealth, positions in occupational hierarchy, and/or ownership of means of production represent the material side. Better economic resources increase individuals' confidence in their power and raise the level of self-identity (Kelley and Evans 1995). In addition to economic resources, cultural capital is also seen as an important source reflecting people's social status (Bourdieu 1984). This includes educational qualifications and tastes in cultural activities, life choices, and entertainment selections. More advanced school degrees, appreciation of high-end arts, and possessing sophisticated tastes positively affect self-evaluation. A recent study on the characteristics of the middle class in China includes consumption in addition to socio-economic status in the definition (Li 2010). Lifestyle and standard of living are the main components of the consumption pattern in the empirical analyses (ibid: 140). These things are also symbolic capital for individuals.

In studies of social stratification, educational achievement is viewed as human capital that enhances occupational status and other labor market outcomes. In the following section, we discuss the cultural and economic aspects of social identity. We then explain the significance of conducting a comparison study of social identity in East Asia.

3 Economic and Cultural Capital

Most people earn their living by working in formal labor markets. While some people own the means of production, many more have to fulfill other job requirements, such as skill, expertise, and/or knowledge. Ownership of property or job characteristics determines earnings or profits, prestige, and power for individuals. For those who are not active in the labor markets, their status identity might still be influenced by the economic achievements of other members in the household, and their social or cultural resources may also play an important role. This paper treats class and occupational positions, as well as labor market outcomes such as family income, as material sources in the determination of social identity.

In social stratification research, socio-economic achievements are seen as primary results of social inequality as well as being factors that account for other stratification outcomes such as career prospects or social identity. Studies have demonstrated the strong, positive effects of education on social mobility, either across different nations or over time (e.g., Ganzeboom et al. 1991). For Bourdieu (1984), education also creates distinction among people, serving as a symbol of elite status and/or higher-class tastes.

The concept of cultural capital as developed by Bourdieu (1984) concerns the consumption of cultural activities representing individual dispositions, tastes, and/or hobbies. People with different cultural capital can be distinguished by: genres of music listened to, museums visited, sports activities, and collections of books in the household. Following the concept of homology proposed by Bourdieu (1984; Swartz 1997), Coulangeon and Lemel (2010: 85) argued that cultural consumption reflects "people's taste and aesthetic judgment." By the same logic, in addition to sharing the same tastes, a social class or status group will have similar dislikes too. Coulangeon and Lemel thus specifically state that "…in the area of music, the contrast is between the preference of the upper class for elite music—i.e. classical music, opera and, to some extent, jazz—against the preference of the working classes for popular genres, such as pop music, rock, rap and dance" (ibid). Thus, people's taste and distaste for certain music types both predict levels of social status. For instance, those who appreciate listening to classical music may naturally think highly of themselves, and those who prefer traditional or popular music may rank themselves in the lower positions of the social hierarchy.

4 Comparative Approach

4.1 *Cross-National Studies*

Several studies have adopted the comparative approach to analyze class identity. Comparing capitalist with socialist regimes, Evans et al. (1992) found respondents from Australia and Hungary all subjectively center their positions in the middle of the class structure. Using ISSP (International Social Survey Programme) data conducted between 1987 and 1988 by member countries, Kelley and Evans (1995) found a similar concentration pattern in six western countries, including Australia, using a 10-point scale. They also found income and education to have significant effects on the subjective evaluation of social positions. Objective class positions are less important than these two factors. Evans and Kelley (2004) used data of the World Inequality Study (covering data from 34 surveys conducted between 1987 and 1997, including the ISSP) to explain differences of subjective social position (a 10-point scale) among 21 countries by using a multi-level regression model. According to their findings, economic prosperity (measured by per capita GNP) positively affects social identity at the aggregate level. However, respondents from former communist countries in central or eastern Europe had a higher regard of their class positions than those in western and northern European countries, and no satisfactory explanation could be found for the country-wide difference. As to individual characteristics, Evans and Kelley (2004) found significant effects of education on class identity, especially in western, more affluent countries. Older people and men tend to rate themselves higher in class hierarchy than younger cohorts or women.

4.2 *East Asian Societies*

East Asia has become an important force in the world economy, especially after the rapid industrialization of Korea and Taiwan since the 1970s and the emerging power of China since the 1990s. All of this region has been affected by Chinese culture to some extent. However we also observe a heterogeneity of gender practices at the workplace and prominent gender wage gaps within the region (Chang and England 2011). Previous studies have demonstrated how economic and social dimensions affected subjective class identity (e.g., Evans and Kelley 2004). However no studies have systemically examined this issue in East Asia, which includes societies with cultural similarities but some political and economic diversity. We hope that studying social identification of people in East Asia will shed light on status study. In the following, we review previous studies researching class identification in specific societies and then propose our hypotheses.

China was once described as a society that had "more equality and less stratification" than any other country. This was before it initiated its market-oriented economic reform in 1978 (Whyte 1975: 684). Under the socialist planned system, all resources were controlled and distributed by the state. The state built a relatively egalitarian society via various political and economic measures, or so-called "de-stratification" mechanisms, in the 1970s (Whyte

1975; Parish 1984). Even though the society was divided into different status groups based on residential status, ownership of work units, and/or cadre or status at the workplace, income inequality was less of an issue than in most other countries in the world, including other socialist regimes. Consumption patterns and life style also appeared to be homogenous among the Chinese at that time (Whyte 1975; Bian 2002).

Market transition not only introduced more mechanisms of surplus accumulation in China, but also brought about a more stratified society. On the one hand, the economic status of most people has on average improved dramatically after marketization, as has the average education level. In China, GDP per capita increased by about 11 times, from 463 yuan in 1980 to 23,708 yuan in 2008, or from 774 yuan to 7,825 yuan, using 1990 as the base year. The illiteracy rate (among the population aged 15 and above) dropped from 22.8 percent in 1982 to 4.1 percent in 2010, while the proportion of people who received junior college and above education rose from 0.6 percent in 1982 to 8.9 percent in 2010 (National Bureau of Statistics of China 2009, 2010, 2011). On the other hand, the distribution of national wealth became more unequal, as the Gini coefficient increased from 0.31 in 1981 to 0.45 in 2003 (World Bank 2009: 33). China seems to have changed from one of the most equal societies in the world to one of the most unequal during the past 30 years of reform.

During the transition period, more and more urban Chinese tended to identify themselves with the lower class. Research shows that about 23 percent of respondents identified themselves as lower class in 2006, compared to 15 percent in 2002 (Li and Zhang 2008).[2] In one survey conducted in Wuhan of Hubei Province in 1996, the respondents were asked about the criteria they used in their class identification. The most chosen item was income, followed by power and education (Liu 2001). Statistical analysis also shows that income (or economic status) is the most important factor in determining people's class identification in China (Li and Zhang 2008; Liu 2001).

In Japan, income is also the most important factor in status identity, as in China, (Arita 2011). However, there is some debate over the effects of education and occupational status. Using the nation-wide data (Social Stratification and Social Mobility, SSM), Kikkawa (2000, 2006) showed that the effect of education on a 5-scale status identity score has become stronger, and that of occupational prestige has become weaker. His recent study (Kikkawa 2011) using a

2 Two data sets were used in their analyses. One is the Survey on Chinese Urban Residents' Attitude toward Social Conflicts conducted in 2002. The other one is the Chinese General Social Survey in 2006. Both surveys were conducted using nation-wide representative sampling under the supervision of the Institute of Sociology, China Academy of Social Science.

10-level status identity scale showed that income and education are the two most important factors on status identity. However, Arita (2011), using the same data as used in Kikkawa (2011), showed that the effect of education for Japanese men is not so strong compared to Taiwanese and Korean men. In addition, Kobayashi (2011), using a 5-level scale, showed that the impacts of occupational prestige and employment status on status identity were significant. The findings in Arita (2011) and Kobayashi (2011) are limited to the respondents who had paid-work at the time of survey. Yamato (2008) showed that being a housewife does not have a significant effect on status identity, after controlling for household income and other factors.[3]

Regarding the impact of cultural capital in Japan, cultural activities also have significant effects on status identity. Kabayashi and Hoshi (2011) examined the relationships between a 5-level point scale of status identity and cultural activities (such as going to classic music concerts, going to museums, joining karaoke clubs, attending sports activities, and reading books) based on the SSM data in 1995 and 2005. They found that joining karaoke clubs, attending sports activities, and reading books had significant effects on status identity.

Arita (2011) used SSM survey data gathered in 2005 to examine the impacts of job- and organization-related variables and individual characteristics on status identity, using a continuous measure. He found that Japanese have on average a higher score of self-identity than Koreans and Taiwanese. Occupational structure is important in explaining variations of status identity in Taiwan but not in the other two societies. However, the sample used in his analysis excludes people not in any paid jobs, and the results provide an incomplete picture of stratification pattern in East Asia. In particular, it excludes many women from the analysis. China is also not included.

Koreans in general show patterns similar to those in other East Asian societies regarding determinants of class identity. Using data from a nation-wide representative sampling survey in 1990 (National Survey of Equity and Social Inequality), Yoon and Seok (1996) found that education has the strongest effect, followed by household income, on self-identity among all variables. They used a 7-point scale in their analysis. A recent study confirmed some other findings in their paper focusing on education and material resources (Arita 2011).

3 Yamato (2008) further divided not-working housewives withdrawing from labor markets and others still looking for paid-jobs. She found that the former have significantly higher status identity than the latter.

Class identity can be affected by external political and economic changes too. Korea is a case in point. According to Hong (2003: 47), around 60 percent of respondents identified themselves as middle class in the early 1990s. However, mainly due to the impacts of the financial crisis in 1997, the proportion declined to 55 percent in 1999. Using a different data set, Han (2009) reported similar findings. He found that people who identified with the middle class (the *joongsan* stratum) comprised 54 percent in 1987, and 64 percent in 1995, but dramatically declined to 35 percent in 1997. Since the financial crisis, the collapse of the middle class has become an overriding theme in journalism, and political party and academic discourse in Korea.[4]

The findings regarding Taiwan do not differ greatly from the other three societies in the region. Asking respondents to choose elements characterizing class identity from their point of view, Wu (1996) found that the most chosen items were income and ownership of property, followed by occupation. Tsai (1998) and Marsh (2002) examine class identification of Taiwanese using a different scheme of class, both using the Taiwan Social Change Survey data. Using a continuous measure ranging from 1 to 10, Tsai (1998) showed that class identification is better represented by respondents' objective class position than by perceived social status in the early 1990s in Taiwan. She found that education, socio-economic status, and income had consistent effects on class identification. The findings reported in Marsh (2002) are generally consistent with Tsai's work. Although his measure of class identification consists of 6 distinct categories—upper, upper middle, middle, lower middle, working and lower class—he treated these categories as a continuous variable in his analyses.

Taking due cognizance of the literature reviewed above, we here present our hypotheses for this paper.

Regarding the differences among societies, we expect that economic resources measured at the individual level will have positive effects on the mean value of social identity among societies, based on Evans and Kelley (2004). Since Japan has the highest per capita income among the four, followed by Taiwan, Korea, and China,[5] we hypothesize that:

> Social identity is higher in Japan than in Taiwan, Korea, or China.

4 For an overview of the effect of the financial crisis on the Korean middle class, see Koo (2007).

5 The per capita gross domestic product (GDP; based on purchasing power) was $32,680 (USD) for Japan, $31,834 for Taiwan, $27,978 for Korea, and $6,567 for China in 2009 (International Monetary Fund 2010). See Chapter 1 for an overview of cross-national differences of social stratification in those societies.

The main contending hypotheses of this paper concern the competing impacts of economic and cultural capital on individual status identity. Explanations that stress the material side represent an orientation toward extrinsic values. Higher income means a higher ability to purchase favorite goods and services, while owning property or being in a higher class position means enjoying higher authority and prestige. The emphasis on cultural capital symbolizes intrinsic values. Good taste in cultural activities represents an aesthetic disposition and the ability to appreciate artistic products. The accumulation of cultural capital will not appear in a bank account or span of control at the workplace but rather in personal intrinsic values. Even though material capital and cultural capital are related to each other, this paper intends to examine and compare the independent explanatory power of these two types of capital.

Following the previous reviews of findings in various societies, we hypothesize that:

1. *Higher income, higher education, and higher ranking in the occupational structure will have positive effects on self-identity.*

However, following the arguments made by Bourdieu (1984; Swartz 1997) and other researchers (Chan 2010), we expect cultural capital to have significant effects too. We therefore hypothesize that:

2. *Individuals with high-end cultural taste, foreign language skill, and global experiences will have higher self-identity than other respondents.*[6]

In contrast to previous studies, we also expect that knowing someone in upper non-manual positions, an indication of resourceful social capital, may raise self-esteem in the social hierarchy. Knowing someone in a high-ranking position may signal the importance of respondents themselves, even when they are not in the same profession. Thus:

3. *An individual knowing people of diverse higher white-collar occupations is expected to have higher self-identity in social hierarchy than others who do not know any people in those positions.*

---

6 We also include several background and other attitudes variables in the analyses. Since their impacts on social identity are not the focus in this paper, we do not speculate on the directions of these variables. We still report the results of these variables in the relevant Tables.

We expect the effect to sustain even after controlling for respondent's own class. Nevertheless, the focus of this paper is to compare the differences of impacts between material capital and cultural capital in predicting social identity of respondents. Social capital is mainly used as a controlling factor in the analysis.

5 Data and Variables

5.1 *Data*

This paper uses the data of the East Asian Social Survey (EASS), conducted in four societies, China, Japan, Korea, and Taiwan, in 2008.[7] A nation-wide stratified random sampling survey was conducted every two years in these four societies respectively in the same year. All the national surveys used national representative sampling and the same questionnaire. The face-to-face interview was adopted in all societies except Japan, where some of the answers were self-written by respondents. The original sample size was 3,010 persons in China, 2,160 in Japan, 1,508 in Korea, and 2,067 in Taiwan.

5.2 *Variables*

The dependent variable—social identity—is measured based on the following question:

> In our society, people have either a high or low status. If "1" represents the lowest status and "10" the highest, how would you grade your social status?

This variable is used as a continuous variable in the multiple regression analysis.

This study aims to compare the explanatory power of material and cultural capital in predicting the social identity of respondents. The material capital consists of two elements in our analysis: class positions and income. The class structure consists of employers (hiring employees), petty bourgeoisie (without employees), the employed, and those without jobs. Wage-workers are further classified as higher non-manual, lower non-manual, skilled manual, and

7 EASS is a collaborative questionnaire survey project among four research teams in the region: CGSS (Chinese General Social Survey), JGSS (Japanese General Social Surveys), KGSS (Korean General Social Survey), and TSCS (Taiwan Social Change Survey), starting from 2005. For information about EASS, please refer to its official website: http://www.eassda.org.

unskilled manual according to respondents' occupational categories. However, holding a job is not the only source of social identity. Many respondents were full-time homemakers, devoted to "reproduction labor." Others were temporarily out of jobs, retired, or unable to work due to various reasons. Together these people are treated as a separate group in the analysis.

The measures for materialism also include income. As wage income is not the only source of income for many people, and those who are not in labor markets do not receive a wage or salary, we use monthly household income in the analysis. The China and Korea surveys directly asked respondents about the amount of household income, while the Japan and Taiwan questionnaires listed a series of income intervals for respondents to choose from. For the latter two cases, we take the midpoint of each category to create a continuous measure of income. For the highest income category, which has no upper limit, we add 30 percent of the lower limit to make the midpoint for this category. In the analysis the natural log of income is used to make the cross-cultural comparisons.

Education is the indicator for the social dimension of status identity. To make the educational institutions comparable, EASS adopts a 7-level scale. The seven levels are: no formal qualification, elementary school, junior high school, senior high school, junior college, university, and a more advanced degree. We combine the last two as one category—university or above. There were no respondents who did not receive any formal qualification in Japan. We thus used those with only elementary school education as the reference group. The coefficients for the group "no formal qualification" applies to China, Korea, and Taiwan only. Another indicator of educational capital is the self-assessment of fluency in using English to communicate with foreigners. The scale ranges from very good (5 points) to very poor (1 point). This is used as a continuous variable too.

Several variables are used to represent the cultural capital of respondents. They include the extent to which the respondents like different genres of music, including western classical music, rock, jazz, blues, popular, or traditional music. For each type, the scale ranges from 6 (Like it very much) to 1 (Never listen to it). All these variables are used as continuous measures in the analysis. We also include overseas travelling experiences as another measure of cultural capital. If respondents had visited at least one foreign place, the coding is 1. If they had visited all the places listed in the questionnaire other than their own countries, the coding is 2. The places listed in the questionnaire include China, Japan, Korea, Taiwan, southeastern Asia, Europe, and North America. Those who had never gone abroad are coded as 0.

In the EASS survey the respondents were asked to check the occupations of families, relatives, or acquaintances they had frequent contact with. These occupations were listed in the questionnaire and the respondents answered Yes or No for each of them. Among the occupations on the list, professionals, managers, legislators, and senior officials belong to the category of upper non-manual. We hypothesized that knowing more professional people would increase one's own self esteem. If the respondent checks Yes for at least one of these four categories, the case is coded as 1. If he or she knows all these categories, the case is coded as 2. The answer would be coded as 0 if the respondent's families or acquaintances are not in any of these categories.

Age, gender, and marital status are socio-demographic variables, which are included as controlling factors in the analysis. Family background variables include parents' education measured in years of schooling. The self-assessed type of residence type is used to control the residential effect. The residence is ranked according to the degree of urbanization: a single farm or home in the country (1 point), a village (2), a town or small city (3), the suburbs or outskirts of a big city (4), or a big city (5). This is used as a continuous variable.

We also include an attitude variable to control respondents' general feelings at the time of being surveyed: feeling of happiness. One study had shown the positive correlation between higher class positions and stronger life satisfaction (Wang and Davis 2010: 168). The question of happiness is addressed as: *How happy or unhappy would you say you are, on the whole?* We regroup the five categories into three: (1) those answering "Very happy" and "Fairly happy" (3 points), (2) answering neither happy nor unhappy (2 points), and (3) answering "Not too happy" and "Not happy at all" (1 point).

6 Findings

Figure 8.1 shows graphs of the distribution of social identity by country.[8] Judging from the means and medians, the results partly support the findings in Evans et al. (1992) and Kelley and Evans (1995). People of East Asia also tend to position themselves in the middle levels of social hierarchy, in the same way as in other countries. Evans and Kelley (2004) reported a positive relationship

8 About 2.5 percent of Taiwanese respondents did not answer this question. The comparable figures for Japan and Korea are 0.8 percent and 0.3 percent respectively. Every respondent answered this question in China. Together these percentages are lower than the figure (4 percent on average) found in Evans and Kelley (2004: 11). However, this does not mean that Taiwanese avoid all attitude questions. Respondents in the other three surveys had high proportions of missing cases in different questions.

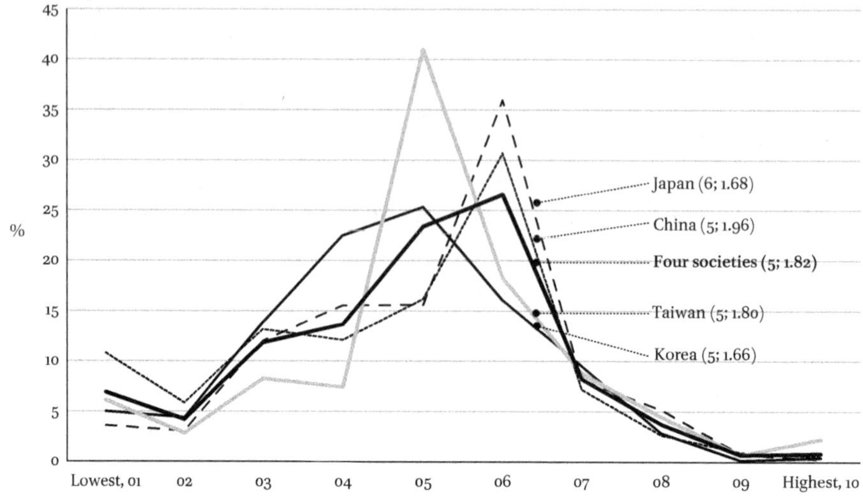

FIGURE 8.1 *Distribution of status identity in respective East Asian society*
SOURCE: 2008 EAST ASIAN SOCIAL SURVEY. NOTE: NUMBERS IN PARENTHESES ARE MEANS AND STANDARD DEVIATIONS OF STATUS IDENTITY

between economic wealth and social identity. Our findings seem to confirm the association in East Asia too. Figure 8.1 shows Japanese people to have higher self-identity than other, less wealthy societies, which is also similar to the ranking pattern found in Arita (2011). However, per-capita income is several times higher in Korea and Taiwan than in China (see above). The latter three societies have the same mean value, but Chinese had more variations. We compare the results among the four societies in detail below.

Koreans show more peaks in their attitudes than the other three societies. The distribution of identification scatters mostly from level 7 to 3 in Korea. However, they also seem to be the most humble, as the majority chose levels 5 or 4. Overall, more than 70 percent of Korean respondents identify themselves in levels below 6. In contrast, Taiwanese respondents have the least variation in their identity among the four societies, since their answers concentrate in one single level, with more than 40 percent of them choosing level 5. Close to 60 percent of Chinese respondents identify themselves with lower positions (below level 6). The pattern of frequency distribution is similar between Chinese and Japanese, except that the latter consistently have higher percentages of respondents identifying with level 6 and above. The degree of economic advancement may explain the difference. Even though the proportion of Chinese respondents identifying with level 6 is higher than that of Korea and Taiwan, the figures are higher in lower levels in China too. Since the shape may reflect subjective evaluation of social inequality, Chinese seem to be more polarized than other three societies. We use a regression model to make the within-regional comparison more precise and to detect the effects of material and cultural variables on social identity. The results are discussed in Table 8.2.

Table 8.1 lists descriptive statistics of independent variables used in the regression model. We will briefly report some of the results. Nearly 84 percent of respondents are married or cohabitating in China, which is higher than the percentages for Japan (71 percent), Korea (66 percent), or Taiwan (62 percent). Educational differences also appear among the four societies. About 84 percent of Japanese respondents have obtained at least a high school degree, which is higher than Korea (76 percent), Taiwan (63 percent), and China

TABLE 8.1 *Descriptive statistics of respondents' characteristics*

Respondents' characteristics	**Chinese**	**Japanese**	**Koreans**	**Taiwanese**	**χ^2-value**
Gender	(3,010)	(2,160)	(1,508)	(2,067)	6.9^{+}
Male	48	46	46	50	
Female	52	54	54	50	
Age (mean; S.D.)	43 (14)	52 (17)	45 (16)	45 (17)	–
Marital status	(3,009)	(2,160)	(1,506)	(2,067)	415.3^{***}
Single	11	16	22	28	
Married or cohabiting	84	71	66	62	
Divorced, separated or widowed	5	13	13	10	
Father's schooling years (mean; S.D.)	5 (4)	11 (3)	8 (5)	7 (5)	–
Mother's schooling years (mean; S.D.)	3 (4)	10 (3)	7 (5)	5 (5)	–
Self-assessed community scale[#]	(2,990)	(2,155)	(1,504)	(2,062)	$1.7E+3^{***}$
Farm in the country (=1)	0	5	1	0.4	
Country/village (=2)	35	32	13	20	
Town or small city (=3)	47	44	31	27	
Suburbs of big city (=4)	2	15	25	25	
Big city (=5)	16	5	30	28	
Education level	(3,005)	(2,139)	(1,503)	(2,067)	$1.6E+3^{***}$
No formal qualification	9	0	6	8	
Elementary school	24	2	10	15	
Junior high school	29	15	8	13	
Senior high school	23	48	40	30	
Junior college	9	13	9	13	
University or higher	6	23	27	20	

TABLE 8.1 *Descriptive statistics of respondents' characteristics* (cont.)

Respondents' characteristics	Chinese	Japanese	Koreans	Taiwanese	χ^2-value
Like classical music#	(3,005)	(2,137)	(1,500)	(1,969)	1.9E+3***
Never listened (=1)	0	0	9	0	
Dislike very much (=2)	11	2	8	3	
Dislike (=3)	39	10	12	25	
Neutral (=4)	29	47	42	29	
Like (=5)	18	35	24	38	
Like very much (=6)	2	6	6	5	
Like rock music#	(3,008)	(2,132)	(1,501)	(1,976)	1.3E+3***
Never listened	0	0	9	0	
Dislike very much	12	5	13	5	
Dislike	40	21	23	37	
Neutral	27	50	32	32	
Like	18	20	18	24	
Like very much	2	5	4	2	
Like jazz and blues#	(3,007)	(2,127)	(1,501)	(1,950)	1.7E+3***
Never listened	0	0	9	0	
Dislike very much	12	3	7	3	
Dislike	42	13	16	28	
Neutral	34	53	38	35	
Like	10	27	26	31	
Like very much	2	4	4	4	
Like popular music#	(3,007)	(2,132)	(1,503)	(2,034)	1.0E+3***
Never listened	0	0	2	0	
Dislike very much	5	2	1	1	
Dislike	18	6	2	9	
Neutral	22	34	14	18	
Like	45	48	55	60	
Like very much	10	10	25	12	
Like traditional music#	(3,007)	(2,152)	(1,504)	(2,042)	441.1***
Never listened	0	0	2	0	
Dislike very much	3	4	2	3	
Dislike	21	14	9	23	
Neutral	26	40	37	31	
Like	39	32	37	38	
Like very much	12	11	14	5	

Respondents' characteristics	Chinese	Japanese	Koreans	Taiwanese	χ^2-value
Fluency in chatting with English speakers[#]	(3,010)	(2,151)	(1,506)	(2,065)	604.5***
Very poor (=1)	71	68	44	48	
Poor (=2)	21	20	38	28	
Fair (=3)	6	10	14	16	
Good (=4)	1	1	3	6	
Very good (=5)	1	0.2	1	1	
Has the respondent ever been to China, Japan, Korea, Taiwan, Southeast Asia, Europe or North America for tourism?[†]	(3,010)	(2,148)	(1,505)	(2,067)	2.4E+3***
Has never been to these places	97	50	52	36	
Has been to at least one place	3	48	47	61	
Has been to all these places	0.1	1	1	3	
Class structure	(2,957)	(2,151)	(1,507)	(2,066)	943.7***
Jobless, house-wives or -husbands, or students, etc.	35	37	41	35	
Wage employee: higher non-manual	8	6	4	9	
Wage employee: lower non-manual	12	26	24	22	
Wage employee: skilled manual	4	5	5	5	
Wage employee: unskilled manual	6	12	9	9	
Petty bourgeoisie	34	8	13	13	
Employer	2	6	4	7	
Monthly household income (mean)[††]	374	5,335	2,882	2,495	–
Any respondent's family members or acquaintances professional, manager, or legislator/senior official?	(3,010)	(2,108)	(1,505)	(2,045)	75.3***
None	40	37	45	32	
At least one of these categories	48	51	45	52	
All categories	12	12	10	16	
Degree of general happiness[#]	(3,010)	(2,151)	(1,484)	(2,062)	714.2***
Unhappy (=1)	12	8	26	10	
Neither happy nor unhappy (=2)	24	32	0	24	
Happy (=3)	64	60	74	65	

Unit: % (persons).

$^+p < 0.1$; $^*p < 0.05$; $^{**}p < 0.01$; $^{***}p < 0.001$.

[#]Being treated as continuous variables in the regression.

[†]Excluding respondents' own country.

[††]Been converted to US dollars at the exchange rate of the end of 2008.

SOURCE: SEE FIGURE 8.1

(38 percent). Compulsory education in Japan started much earlier than in the other three societies. Since 1947, Japanese children aged from six to 15 have to receive mandatory education for nine years. Today, approximately 98 percent of junior high school graduates choose to go to high school after graduation (Ministry of Education, Culture, Sports, Science and Technology [Japan] 2011). In contrast, the nine-year compulsory education was not implemented until 1959 in Korea, 1968 in Taiwan, and 1986 in China.

As to distributions of employment status/class, more than 35 percent of respondents do not have paid jobs in all four societies during the survey period. The percentage is the highest in Korea, about 41 percent. In China, where the economy has been booming since the 1980s, many people have started up their own business, taking the opportunity to make their fortunes. About 34 percent of respondents belong to the class of the petty bourgeoisie in China, which is much higher than Japan (8 percent), Korea (13 percent), or Taiwan (13 percent). One possible explanation for China's high percentage might be due to the large proportion of peasants (in 1978, each peasant was assigned a small piece of land, which they were not allowed to sell on the market). As Japan, Korea and Taiwan entered the post-industrial stage, the service sector employed the highest percentages of workers. While about 22 to 26 percent of respondents work in the lower non-manual group in Japan, Korea, and Taiwan, the comparable figure is only 12 percent for China, according to our sample.

Popular and traditional music seem to be the most preferred music genres in all four societies. As to country-wide differences, Japanese respondents seem to be the most accepting of all genres of music of the four societies; Chinese seem to only like pop or traditional music. Taiwanese respondents, on the other hand, appear to have polarized views about Western-style music. About 28 percent dislike classical music or dislike it very much, while 43 percent like it or like it very much. The comparable percentages for rock music are 42 percent versus 26 percent and 33 percent versus 35 percent for jazz and blues. As to travelling experience, Taiwanese are the most frequent travelers of the four societies; Chinese are the least likely to travel abroad. Geographically Taiwan is the smallest country of the four, and it is likely that many Taiwanese go abroad once in a while out of the desire to "get out" and enjoy larger spaces.

As the chief aim of this paper is to compare the effects of different types of capital, in Figure 8.2 we list the increase of adjusted R-square after adding every new block of variables in the regression models. Model 1 shows the results of including nation dummies only. It explains about 1.6 percent of the total variance of social identity in East Asian societies. Individual and family backgrounds add about 5.4 percent of explanatory power (Model 2). The variable of educational achievements alone explains the close to 3 percent more

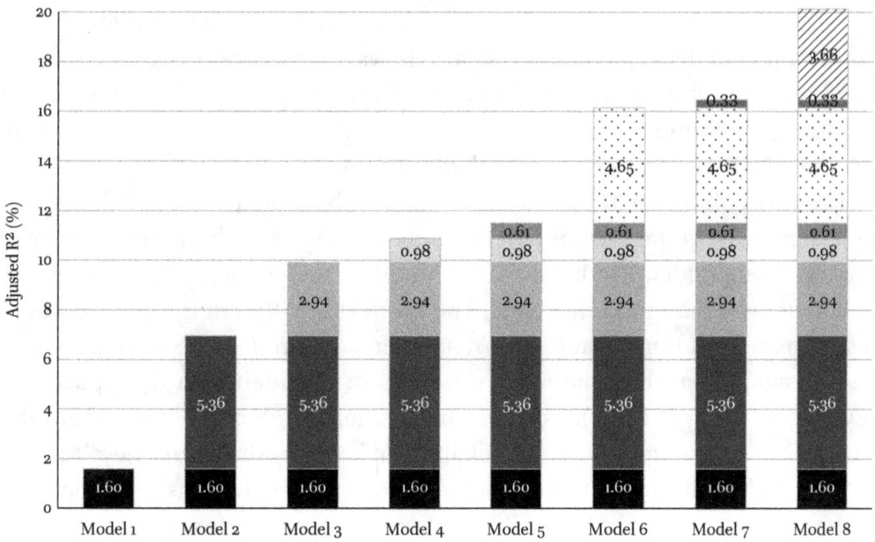

FIGURE 8.2 *Increase of explanatory power from regressions of status identity on different blocks of variables*

Model 1: Society.

Model 2: Model 1 + background characteristics (including male, age, age^2, marital status, parents' schooling years, and community scale).

Model 3: Model 2 + education level.

Model 4: Model 3 + cultural capital (including liking different genres of music, fluency in chatting with English speakers, and experience of travelling abroad).

Model 5: Model 4 + class structure.

Model 6: Model 5 + household income.

Model 7: Model 6 + social capital.

Model 8: Model 7 + general happiness.

SOURCE: SEE FIGURE 8.1

variance in the analysis (Model 3). The impact of cultural capital explains little of the variation of social identity, as it adds only 1 percent of explanatory power in Model 4. Objective class positions have even less explanatory power than cultural capital (about 0.6 percent), as shown in Model 5 of Figure 8.2. In contrast, adding household income significantly increases the value of the adjusted R-square to about 4.6 percent (Model 6). Combining the effects of class positions and income together, material capital explains 5.2 percent of the variations in the model, equivalent to the extent of background variables. Social capital contributes little (0.3 percent) to explaining the variations of social identity as shown in Model 7. Surprisingly, respondents' subjective attitudes, namely the evaluation of happiness, add 3.7 percent more to the explanatory model. In total, as Model 8 shows, our analytical model explains roughly 20 percent of variation of social identity among people in East Asia.

To summarize the results of Figure 8.2, the blocks of variables that contribute the most to the explanations are as follows, from largest first: personal and family backgrounds, economic capital, and self evaluation of happiness. The results of regression analysis for Model 8 as well as the results for each society are listed in Table 8.2, which we shall discuss next.

The first column of Table 8.2 shows the results of analyzing the data of all four societies together. Let us first examine the results of dummies of the four societies. Respondents in Japan, Korea, and Taiwan have a significantly higher social identity than those in China. The results are different from those which researchers found in former eastern and central European countries about a decade ago, where respondents showed more confidence in their positions (Evans and Kelley 2004: 17). As mentioned earlier, the ideology of an egalitarian society in China might mean that claiming a lower position for oneself might be both politically correct and a sign of modesty. The findings are consistent with the results found in Li and Zhang (2008) in a recent survey.

In Figure 8.2 we show that background variables as a whole explain a relatively large proportion of variations of social identity in the regression. According to Table 8.2, gender, marital status, and father's education are shown as specifically the most important factors. Women have higher identity of social positions society than men.[9] This differs from the findings in Evans and Kelley (2004). We suspect that as women achieved higher education, and found more job opportunities and economic independence, their self-identity in class structure also increased. In Evans and Kelley (2004), the data were collected during the late 1980s and before the late 1990s, when women's status worldwide was not as high as at present. Married or cohabitating women possess higher social identity than those who are single or those with other marital status: being in a marriage or a relationship seems to increase one's confidence and self regard of social status. Father's educational qualifications also have positive effects on increasing respondents' self-assessment.

As noted when discussing Figure 8.2, education is an important determinant of social identity in the EASS survey. Respondents obtaining education equal to or higher than senior high school level have a significantly higher social identity than those with lower education.[10] The coefficients for these

9 Gender differences in self-identity are an important issue in social stratification studies (e.g., Baxter 1994). Analyses on gender differences and self-identity have focused on marital status and information concerning both respondent's and the spouse's socio-economic characteristics. The models were different from the ones we use in this study.

10 No respondents in Japan were without any formal education. We thus use the level of elementary school as the reference group. The coefficient for the group "no formal qualification" applies to Chinese, Koreans, and Taiwanese only.

TABLE 8.2 *Multiple linear regression of status identity in East Asia*

Independent variables	Regression coefficients (S.E.)				
	Four societies	China	Japan	Korea	Taiwan
Society (China = 0)					
Japan	3.27 (0.22)***				
Korea	1.46 (0.13)***				
Taiwan	3.23 (0.21)***				
Individual Socio-Economic Variables					
Male (=1)	−0.11 (0.04)**	−0.15 (0.07)*	−0.10 (0.10)	0.03 (0.08)	−0.15 (0.08)+
Age	−0.01 (0.01)	−0.05 (0.02)**	0.4E−2 (0.02)	−0.04 (0.02)*	0.03 (0.02)
Age^2	0.2E−3 (0.00)*	0.6E−3 (0.00)**	0.8E−4 (0.00)	0.5E−3 (0.00)**	−0.2E−3 (0.00)
Married or cohabiting (=1)	0.16 (0.06)**	0.21 (0.11)+	0.09 (0.12)	0.13 (0.11)	0.07 (0.10)
Father's schooling years	0.01 (0.01)*	0.01 (0.01)	0.02 (0.02)	0.02 (0.01)	0.01 (0.01)
Mother's schooling years	0.3E−2 (0.01)	0.01 (0.01)	0.01 (0.03)	0.01 (0.01)	−0.01 (0.01)
Self-assessed community scale	0.02 (0.02)	0.02 (0.04)	0.02 (0.05)	0.02 (0.04)	0.06 (0.04)
Educational Capital					
Education level (elementary school = 0)					
No formal qualification	−0.07 (0.10)	−0.13 (0.14)	(dropped)†	0.08 (0.23)	0.01 (0.22)
Junior high school	−0.2E−3 (0.07)	0.06 (0.10)	−0.24 (0.53)	−0.16 (0.20)	0.16 (0.16)
Senior high school	0.21 (0.08)**	0.26 (0.12)*	0.29 (0.52)	0.08 (0.17)	0.44 (0.16)**
Junior college	0.25 (0.10)**	0.30 (0.17)+	0.29 (0.54)	0.04 (0.21)	0.55 (0.18)**
University or higher	0.33 (0.10)**	0.33 (0.20)+	0.37 (0.54)	0.35 (0.19)+	0.39 (0.19)*

TABLE 8.2 *Multiple linear regression of status identity in East Asia* (cont.)

Independent variables	Regression coefficients (S.E.)				
	Four societies	China	Japan	Korea	Taiwan
Cultural Capital					
Like classical music	0.05 (0.02)$^{+}$	0.06 (0.05)	−0.07 (0.07)	0.09 (0.04)*	0.02 (0.05)
Like rock music	0.04 (0.03)$^{+}$	0.08 (0.05)	−0.02 (0.06)	−0.01 (0.04)	0.05 (0.05)
Like jazz and blues	−0.03 (0.03)	−0.02 (0.06)	−0.2E−2 (0.07)	−0.04 (0.04)	−0.03 (0.05)
Like popular music	0.01 (0.02)	−0.06 (0.04)	0.04 (0.07)	0.03 (0.04)	0.13 (0.05)*
Like traditional music	0.04 (0.02)$^{+}$	0.05 (0.04)	0.08 (0.06)	0.02 (0.04)	0.01 (0.04)
Fluency in chatting with English speakers	0.11 (0.03)***	0.12 (0.06)*	0.16 (0.07)*	0.14 (0.06)*	0.09 (0.05)*
Has ever been to China, Japan, Korea, Taiwan, Southeast Asia, Europe or North America for tourism (excluding respondents' own country) (=1)	0.08 (0.05)	−0.37 (0.21)$^{+}$	0.04 (0.10)	0.12 (0.09)	0.07 (0.09)
Economic Capital					
Class structure (jobless, house-wives or -husbands, or students, etc. = 0)					
Wage employee: higher non-manual	0.20 (0.09)*	0.14 (0.15)	0.12 (0.21)	0.10 (0.20)	0.39 (0.16)*
Wage employee: lower non-manual	−0.03 (0.06)	−0.10 (0.12)	−0.09 (0.13)	−0.15 (0.11)	0.11 (0.12)
Wage employee: skilled manual	−0.14 (0.10)	0.04 (0.19)	−0.27 (0.23)	−0.71 (0.21)**	0.05 (0.20)
Wage employee: unskilled manual	−0.18 (0.08)*	−0.13 (0.15)	−0.24 (0.18)	−0.47 (0.16)**	−0.07 (0.16)
Petty bourgeoisie	0.19 (0.06)**	0.27 (0.10)**	−0.34 (0.18)$^{+}$	−0.06 (0.13)	0.24 (0.14)$^{+}$

Employer	0.27 (0.11)*	0.57 (0.28)*	0.22 (0.21)	−0.12 (0.21)	0.16 (0.17)
Household income (natural log)	0.37 (0.02)***	0.28 (0.04)***	0.68 (0.08)***	0.60 (0.05)***	0.26 (0.06)***
Social Capital and Quality of Life					
Any respondent's family members or acquaintances professional, manager, or legislator/senior official? (None = 0)					
At least one of these categories	0.17 (0.05)***	0.23 (0.08)**	−0.09 (0.11)	0.10 (0.09)	0.30 (0.10)**
All categories	0.31 (0.07)***	0.37 (0.12)**	0.10 (0.15)	0.14 (0.14)	0.54 (0.13)***
Degree of general happiness	0.51 (0.03)***	0.74 (0.05)***	0.45 (0.07)***	0.27 (0.05)***	0.41 (0.06)***
Constant	−1.28 (0.33)***	−0.27 (0.57)	1.63 (0.86)*	0.14 (0.57)	0.93 (0.55)+
Sample size	6,877	2,768	1,142	1,271	1,696
Adjusted R^2 (%)	20.13	18.05	19.17	32.80	14.23

+$p < 0.1$; * $p < 0.05$; ** $p < 0.01$; *** $p < 0.001$.
†The Japanese respondents all have formal educational qualification.
Note: The measure of status identity ranges from 1 (lowest) to 10 (highest).
SOURCE: SEE TABLE 8.1

different educational categories also show a linear relation between educational degrees and self-identity: the higher the levels of education, the larger the coefficients or the more positive subjective evaluation of social positions. Language capital is another important factor in the model. Fluency in English conversation helps to increase respondents' social identity.

The impacts of cultural capital are, however, limited. Though respondents who are fond of classical music, rock, or traditional music show a significantly higher self-identity, the significance level is not too strong, according to the statistical testing. Travel experiences do not help increase one's self-identity.

For economic capital, we include both class structure and family income in the analysis. There are three categories to represent class in our model. One category includes those people with ownership of means of production: employers and petty bourgeoisie. The second category consists of those not holding any paid jobs at the time of survey. The third category consists of those who are employed. The employed are further classified into four categories based on occupational characteristics. Using those not in the job markets as the reference group, we find that owning means of production or being in upper non-manual positions significantly raises the level of social identity. In contrast, unskilled manual workers have a lower social identity than those without paid jobs. In sum, the ownership of means of production still has a strong influence on how people evaluate their social status in East Asia, even after controlling for education and income (see below).[11]

Table 8.2 shows that the higher the family income of the respondents, the stronger the positive identity of their positions in the society. Although status identity seems to be more a social than an economic concept, we find that materialism, especially the absolute amount of income in the household, stands as an important factor in determining social identity.

Further, we find that knowing people in upper non-manual positions significantly increases the subjective evaluation of social positions. Having kin or acquaintances in the privileged class produces a direct effect on people's self-esteem in East Asia. The other attitude variable we included to control the effects of emotional reactions during the survey was happiness. The feeling of happiness has significant effects on status identity. The happier the respondents are, the more likely they are to have higher social identity than those expressing less happiness. This shows that identity in the social hierarchy has

11 EASS includes variables distinguishing between full-time and part-time jobs, regular and non-regular, and public and private sectors. We included these variables in the analyses but found them to be insignificant. The results are not reported here.

an emotional side, and is not decided by objective achievements or conditions only.

Table 8.2 lists the results of analysis of social identity in the respective societies. The impact of individual background on social identity is considerable in China. Chinese women's self-assessment is higher than men's, young people's is higher than older people's, and married or cohabiting people's is higher than that of people who are single. We speculate that the advancement of women's socio-economic status and aggregate economic development in recent decades may explain why gender and age show such differences in subjective self-identity.

In China, both education and economic capital are important determinants of raising social identity. People with senior high school or more advanced levels of education have a significantly higher social identity than those with elementary school education. According to the coefficients, the higher the levels of education, the higher the self-assessment. English fluency also significantly raises self-assessment in China. Capitalists and the rich tend to have higher status identity. The impact of cultural capital is rather limited in China. Similar to what the general model shows, kinship and social networks and degree of general happiness significantly improve people's social identity.

The results for Japan show a different story from those for China. None of the family background variables have significant effects in Japan. Education, cultural capital, class structure, and kinship and social network do not show any impact either. That small business owners have a lower social identity may be related to their inability to compete with large capitalists or in unstable financial conditions. The similarities between the two societies are rather limited. Command of English has a positive effect on status identity in Japan, as we find in China. As Matsushige (2001) suggested, Japanese people who have a command of English have a better chance of finding jobs and also of getting promoted in this era of globalization. And the degree of general happiness improves status identity in Japan too.

In Korea, we also find age to have a significantly negative effect on status identity, as we find in China. We believe that the negative effect of age on status identity in Korea needs to be considered in the context of the financial crisis, which resulted in many elderly people losing their public pension and the family support necessary to survive in precarious jobs, and living in poverty. On the other hand, the effect of education is limited in Korea, as it is in Japan. Educational differences occur only at the university level. Respondents with other levels of education do not show significantly higher self-identity than those with only elementary school background. Economic capital, measured by household income, has a strong effect on social identity in Korea too. It is also noteworthy that the effect of objective class position is the strongest in Korea among the four societies. The biggest input is due to the negative effects of belonging to the manual class. Both skilled and unskilled manual workers tend to evaluate their class status lower than those not in formal labor markets in Korea. Since income was controlled in the model, the interpretations of the class differences may lie in the relative deprivation of the working class in Korea. Cultural capital as a whole shows a significant effect in Korea, but only for the genre of classical music. In this country, listening to classical music has a positive effect on an individual's social identity.

The findings on Taiwan show some differences and similarities to those of the other three societies. Individual and family background factors play a less important role in Taiwan than in Korea or China. Gender shows significant effects, as in China. Women have higher self-identity than men in these two Chinese societies. Another similarity occurs in the factor of education. Both Taiwanese and Chinese respondents with senior high school level or higher educational degrees put themselves in higher positions in the social stratification system than those with primary school education only.

The positive impact of cultural capital for listening to popular music exists only in Taiwan, something that distinguishes it from the other three societies. Respondents who hold upper non-manual jobs or who are self-employed in Taiwan have a higher social identity than those of the contrasting groups. In a similar way to the findings for China, having acquaintances in professional jobs also raises people's self-identity. The model explains the most variations in Korea (adjusted R-square close to 33 percent), followed by Japan (19 percent), China (18 percent), and Taiwan (14 percent).[12]

7 Discussion

If we compare our study to previous studies, it shows a similar pattern of middle-class identification to theirs. Respondents in Australia (Evans and Kelley 2004), Europe (Kelley and Evans 1995), and the United States (Evans et al. 1992) tend to identify themselves in the middle or just below the middle positions in the social hierarchy. Our findings demonstrate that the majority of respondents choose class levels of 6 in China and Japan, 5 in Taiwan, and 5 or 4 in Korea. These results represent a general middle class identification by respondents in the region. Here we seem to find a convergence between the East and

12 High-end cultural capital was also affected by education, income and occupation in Japan (Kikkawa 2011). This suggested that economic status (measured by income and occupation in this study) absorbed the effect of cultural capital on status identity in Japan.

West since our results are consistent with what the above researchers found in other regions. However, our work includes measures of cultural capital, social and kinship network, and detailed occupational positions. Thus, in addition to presenting particularities of East Asian societies, our findings provide more rigorous testing of the effects of material capital on social identity.

Several findings in our paper differ from those found in Evans and Kelley (2004). First and foremost, Evans and Kelley concluded that East Europeans viewed themselves higher in the social hierarchy than respondents in other countries. They did not find a good explanation for the results. According to the regression analysis provided in this paper, Chinese show a lower status identity than the other three East Asian societies. Statistically speaking, the distribution of subjective social identity is rather diverse, and many respondents chose the bottom levels in China (Figure 8.1). This paper does not control for other stratification dimensions, such as political power, in the analysis. We suspect that this might be a factor, since belonging to the party or having *hukou*, or residential status, in the cities benefits Chinese in numerous ways, including in finding jobs and obtaining housing arrangements (Wu 2006; Wu and Treiman 2007). Including the occupation of farmers might improve the model specification, as well.

This paper also differs from Evans and Kelley (2004) in its analysis of the impact of education in studied countries. Their work showed that education has stronger effects on self-identity in Western-capitalist regimes, but weaker effects in eastern Europe, using interaction terms. Analyzing the same model in our respective societies, we found that education had no effect in Japan but does play an important role in Taiwan and China. We think that the divergence between our findings and those mainly based on Western, industrialized societies may be explained from a cultural perspective. Both societies (those of Taiwan and China) have a long history of holding education in high regard. There is an old saying in Chinese tradition: The worth of other pursuits is small; the study of books excels them all. In other words, persons who have knowledge are the most respected. We find that there is a linear relationship between educational achievements and status identity in these two societies, based on our analyses.

The results of our findings show that the determinants of social identity are more based on material rewards of individuals or households than cultural taste in East Asia. In this aspect, our results seem to be consistent with findings in previous literature about the impacts of personal income (e.g., Wu 1996; Tsai 1998; Kikkawa 2000). However, even though the explanatory power of education is lower than that of household income, it is still an important factor in the model. The significance of education is stronger than that of class structure.

Economic well-being and educational expansion provide for relatively strong confidence for most East Asians in their social position.

Our findings, however, do not simply add to previous research. There are some results that are unique to this study. Firstly, as we reported above, even though materialism matters in the determination of social identity, the influence of education remain strong. In Asian societies, education remains a symbol of honor regardless of occupation or economic circumstances. Intellectuals living a modest life receive more respect than those who are rich but have little education. At the very least, this points to the need for further testing in different cultures on findings that focus only economic resources as determinants of status positions, as Lamont (1992) argued.

Secondly, the importance of cultural tastes in affecting identification of social positions should not be overemphasized. Our results show that measures such as musical taste and travel experience play a rather minor role in explaining variances of social identities in the region. Listening to classical music does little to increase an individual's sense of self-worth. It is still possible that the indicators of cultural capital used in the analyses are not conclusive, as suggested by Bourdieu (1984; Swartz 1997). For instance, EASS does not ask about other indicators suggested by Bourdieu, such as the frequency of visiting museums or art galleries, in its questionnaire. However EASS asks questions about several genres of music in the survey. We also included travel experience and English fluency in the analysis. These two indicators are related to varieties of and access to cultural consumption. Conspicuous consumption has been an important aspect of symbolic capital for a long time. Spending on luxury goods has been taken as a symbol of middle-class status in East Asia, especially in Japan and China (New York Times, March 26, 2011). Even though our findings cast some doubt on the strength of the association between cultural activities and subjective evaluations of social positions, a more sophisticated method may improve the explanatory power of the statistical model.

Thirdly, our findings show the heterogeneity of social identity among East Asian societies, which are still widely assumed to be culturally homogeneous. We find that the distribution pattern of social identity is similar between China and Taiwan. The bottom-heavy distribution of subjective ranks in Korea may be the result of a shrinking middle social identity after the 1997 financial crisis (Han 2009; Hong 2003). This appears not to have returned to the previous level even a decade after the event. The experiences of the massive downward mobility at that time seem to have exerted a long-standing, negative effect on Koreans' self-identity.

Our study further shows that the determining power of economic condition on one's subjective social identity is strong in East Asian countries, and the role of cultural capital that diverts the effect of material resources is limited. In other words, the gap between objective and subjective class is narrow in this region.

What are the implications of our findings? During their period of rapid industrialization, East Asian societies have maintained relatively low levels of economic inequality, engendering a large group of affluent workers and small shop owners. East Asian countries are generally seen as societies where internal homogeneity is relatively high, and consensus on social hierarchy strong. This means that cultural diversity, which may provide people with diverse sources of identity, is relatively low. In such societies, where material resources translate directly into subjective identity, mid-level social identity is easily formed but also easily destroyed, depending on economic situation. Where the importance of the economic dimension overrules other possible sources of identity, subjective status tends to be greatly affected by economic fluctuation. As economic inequality increases, people's subjective identity is adjusted to their changed position in the economic hierarchy. In sum, the foundation of the strong mid-level social identity in Eastern Asia is rather fragile, and likely to undergo change in the future as inequality in this region increases.

References

Arita, Shin. 2011. "A Comparative Analysis of Social Stratification in Japan, Korea and Taiwan: Where is the Locus of Social Inequality?" In Yoshimichi Sato, ed, Elucidation of Social Stratification in Contemporary Japan: Vol. 1, A Report of Grants-in-Aid for Scientific Research (Basic Research A, Principal Investigator: Yoshimichi Sato), pp. 323–342, March 2011.

Baxter, Janeen. 1994. "Is Husband's Class Enough? Class Location and Class Identity in the United States, Sweden, Norway, and Australia." *American Sociological Review* 59(2): 220–235.

Bian, Yanjie. 2002. "Chinese Social Stratification and Social Mobility." *Annual Review of Sociology* 28: 91–116.

Bourdieu, Pierre. 1984. *Distinction: A Social Critique of the Judgement of Taste*. Cambridge: Harvard University Press.

Chan, Tak Wing. 2010. "The Social Status Scale: Its Construction and Properties." In T.W. Chan, ed., *Social Status and Cultural Consumption*, 28–56. Cambridge: Cambridge University Press.

Chan, Tak Wing and John H. Goldthorpe. 2010. "Introduction: Social Status and Cultural Consumption." In T.W. Chan, ed., *Social Status and Cultural Consumption*, 1–27. Cambridge: Cambridge University Press.

Chang, Chin-Fen and Heng-Hao Chang. 2010. "Who Cares for Unions? Public Attitudes toward Union Power in Taiwan, 1990–2005." *China Perspectives* 2010(3): 64–78.

Chang, Chin-Fen and Paula England. 2011. "Gender Inequality in Earnings in Industrialized East Asia." *Social Science Research* 40(1): 1–14.

Coulangeon, Philippe and Yannick Lemel. 2010. "Bourdieu's Legacy and the Class-Status Debate on Cultural Consumption: Musical Consumption in Contemporary France." In Tak Wing Chan, ed., *StatusSocial and ConsumptionCultural*, 84–108. Cambridge: Cambridge University Press.

Davis, Nancy J. and Robert V. Robinson. 1988. "Class Identification of Men and Women in the 1970s and 1980s." *American Sociological Review* 53(1): 103–112.

Evans, Mariah D.R. and Jonathan Kelley. 2004. "Subjective Social Location: Data from 21 Nations." *International Journal of Public Opinion Research* 16(1): 3–38.

Evans, Mariah D.R., Jonatha Kelley and Tamas Kolosi. 1992. "Images of Class: Public Perceptions in Hungary and Australia." *American Sociological Review* 57(4): 461–482.

Ganzeboom, Harry B.G., Donald J. Treiman and Wout C. Ultee. 1991. "Comparative Intergenerational Mobility Research: Three Generations and Beyond." *Annual Review of Sociology* 17: 277–302.

Gerth, Hans H. and C. Wright Mills, eds. 1958. *From Max Weber: Essays in Sociology*. New York: Oxford University Press.

Han, Sang-Jin. 2009. "The Dynamics of Middle Class Politics in Korea: Why and How Do the Middling Grassroots Differ From the Propertied Mainstream?" *Korea Journal of Sociology* 43(3): 1–19.

Hong, Doo-Seung. 2003. "Social Change and Stratification." *Social Indicators Research* 62: 39–50.

International Monetary Fund (IMF). 2010. World Economic Outlook Database, Available at http://www.imf.org/external/pubs/ft/weo/2015/01/weodata/index.aspx (accessed 11 January 2011).

Kanbayashi, Hiroshi and A. Hoshi. 2011. "Middle Status Identity and Lower Status Identity: Psychological and Behavioral Pattern Analysis." In Y. Saito and K. Misumi, eds., *Values and Attitudes in a Time of Destabilization* (Contemporary Stratified Society 3), 31–61. Tokyo: University of Tokyo Press. (in Japanese)

Kelley, Jonathan and Mariah D.R. Evans. 1995. "Class and Class Conflict in Six Western Nations." *American Sociological Review* 60(2): 157–178.

Kikkawa, Toru. 2000. "Changes in the Determinants of Class Identification in Japan." *International Journal of Sociology* 30(2): 34–51.

Kikkawa, Toru. 2006. *Education and Social Inequality: Contemporary Educational Credentialism in Japan*. Tokyo: University of Tokyo Press (in Japanese).

Kikkawa, Toru. 2011. "The Present and Future of Class Consciousness." In Yuriko Saito and Kazuto Misumi, eds., *Values and Attitudes in a Time of Destabilization*, 63–77. Tokyo: University of Tokyo Press. (in Japanese)

Kobayashi, Daisuke. 2011. "Work and Status Identity in the Fluidity of Employment." In Yuriko Saito and Kazuto Misumi, eds., *Values and Attitudes in a Time of Destabilization*, 95–110. Tokyo: University of Tokyo Press. (in Japanese)

Koo, Hagen. 2007. "The Changing Faces of Inequality in South Korea in the Age of Globalization." *Korean Studies* 31:1–18

Lamont, Michèle. 1992. *Money, Morals and Manners: The Culture of the French and American Upper Middle Class*. Chicago: University of Chicago Press.

Li, Chunlin. 2010. "Characterizing China's Middle Class: Heterogeneous Composition and Multiple Identities." In Cheng Li, ed., *China's Emerging Middle Class: Beyond Economic Transformation*, 135–156. Washington: The Brookings Institution.

Li, Peilin and Yi Zhang. 2008. "The Scope, Identity, and Social Attitudes of the Middle Class in China" *Society* 28(2): 1–19 (in Chinese).

Liu, Xin. 2001. "Strata Consciousness in Transition-Era Urban China." *Sociological Studies* 3: 8–17. (in Chinese)

Marsh, Robert T. 2002. "Social Class Identification and Class Interest in Taiwan." *Comparative Sociology* 1(1): 17–41.

Matsushige, Hisakazu. 2001. "English-Language Skill, Promotion, and Income: Is There an English Divide?" In H. Matsushige, *The Empirical Analysis of the Effects of College Education*, 29–48. Tokyo: Nippon Hyoronsha. (in Japanese)

Ministry of Education, Culture, Sports, Science and Technology (MEXT). 2011. *School Basic Survey Report*. Tokyo: Analytical Research Planning Division, Lifelong Learning Policy Bureau, MEXT. (in Japanese)

National Bureau of Statistics of China. 2009. *China Population and Employment Statistical Yearbook 2009*. Beijing: China Statistics Press.

National Bureau of Statistics of China. 2010. *China Statistical Yearbook 2010*. Beijing: China Statistics Press.

National Bureau of Statistics of China. 2011. *China Statistical Yearbook 2011*. Beijing: China Statistics Press.

Parish, William L. 1984. "De-stratification in China." In J.L. Watson, ed. *Class and Social Stratification in Post Revolution China*, 84–120. Cambridge, UK: Cambridge University Press.

Simpson, Ida H., David Stark and Robert A. Jackson. 1988. "Class Identification Processes of Married, Working Men and Women." *American Sociological Review* 53(2): 284–293.

Swartz, David. 1997. *Culture and Power: The Sociology of Pierre Bourdieu*. Chicago: University of Chicago Press.

Tsai, Shu-Ling. 1998. "Class Identification in Taiwan: 1992–1996," Paper presented at the Publication Ceremony of *National Science Council Research Project on Sociology, 1995–1997*, Institute of Sociology, Academia Sinica, Taipei, Taiwan, January 16–17.

Wang, Jianying, and Deborah Davis. 2010. "China's New Upper Middle Classes: The Importance of Occupational Disaggregation," in Cheng Li, ed., *China's Emerging Middle Class: Beyond Economic Transformation*, Washington: The Brookings Institution, 157–178.

Whyte, Martin K. 1975. "Inequality and Stratification in China." *China Quarterly* 64: 684–711.

World Bank. 2009. *From Poor Areas to Poor People: China's Evolving Poverty Reduction Agenda: An Assessment of Poverty and Inequality in China*, http://www.worldbank.org/research/2009/03/10444409/china-poor-areas-poor-people-chinas-evolving-poverty-reduction-agenda-assessment-poverty-inequality-china-vol-1-2-main-report (accessed 8 October 2011)

Wu, Nai-The. 1996. "Class Identity without Class Consciousness? Working-Class Orientations in Taiwan." In E.J. Perry, ed., *Putting Class in Its Place: Worker Identities in East Asia*, 77–102. Berkeley: Institute of East Asian Studies, University of California.

Wu, Xiaogang. 2006. "Communist Cadres and Market Opportunities: Entry into Self-Employment in China, 1978–1996." *Social Forces* 85(1): 389–411.

Wu, Xiaogang and Donald J. Treiman. 2007. "Inequality and Equality under Chinese Socialism: The Hukou System and Intergenerational Occupational Mobility." *American Journal of Sociology* 113(2): 415–445.

Yamato, Reiko. 2008. "Do Full-Time Housewives and Their Husbands Have Higher Social-Status Identification than Working Wives and Their Husbands?" In M. Todoroki, ed., *Social Stratification and Social Psychology in Contemporary Japan*, 87–102. Kyoto: Doshisha University. (in Japanese)

Yoon, Jeongkoo and Hyun-Ho Seok. 1996. "Conspicuous Consumption and Social Status in Korea: An Assessment of Reciprocal Effects." *Korea Journal of Population and Development* 25(2): 333–354.

Name Index

Subject Index

www.ingramcontent.com/pod-product-compliance
Lightning Source LLC
LaVergne TN
LVHW050650051026
849532LV00002B/587